HEROES, HIGHBROWS AND THE POPULAR MIND

Heroes, Highbrows

and the

Popular Mind

by

LEO GURKO

THE BOBBS-MERRILL COMPANY • INC.

PUBLISHERS

INDIANAPOLIS   NEW YORK

E
169.1
G955

First Edition

To my wife, Miriam Gurko, whose creative sense, editorial skill and powers of endurance helped make this book possible.

ACKNOWLEDGMENTS

I WISH to express my thanks to the following authors, publishers, newspapers and magazines for granting me permission to quote excerpts from their works:

American Association of University Professors BULLETIN and
>   H. W. Prentis, Jr.
>> H. W. Prentis, Jr., "Liberal Education for Business and Industry"

THE AMERICAN SCHOLAR
>   Christian Gauss, "Can We Live with Our Enemies?"

THE ATLANTIC MONTHLY
>   George W. Gray, "No Hitching Posts"
>   Budd Schulberg, "Movies in America: After Fifty Years"
>   Gilbert Seldes, "How Dense is the Mass?"
>   André L. Simon, "U. S. A. Retasted"

COLLIER'S
>   Vera Caspary, "Marriage '48"
>   John E. Gibson, "It's Smart To Be Stupid"
>   Howard Whitman, "Merchants of Luck"

CORONET
>   Ezra Goodman, "Are the Movies a Menace?" From CORONET, July 1948, copyright 1948 by Esquire, Inc.

Mary Ellen Chase
>   "Are We Afraid To Be Alone?" WOMAN'S DAY

Thomas Y. Crowell Company
>   William A. Lydgate, WHAT AMERICA THINKS

E. E. Cummings
>   Lines from "conversation with my friend is particularly"
>   "you shall above all things be glad and young"

From CIVILIZATION IN THE UNITED STATES, ed. by Harold
E. Stearns:
Ernest Boyd, "As An Irishman Sees It"
J. Thorne Smith, "Advertising"
Harper & Brothers
Merle Curti, THE GROWTH OF AMERICAN THOUGHT
Thomas Wolfe, THE WEB AND THE ROCK and YOU CAN'T
GO HOME AGAIN
Henry Holt and Company
Henri Bergson, CREATIVE EVOLUTION
Frederick Jackson Turner, THE FRONTIER IN AMERICAN
HISTORY
Houghton Mifflin Company
Ross Lockridge, Jr., RAINTREE COUNTY
Alfred A. Knopf
D. W. Brogan, THE AMERICAN CHARACTER
Bergen Evans, THE NATURAL HISTORY OF NONSENSE
André Gide, THE COUNTERFEITERS
H. L. Mencken, SELECTED PREJUDICES
Oswald Garrison Villard, THE DISAPPEARING DAILY
LIFE
Review of "The Seven Year Itch," December 8, 1952, copy-
right by Time, Inc.
Little, Brown & Company
Jacques Barzun, TEACHER IN AMERICA
Bernard DeVoto, THE LITERARY FALLACY, copyright by
Indiana University
Leonard Lyons
Anecdotes from "The Lyons Den," New York POST
The Macmillan Company
Jack London, THE CALL OF THE WILD
Frank Luther Mott, AMERICAN JOURNALISM
NEW REPUBLIC

New York HERALD TRIBUNE
    Articles by John Crosby and James S. Barstow, Jr.
The New York TIMES
    Articles by Alexander Cowie, Bosley Crowther, Kenneth
        S. Davis, David Dempsey, Benjamin Fine, Ezra Good-
        man, Jack Gould, Seymour E. Harris, Gladwin Hill,
        Aline B. Louchheim, Gian-Carlo Menotti and Russell
        Porter; and various news items
    Letters from Edwin R. Embree and Sylvester Weaver, Jr.
The New York WORLD-TELEGRAM AND SUN
    Column by Frederick C. Othman, reprinted by permission
        of United Feature Syndicate, Inc. and The New York
        World-Telegram and Sun
W. W. Norton & Company
    Karen Horney, NEUROSIS AND HUMAN GROWTH
    H. A. Overstreet, THE MATURE MIND
Random House
    William Faulkner, GO DOWN, MOSES AND OTHER STORIES
    Budd Schulberg, WHAT MAKES SAMMY RUN?
Rinehart & Company
    Charles Jackson, THE OUTER EDGES
    Philip Wylie, OPUS 21
The Ronald Press Company
    Ralph Henry Gabriel, THE COURSE OF AMERICAN DEMO-
        CRATIC THOUGHT, 1940
    James Playsted Wood, MAGAZINES IN THE UNITED STATES,
        1949
V. Sackville-West
    ALL PASSION SPENT, Doubleday & Company. Copyright
        1931 by V. Sackville-West and reprinted by permission
        of the author.
THE SATURDAY REVIEW
    Editorial by Norman Cousins

Charles Scribner's Sons

    Ernest Hemingway, THE SUN ALSO RISES

    Dixon Wecter, THE SAGA OF AMERICAN SOCIETY

    Thomas Wolfe, OF TIME AND THE RIVER

Simon and Schuster

    John Crosby, OUT OF THE BLUE

    Quincy Howe, THE NEWS AND HOW TO UNDERSTAND IT

The University of Chicago Press

    Richard M. Weaver, IDEAS HAVE CONSEQUENCES

The Viking Press

    Malcolm Cowley, EXILE'S RETURN

THE WORLD BOOK ENCYCLOPEDIA

    Copyrighted by Field Enterprises, Inc. Used by special permission.

I wish to thank also any other authors and publishers whose names may have been inadvertently omitted.

FOREWORD

It has long been the fashion to regard Americans as materialists, pursuers of the "fast buck," emotional adolescents and producers of a shoddy and vulgar culture. We have been accused of being anti-intellectual, interested only in physical comforts, a nation of cultural ignoramuses.

But Americans are not that simple. We are also a nation of idealists, humanitarians, independent thinkers, and the producers of a vigorous, creative and maturing society. We number among our great men writers, scholars and statesmen who have been acclaimed abroad as well as at home. American life, far from being stereotyped, consists of many complex and opposing elements: idealist and materialist, highbrow and lowbrow, liberal and conservative, cutthroat competition and enlightened co-operation, individualism and conformity.

This book is an inquiry into the nature and direction of these contending forces. It explores the prevailing American distrust of thinking and culture, and the antipathy to the creative artist and man of ideas. Thought and action, instead of being integrated parts of our national life, have been frequently driven apart by this distrust—a division which has injured the democratic concept of the whole man. As a people we are wary of theorizing. We look askance at scientists engaged in "pure" research, at writers and artists involved in their essentially nonutilitarian pursuits, and at college professors with their academic viewpoint. Despite the greater participation of women in political and professional activity, we still tend to regard with patronizing amusement those who in their leisure time branch out into anything more serious than needlework, canasta and the Ladies' Aid. Side by side with our growing interest in music, composers are still largely rewarded in terms of their commercial capacity to "entertain."

The position of the intellectual man has often been a difficult one in the United States, in modern times especially. Unless his ideas have had an immediately practical use, they have been generally regarded as wasteful and even unmanly. An early articulation of this attitude was made by Benjamin Franklin, one of America's great folk heroes, himself a man of ideas that were put to immediate use. "Time is money," declared the inventor of the lightning rod, thereby reducing even that intangible dimension to specific and manageable terms. Most of our historical experiences since Franklin's day, including the frontier, the immense growth of industrial technology, and the global wars of the twentieth century, have confirmed and solidified our attachment to the practical.

Yet the forces pulling the other way are also a vital part of the scene and as deeply rooted in our tradition. There was a time when preachers and scholars, writers and philosophers, were among the acknowledged leaders of the community and enjoyed the prestige accorded them to this day in most other Western countries. The frontier, to be sure, glorified the physical virtues but it also had much to do with the growth of democratic education. The phenomenal rise of our factory civilization after the Civil War made the pursuit of money and the acquisition of property dominant ideals for most Americans, but it also prepared the way for the new ideas and social directions of the New Deal and its economic reforms now so generally accepted. The wars of our century placed an enormous premium on industrial equipment, arms and the "know-how" that went into making them, but they have also created vast moral dilemmas which the man accustomed to thinking in terms of basic principles is peculiarly fitted to solve. And our popular arts, for all their false romanticism, escapist fantasies and frequent vulgarity, have stimulated a love of music, a desire for adult films, a demand for serious books and an intelligent awareness of world events, undreamed of in previous generations.

In nearly every area of culture, the impulse toward more mature attitudes and forms of entertainment is becoming articulate. The outcries against the flood of banal movies and insipid radio programs have grown louder in recent years. The young art of television, already exhibiting discouraging marks of infantilism, is being held up to searching examination not simply by sections of the public at large but by critics and producers closely allied with its fortunes.

While there are, then, forces against culture, there are also movements toward it. Indeed, antithesis of one kind or another reaches into every aspect of our life: into our social and political behavior as well as our literature and mass-communication media. A unique feature of American political life, for example, is that neither of the two great parties can be ticketed as all conservative or all liberal, but that within each there are contending liberal and conservative wings. And it is within ourselves as individuals that we sense most strongly impulses pulling us in different directions at the same time: toward materialism and yet toward spirituality, preoccupation with ourselves and concern for others, the response to emotion and the call to reason.

Ultimately it is the fusion of these opposite tendencies within the individual, within political parties, within the social and intellectual groupings of the country as a whole, that leads us toward the full realization of the democratic premise: the achievement of self-rule by men accepting and harnessing the divergent elements within themselves and their institutions. It is not by the triumph of one faculty at the expense of others that this can be done, but by their working together toward the common end of civilized maturity. Pressures are at work to prevent this fusion by seeking to force us into narrowing conformity of one kind or another. But these pressures generate a mounting resistance which in the long run thwarts the rigid uniformity they would impose.

This book seeks to clarify the sources and present status of these conflicting tendencies, whose resolution promises to cement the divisions in our culture. Signs of it, even in this difficult century, are already in evidence, and lead us to the reaffirmation of the whole man and his triumphant emergence in American democracy.

CONTENTS

Part I

The Intellectual Man in American Life

Chapter I

Thinkers and Doers

"AMERICA IS THE ONLY COUNTRY IN THE world," a columnist once observed, "where a man who uses a word that isn't understood by another man, is made to feel inferior to that other man."[1] To be suspected of learning or, what is worse, to display it publicly, is to invite ridicule. In our national stereotype, college professors are looked on as fogies, usually old, so wrapped up in musty and useless books that they have lost touch with life. Artists—of every genre—are supposed to be unconventional fellows, to be envied perhaps in one's duller moments, but kept firmly outside the pale of respectable society. Many people regard the intellectual as a snob, and the word itself has acquired an unpleasant flavor. Women especially are sensitive to it. Call a woman an intellectual and she is likely to feel insulted. You have as much as said that she is without feminine charm, must make up in brains what Nature denied her in beauty, and cannot be expected to lead a full life. Here, as so often elsewhere, cultivation of mind is regarded as a poor substitute for living.

The same generalized associations are carried over to culture

---

[1] Samuel Grafton, former columnist on the New York *Post*.

itself. Culture is a heavy and formidable something locked up in libraries and museums, or it is a collection of unfamiliar facts which ladies' literary clubs are forever pursuing in order to set themselves above "ordinary folks." In some parts of the country art is still looked on as foreign and un-American, tied up in a vaguely licentious way with France, and culture generally is denied any sort of usefulness in dealing with the problems of everyday existence. Or it is regarded as a luxury that the very rich perhaps can afford, but that is hardly relevant to the aims of plain people and is utterly alien to the peculiarly American phenomenon summed up under the headings of "just folks," "the average man," or "the common man." An interview with Gary Cooper, as reported in the New York *Times,*[2] illustrates this. When asked to what he attributed his success, the popular movie star replied, speaking in the same patois as his screen characters:

Shucks, . . . I guess I've just been lucky. I always try to stick pretty much to the type of stuff in which people are accustomed to seeing me—typical, average-guy roles like Mr. Deeds, Sergeant York and Dr. Wassell—people from the middle of the U.S.A. Once in a while I like a good Western—gives me a chance to shoot off guns.

My taste in art and literature is real ordinary. I don't try to pretend I know anything. I don't place myself above other people. I'm the average guy in taste and intelligence. If there's any reason for what you would call my success, that's it.

In colloquial usage, culture is synonymous with pedantry, divorce from reality, phoniness, foreignness, unmanliness in men and unattractiveness in women. At best it is regarded as a harmless pastime for idle females. This is reflected in Helen Hokin-

---

[2] Ezra Goodman, "Average Guy," the New York *Times,* December 19, 1948.

son's amusing cartoons of upholstered clubwomen with their synthetic passion for synthetic culture.[3]

When culture cannot simply be laughed out of sight, it is "popularized." Apparently there is no subject so complex that it cannot be reduced to surface terms, none so serious that its impact cannot be cushioned. Every aspect of science, from the atom bomb to cancer research, has been treated in the newspapers and magazines, nearly always shallowly, often misleadingly. And with a rare exception, such as *The Snake Pit,* the movies have used psychiatry, an involved and vital field, as the basis for a long sequence of sensationalized films in which accuracy is frequently sacrificed to the needs of "entertainment." Religious issues have been diluted to inspirationalism. Ethics and philosophy have been strained through the pragmatic sieve, and formulated in terms of *Does it work?* and *Can I get away with it?*[4]

---

[3] All sorts of reasons have been advanced for female predominance in the cultural audience. One of the most original—it might be called the hip-and-shoulder theory—was advanced in an *Esquire* article by Dr. J. B. Rice: "The bodies of men and women are built differently. For not only is a man's upholstery thinner, he also has a differently designed chassis. Women have their greatest weight and girth centered near their hips; while men, designed for heavy duty, have theirs in their shoulders. A woman can be reasonably comfortable in a small straight-backed chair with a hard seat—but a man can't. The dragging weight of his muscular arms and his heavier shoulder girth makes any posture in which he can't lean back to support his shoulders almost intolerable after a few minutes. Like a baby he doesn't know where he hurts or why; all he knows is that he hates concerts and lectures. As long as auditoriums provide only small straight-backed chairs and don't allow sufficient leg room between rows, they're going to have to peddle their precious culture almost exclusively to women." From "Nature of the Human Male," *Esquire,* October 1948.

[4] Some perfect cases of this were the basketball bribery scandals that spread through a variety of colleges in 1950-1, and the expulsion in 1951 of ninety West Point cadets for cheating. The moral issue was perhaps best summed up by Brigadier-General David J. Crawford, commander of the Army's tank-automotive center at Detroit. When relieved of his command and reprimanded for accepting favors from government contractors and building a sailboat for himself out of Army materials, he said: "I did nothing that anyone else wouldn't have done—only someone caught me at it." Quoted in *New Republic,* August 6, 1951.

The process of thinning out culture appears in other fields. Medical investigation of diseases has been funneled into premature announcements of sure cures or overdrawn accounts of sensational cases, dressed up in just enough medical jargon to make them sound authentic. Modern art—resistant to popularizing—has been the target of calumny because, in its rebelliousness, it has been hard to absorb emotionally, and in its experimentalism, it has proved difficult to understand. The same is true of much contemporary music and poetry. When artists have made their way despite this hostility, and have arrived, it is their private lives and the melodramatic sides of their work which have been played up. Culture can be an exotic accessory to brighten dull routine, but it is seldom accepted as an entity in its own right, an experience to be taken on its own terms. In effect, there is little to choose between an outright antagonism to culture and the process by which it is watered down.

Part of the blame for this state of affairs lies with the intellectual himself. He suffers from certain occupational diseases: a sense of superiority; a frequent inability to take a stand on any question because he sees both sides of it too keenly; a tendency to forget that ideas, when divorced from action, can become stuffy and sterile; a contempt for people less educated or attuned than he; an arrogant and dogmatic belief in the rightness of his conclusions; a certain preciousness of attitude with regard to practical problems. All this contributes to the exaggerated conception of him as an ivory-tower resident, a highbrow, an impractical theorist, a person who though "he never met a pay roll" has a pat solution for everything, a philosopher ranging from the amateur of college bull-sessions to the professional operating in the upper echelons of abstract thought. Nor is it surprising that in America he often feels outside the main stream of life, lacking the assured public prestige of the businessman, doctor, engineer, or lawyer; nor that the average American holds him half in awe, half in contempt, and feels generally alienated.

This feeling of alienation is reinforced by the fact that the intellectual is a man who applies himself to disinterested ends, and pursues his profession more for its own sake than for the livelihood to be derived from it. His ranks include writers, artists, teachers, scientists, clergymen, scholars, and nearly everyone who chooses his mode of life for reasons other than the acquisition of money or worldly power. All this in a society dominated by money standards.

By very definition, the man of ideas thinks first and acts afterward, in sharp contrast to the more common American tendency to act first and think afterward. This tendency was brought to a head by the enormous wealth of the country which, in the late nineteenth century especially, was to be won by those who moved most swiftly and were least burdened by a sense of obligation to others. Prompt action, least freighted with reflection on causes and consequences, enabled a man to win the greatest material rewards. Thinking was a bit in the teeth of action, and hence a handicap in the race for success. Contempt for ideas, theories, abstractions, was strong during the middle and late stages of the frontier, when the relatively easy access to free land and forests, to gold and copper mines, through the expenditure of physical energy alone, made anticulturalism inevitable. This easy access helped create the American type, described by Frederick Jackson Turner in *The Frontier in American History:*

. . . self-examination . . . is not characteristic of the historic American. He has been an opportunist rather than a dealer in general ideas. Destiny set him in a current which bore him swiftly along through such a wealth of opportunity that reflection and well-considered planning seemed wasted time. He knew not where he was going, but he was on his way, cheerful, optimistic, busy and buoyant.[5]

We became a nation of busy opportunists, of doers rather than thinkers, devotees of the short-range view rather than the long, who piled up mountains of achievement side by side with mountains of waste. Reflection and the long view, we assumed, had no relevance to the building of the country, and so we consigned them to the sidelines.

The great error, still shared by intellectuals and nonintellectuals alike, is this assumption that a gap must exist between "intellectual" and "physical" affairs. Our whole historical experience shows that, in actuality, no such gap exists, and that when people have acted on the assumption that it does, only damage and confusion have resulted. The very period of the frontier and the tremendous industrial expansion which saw scorn for reflection and the long view at its most intense, witnessed as a result of that scorn the beginning of a disastrous policy in one of the vital national areas of public interest—the conservation of natural resources. For a long time these were regarded as inexhaustible; hence there was no admitting that one could be reckless or profligate in their exploitation. The warnings and efforts of President Theodore Roosevelt went largely unheeded. Deforestation, the unchecked draining-away of topsoil, the impoverishment of petroleum and oil reserves, the denudation of fisheries, did not begin to assume dangerous proportions until the end of the second World War. Industry paid little attention to the problem, partly because it seemed illusory, partly because such attention would have yielded no short-term profit. Professional economists stressed distribution and production as the keys to Utopia, to the virtual exclusion of

---

[5] Frederick Jackson Turner, *The Frontier in American History* (New York: Holt, 1920), p. 290.

conservation. Even the Teapot Dome scandal of the twenties, with its focus on naval oil reserves, did little to arouse public interest in the problem.

The stock-market crash of 1929, however, and the ensuing depression jolted the American out of his buoyancy and optimism, and forced him, whether he wished to or not, to take stock of his stalled society and think. Desperation hastened this process, paving the way for the emergency measures of the New Deal. Whatever may be said about these measures, they represented an attempt by organized intelligence to get the country back on its feet. Certainly this was true of the government's new policy with regard to natural resources, though this policy, like so many of the New Deal's experiments, was carried out in short, uneven bursts. The establishment of the CCC (Civilian Conservation Corps) initiated activity of a sporadic kind. Under the spur of the quickening social consciousness of the middle '30s and the aggressiveness of Harold L. Ickes, Secretary of the Interior during the four Roosevelt administrations, further organized work in conservation got under way. But it was not until the middle '40s, when the tremendous pressures upon steel, oil and food during the second World War revealed the narrowing margin of our reserves, that a growing awareness of the issue was crystallized on a national scale. The various predictions of the exhaustion of the great Mesabi iron range in Minnesota, and of the once vast petroleum reserves of Texas and Oklahoma, sharpened the edge of this consciousness. Some private industries began investing money in conservation along lines parallel to the government's, in the perfectly rational hope that a relatively small amount invested now would yield incalculable future returns. But this rationality arrived late on the scene, and then only fitfully and piecemeal.

The lack of intelligent foresight in the field of natural resources had political results as well. Foreign policy is made up of many complex elements, economics among them. Our dwindling oil resources forced us to look for oil reserves abroad, which spurred our interest in the Arabian peninsula, which in turn helped to formulate the Truman Doctrine regarding Greece and Turkey as buffers to protect that peninsula. Thus shortsightedness with regard to the single issue of conservation at home helped set in motion a whole chain of events around the world. A refusal to think clearly and over the long view produced consequences which in this instance were almost literally beyond calculation. Perhaps our oil problem will be solved at the last minute by the ingenuity of some scientist who will find a practicable means of extracting oil from coal, and harness petroleum to our coal reserves (which are said to be virtually inexhaustible). Or some other synthetic process might be developed to save us from the results of our shortsightedness. Yet it would be compounding the original error to rely blithely on inventiveness always rising up at the right moment to defeat folly. The law of averages aside, this complacency, with its indifference to thinking and planning, creates the very situations in which we are made the enemies of our own self-interest.

A further instance of irrationality in matters vital to the nation has been the frequent reluctance to accept technological change. Often this has been motivated by a narrow zeal for limited profits today at the expense of much larger ones tomorrow, an increase made inevitable by the immense expansion of business activity through technological inventiveness. The whole history of commerce and industry is marked by hostility to new inventions. Suppliers of horses fought against stagecoaches, stagecoaches against canals, canals against railroads, railroads against automobiles, buses and airplanes, each resisting its successor tooth and nail. Great corporations have bought up patents and suppressed them for varying lengths of time. Devices which ultimately brought about the vast expansion of industries like printing and textiles had to struggle against indifference or outright opposition to make their way. The great transformations effected by the steamboat, the railroad, the sewing machine and scores of other inventions were postponed by skepticism and antagonism. When the automobile first appeared, it met with the same laughter, ridicule and distrust that had greeted the steamboat and locomotive—an emotional process repeated with Henry Ford's later application of mass assembly-line techniques and the revolutionary offer of five dollars a day to his workers.

Industrial and technological progress was slowed also by resistance on the part of bankers as well as businessmen and the general public. For a long time many great banking houses tended to look on research and the rapid industrial changes resulting from it as unsettling to the country; and regarded with suspicion and instinctive distaste proposals to launch new contrivances. Bankers even considered labor-saving agricultural machinery as bad for farmers since it might demoralize them with too much leisure time.

The business community has not been alone in failing to foresee the greater benefits that would result from the development of new ideas. Doctors and the medical profession in times past have campaigned against new processes and discoveries in medicine. The history of the great medical researchers in the nineteenth century—Pasteur, Koch, Semmelweiss—tells the same bitter story of organized opposition to the future. Farmers, traditionally the most conservative members of society, greeted the iron plow at its first appearance as an instrument of destruction which would surely poison the ground. They regarded the railroad as a great black puffing monster which would scare the cattle, burn down barns by the flames spouting from the locomotives, and even frighten hens so that they would stop laying eggs. Or else the locomotive was looked on as an agent of the Devil, its grinding wheels, belching smoke and hideous noise seeming to come straight from hell itself. These irrational superstitions blinded many farmers to the real benefits that would accrue to them through the rapid transportation of their products to market and the opening of new consumer areas hitherto out of reach.

Workers, too, have been proverbially opposed to technological change. In its modern phase this opposition began in the 1820s with the Luddites smashing weaving looms in the early textile mills. Since then, workers have wrecked new machines which threatened to displace them, forced employers' associations to curtail the introduction of processes that injured them economically, called for periodic moratoriums on labor-saving inventions, and have in many other cases resisted the advance of technology as vigorously as have agriculture and business. Yet this very advance was the basis in the past half century for the unparalleled rise in the standard of living of the American working population.

These several types of unenlightened self-interest sprang in part from indifference or hostility to thinking and planning in broad perspective. In *The Course of American Democratic Thought,* Ralph Henry Gabriel describes this hostility to scientific progress:

. . . the age of science has been marked by economic and international disaster. . . . A growing school of thought blamed the machine . . . for the fact that civilization was faltering. When in bleak depression millions of American men and women found themselves adrift with no means of earning bread, the idea of the machine as Frankenstein spread among the masses. The inchoate thoughts of the sufferers found expression in a demand for a scientific holiday. . . . A thrill of fear ran through the laboratories of the nation. On February 23, 1934, in the blackest month of a depression winter the New York *Times* published a significant dispatch. "Science struck back at its critics yesterday and with the aid of some of its own inventions—the radio, sound cameras and loudspeakers—it told the world that science makes jobs and does not end them. . . . Two of its leading representatives, Dr. Karl T. Compton . . . and Dr. R. A. Millikan . . . slaughtered with words and refuted with figures those who are pressing for a 'research holiday' and those who contend that science is the root of economic ills."[6]

Resistance, though delaying the advance of science and technology, did not halt it. But the delays caused friction, proved expensive, and were in every way damaging to the public interest. Once again the short-range view triumphed over the long, with injury not only to the country but to the ultimate welfare of the particular groups whose immediate interests seemed threatened.

The waste of natural resources and the resistance to technological change are but two instances of the price we have paid for ignoring the long-range values of the intellectual approach to life. Without the essential elements of that approach, the reflection and well-considered planning of which Turner spoke, we can look forward to the prospect of further penalties induced by heedlessness and waste in whatever fields they may appear. Changes for the better can be effected only when the realization becomes general that the virtues and resources of the thinking mind are not confined to vague theorizings and distant abstractions but operate effectively within the world of everyday matter.[7] As that realization occurs, much of the antipathy to culture and men of ideas will disappear.

---

[6] Ralph Henry Gabriel, *The Course of American Democratic Thought* (New York: the Ronald Press, 1940), p. 382.

[7] On a local scale, this principle was dramatically illustrated by Louis Bromfield in *Malabar Farm*. This absorbing account of the novelist's rehabilitation of a run-down Ohio farm showed what concentrated planning and the intelligent use of the technics of agricultural science could do to reverse the pattern of natural erosion and human neglect.

Chapter II

Culture Through a Cracked Looking Glass

I

IN 1937 LESLIE HOWARD, ONE OF THE MOST
popular and skillful actors of the day, appeared in a Hollywood
movie called *Stand-In*. It was a stereotyped piece which lam-
pooned the films and filmmakers through the use of slapstick
that never quite came off. Its view of culture, however, suffered
from a distortion so characteristic as to give the movie an
importance which its intrinsic merits did not deserve. The central character, played by Mr. Howard, is a mathematical wizard
who has risen to a high place in a great Eastern bank. We see
him at the beginning, a thin, stooped, rather faded young man,
with tortoise-shell glasses which he continually removes and
puts on nervously, walking through the offices of the bank reel-
ing off dictation involving high and complicated numbers to a
harried secretary following him at two paces. His eye has a
remote look, and the pallor of his skin indicates that his life has
been led indoors. In short, Hollywood's conception of an intel-

32

lectual: brainy, but, by God, not normal, not, somehow, right. Too many statistics, too few red corpuscles.

The bank holds a mortgage on a movie company which has been losing money and is now on the verge of going under. To save its investment, it dispatches our bloodless mathematical friend to Hollywood. Figures should do the trick, he believes, it's all a matter of figures. Life itself is really only a bookkeeping operation. In Hollywood, however, his real education begins. And what an education it turns out to be! First, he meets an attractive young lady who is a stand-in for the temperamental star. After lecturing him on how the employees of the company are human beings and not numbers on an accounting sheet, she consents to act as his secretary and show him the ropes. The president of the company is a suave crook who is deliberately driving the firm on the rocks so that its assets may be sold cheap to a dummy company secretly owned by himself. The female star is in cahoots with him and starts to vamp our hero in a style that would make Theda Bara look like a model of subtle artistry. The ace producer, in love with the star, really knows his business but has begun hitting the bottle because of her disgraceful conduct. The director is a phony who assumes a Viennese accent and stands around ready to pick up whatever illegal profits the big boss consents to throw his way. Into this unsavory and unpromising setup barges our hero, with his paper armament and wistful ignorance of the ways of the world. His only asset is the hardheaded, somewhat cynical young lady who knows the score but who, we can see, is going to have trouble teaching it to her new employer. To him she has taken an unaccountable liking, so far strictly maternal; the babe-in-the-woods in him calls out to the mother in her.

His initiation into the realities of life proceeds rapidly. The director blackens his eye with one well-directed punch, whereupon his girl friend teaches him judo, which enables him thereafter to knock down men twice his size. The president of the company issues discharge notices to everyone just when our hero is within sight of a solution. This forces him to take off his coat, address the dismissed employees, persuade them to return to work for just one more week end. By this time his whole appearance has changed. He has shed his spectacles and straightened up noticeably; his eye, once glazed, is now bright; his complexion, even on the black-and-white screen, has acquired a healthy tone. His speech is no longer a monotonous jumble of abstruse computations, but vigorous and direct. In short order, he tosses the president off the premises, dismisses the star, persuades the producer to stop drinking and turn out a smash hit that saves the company, puts all the employees, whom he now acknowledges to be real people, permanently back to work, and marries the girl. He kisses her with authority, a sign that he has acquired the confidence and "know-how" no American male can do without. His transformation from bookworm to man is complete.

The movies have hugged this concept of the man of abstract ideas, his deficiencies and salvation, tenaciously. The variations on it have been numerous, but certain common elements are retained intact: he is impractical; his brains have interfered with his participation in life; he is, if not sexually unattractive or impotent, timid and gauche; his rescue from these limitations is most quickly effected by a charming young lady who knows all the answers and teaches them to him in circumstances that begin with pity and end with love.

In 1948, eleven years after *Stand-In,* Hollywood was still ringing the same changes on this emotional equation. Ray Milland, a popular actor, starred during that year in a movie called *The Trouble with Women,* which followed, with a few mechanical alterations, a familiar script. The central figure is not a mathematician but a professor of psychology who has just written a best-selling book attacking women as ruthless and dominating. He himself shies away from women and refuses to have anything to do with them. Since he teaches, he naturally wears tortoise-shell glasses, never can find his socks, shoes or ties, and has difficulty saying hello to casual passers-by without stumbling and stammering. His rejuvenation begins when an enterprising and beautiful young female reporter is sent by her hard-boiled city editor to get an interview with him. He has sworn never to be interviewed, certainly not by women; so half the picture is devoted to juvenile shenanigans in which he seeks to avoid her and she seeks to corner him. When she succeeds, an outcome never in doubt, his metamorphosis proceeds at a breakneck pace. Off come the glasses. One kiss is all he needs to become a master at the art of making love. His bumbling manner disappears and is replaced by a casual nonchalance that would arouse the envy of a *boulevardier*. His ideas about women grow much more tempered and sensible. By the last reel he has become a composite of all the traits comprising the male movie hero: he is manly, good-looking, easy-mannered, equally at home in an alley brawl and a drawing room, daunted by nothing. It is difficult to say which portrait is less real: the intellectual or the intellectual after his conversion to the type of American male glorified by Hollywood.

Nor is this portrait limited to the male of the species. "In a recent motion picture," Alexander Cowie recalled, "a comedy sequence shows an obviously cultivated young woman making out very badly in the rehearsal of a song-and-dance act. Well, she is so inadequate in her attempt that the other performers laugh. Whereupon heart-of-gold Durante yells: 'Cut that out! The rest of youse wouldn't do no better if you was educated like she is.' "[1]

---

[1] The New York *Times*, August 11, 1946.

Women have undergone the same transformation as the male intellectual, complete with glasses and all. A smoothly finished instance was *A Foreign Affair,* in which Jean Arthur is a congresswoman making a junket to occupied Berlin with a committee of colleagues to investigate the morale of our soldiers. In the opening scene we find the intellectual woman *à la* Hollywood. While everyone else is looking out the airplane windows at the German landscape below, she is busy writing down a series of official notes describing the unimportant statistical details of the journey which she files away in a complex compartment-within-compartment brief case. There is a smug, severely efficient look on her bespectacled face as she does this. Her hair is pulled up in a severe knot. Her clothes are serviceable and dowdy. When the plane lands in Berlin we discover that she is a lady of principle, who wants to make sure that there is no fraternizing with the *Fräuleins* or dealing on the black market, and will not be taken in, as are the others, by the carefully conducted tours arranged by the attendant general. She is regarded by everybody as a pest, a troublemaker and worst of all, a woman with intellectual convictions. In this dilemma there is obviously only one solution. A handsome captain is pressed into service, detailed to make love to the lady, distract her in any way possible in the hope of removing her sting. In one reel flat she begins to assume her other shape, the shape Nature designed for women. Off come the spectacles, down comes the hair knot. The dowdily efficient suit is replaced by a stunning gown bought (as a crowning touch) on the black market. Helped along by some useful hints on female glamour by a German night-club singer who has been the mistress of numerous Nazi bigwigs and American conquerors, our heroine sheds her principles and blossoms into an attractive woman without an idea or conviction in her pretty head except that she is in love and will do anything to get her man. She does everything and gets him. At the end the change is complete. Her flesh has flowered while her brain has receded, or rather because her brain has receded, there being, at Hollywood's insistence, an irreconcilable hostility between them. Since a choice must be made between one and the other, the wise woman (and man) will choose physical attractiveness and let thinking fend for itself.[2]

This is but one of the forms in which woman has been rescued from the tyranny of intellect. The movies have liberated her in other professions: as a business executive making a marvelous administrative success of things but at what a shocking emotional price; as a schoolmistress loved by all the children but beginning to wither around the edges; as a social worker good as can be but drying up visibly; as an office clerk cut off from life by desks, files and papers.

Dozens of films have ground out a similar pattern, and have rescued any number of brainy dodoes from the grave penalties and restrictions imposed on them by their brains. The appearance of *Apartment for Peggy* and *Letter to Three Wives,* the only films in recent memory that defend "intellectuals" (teachers in each case), betokens that Hollywood can revolt against the tyranny of its own clichés. But two movies cannot efface the habits of thirty years, and Hollywood's refracted view of culture and ideas remains integral to its projection of American life.

Even children have not escaped Hollywood's searching eye. There is in every classroom scene a learned little boy. He wears glasses and talks in polysyllables. Usually his clothes are fancier and more "girlish" than his fellows', which mark him off as a sissy. He always flees from fisticuffs and rough play, can't do anything with his hands except write long words, and looks at the world with owlish timidity. Every now and then, by way of

---

[2] Or as actress Vanessa Brown—herself a former Quiz Kid with an I.Q. of 165—put it in a *Life* interview: "In Hollywood having a mind is all right—if you conceal it behind a low-cut bosom." *Life,* December 8, 1952.

showing that it was not temperament that made him that way but a wrong turning in the direction of books, the movies will have him one day goaded beyond endurance, throw away his glasses and beat up the school bully. After which he never again puts on his specs, reduces his language to colloquial English, and becomes a regular fellow. More often, however, he is left the bookworm, to serve as a hideous and permanent example to other boys of the disastrous results of learning.

Hollywood's contempt, pity and scorn for the intellectual life know no age limits, and are equaled only by its passion for freeing persons of both sexes from the mind's fell clutch.

II

The attitude of the mass-circulation magazines toward reason and intellect, in their fiction at least, is scarcely different. In their pages the more a man "feels" and the less he "thinks," the more effective he is in his dealings with others. The formula stories do not as a rule deal with scientists and philosophers, but when they do, their slant on these hapless persons is frankly contemptuous. The following passage from a story in *Collier's* is typical:

Her ardor was becoming. Excitement made her prettier than ever. If Henry Fowler had been a man of sense instead of science, he would have petted her a bit and given her an opportunity to make up her mind about the New York trip. Unfortunately Henry was not the sort to cuddle and cajole his wife into obedience. He used logic, which is undependable, and reason, which is repulsive.[3]

However agile the scientist may be in handling the atom bomb, he cannot handle his wife. He does not know how to coo

---

[3] Vera Caspary, "Marriage '48," *Collier's*, October 9, 1948.

at her caressingly or bellow at her dominatingly, the two most effective ways of controlling women, as is well known to all veteran readers of popular magazine fiction. He employs, instead, undependable logic and repulsive reason, which may be all right with nuclear energy but are poison with the female of the species, especially if she is pretty. There is some question whether this includes homely ladies who may indeed listen to reason and logic, which only proves they are homely. If they were attractive, they wouldn't. Furthermore, there is an absolute hostility not only between reason and emotion, but also between "sense" and "science." By sense is presumably meant common sense or plain ordinary "horse sense," that instinctive faculty praised from Benjamin Franklin to David Harum without which no real success is thought possible in America. It is on no account to be confused with theoretical or intellectual sense, too much of which trips one up and makes failure inevitable.

The same theme, variously elaborated, appears nearly everywhere in popular periodical fiction. On the simplest level the man of ideas seems not only emotionally stupid but socially dull. In one story published in *The Saturday Evening Post,* he is a professor of chemistry so tedious his beautiful wife cannot abide him. "I can't stand being a professor's wife in a college town. It bores me to the point where I could scream. . . . He's a stick. He's just a dull, tiresome stick. Of course, he's kind and even-tempered in a cowlike way. . . ." His cowlike goodness, however, is drowned in a flood of other complaints. "Our friends are incredibly dull. You should listen to their conversation. . . . Formulas and equations. Symbolic reactions and experiments. That's all I hear all day long."[4]

So she leaves him, weeping at her lot. Though he is in line for the chairmanship of the department and so presumably knows

---

[4] Nancy and Norbert Davis, "The Captious Sex," *The Saturday Evening Post,* January 8, 1949.

his formulas, equations and college politics especially well, in all else he behaves like a half-wit. An old flame turns up at this point, beautiful, unmarried, making eighteen thousand a year as a department-store executive, and, for no discernible reason, with a secret yen for our professor. He makes a few feeble passes at her, just as a professor with no idea of courtship would. When his wife hears of this she comes rushing back to claim her man, but before she can say a word, he confesses his inability to live without her and promises to come out of his academic cloud.

He is bumbling throughout, as the inconsiderate husband, the inept lover and the repentant spouse. In all three roles he bears the stigmata of his magazine image: absent-mindedness, impracticality, social naïveté. No overtones of pity or patronizing fondness disguise the fact that in the important areas of living he is a complete and absolute fool.

In our magazine versions of human behavior the antithesis between learning and life extends to more complex situations. Many a scholar—historians and archaeologists are popular professional specimens—has lost his wife to another man because he fails to understand that people, not facts, are important. When he is not the gauche, bumbling type, he is portrayed as dry, inhuman, cold, unfeeling, antisocial. He regards love with the same clinical eye he casts on any laboratory process, and he would no more allow his emotions to run away with him in his relations with his wife than he would while examining some ninth-century palimpsest or a fossil in a "dig." Small wonder that his wife, after her feelings have been on this slow-starvation diet, leaves him altogether for some sturdy businessman or engineer. Or is about to leave him when he comes to his senses, emerges from his bookish fog, and reclaims her before she takes the irrevocable step. He realizes in the nick of time how the life of the mind, by its inherent pull, has carried him away from emotional vitality. Head versus heart again.

In this context the intellectual, as long as he remains one, is impotent; the practical man, significantly, virile. The suggestion is powerfully rendered that books, libraries, abstract ideas, laboratories, museums, the ivy-covered towers of a university, are somehow emasculating, while factories, executive suites, mine shafts, bridges being thrown across dangerous rivers, trucks on long night rides over lonely highways, lend themselves *per se* to the rich full existence. Our fictional scholar is cut off from the life of action by ideas. We come here to the root of the matter: men who think, write or talk too much are emotionally inadequate; faith must be placed in men of action. The strong link that is presumed to exist between thought and impotence has its reverse in the bond that connects practicality and virility. These bonds and links are forged over and over again in the novelettes (complete in one issue), serials, short stories and short-shorts published in vast numbers by the popular magazines of the country.

III

In 1946 the State Department's Office of International Information and Cultural Affairs bought a collection of American paintings for exhibition abroad. Seventy-nine oils and thirty-eight water colors were included at a cost of $56,000, and sent from capital to capital by way of advertising the advanced directions of American art. The principal exhibition was held in Paris during UNESCO month, November 1946.

The purchase involved a very small part of the large funds spent by the United States for propaganda abroad and for a time was scarcely noticed at home. The Hearst newspapers, however, always on the alert for unhealthy alien influences, began a strong campaign against the collection, devoting a full page once a week for several weeks to exposing what they regarded as its "absurdity and Communistic influences," calling it "weird junk" posing as modern art. The exhibit was attacked as unrepresentative of America and the paintings traced to the foreign ideologies and spiritual illness of Europe. Where the artists were not downright absurd or unintelligible, the Hearst articles continued, they appeared to demean American society by portraying it in ugly, sordid, materialistic terms; and they were thus carrying out the Communist line, as plainly visible in oils and water colors as in print.

The furor thus created quickly reached Congress. Various congressmen who had paid no attention to the collection until then took a first look, and began emitting cries of anguish. Washington columnist Frederick C. Othman described the ensuing scene:

They waved in the air reproductions of such paintings as Gregorio Prestopino's "Trolley Car," Philip Evergood's "Girl with Cock," Loren MacIver's "Blue Landscape" and Abraham Rattner's "Yellow Table." They said that if these squiggles were art, then they (the Congressmen) were nearsighted crawfish.[5]

The hubbub grew. Several congressmen were violently upset by Yasuo Kuniyoshi's fleshly "Circus Girl Resting," and muttered imprecations about obscenity paid for by taxpayers' money. Many of the arguments used against the WPA projects a decade before were taken out of cold storage, dusted off, and tossed at the target. The *coup de grâce* was delivered by President Truman who, after glancing at reproductions of the collection, remarked that they looked to him like scrambled eggs. These broadsides brought quick action. Secretary of State Marshall

---

[5] New York *World-Telegram*, May 15, 1948.

ordered the exhibit closed on the grounds that it had become a matter of public controversy. The pictures were removed from walls in Prague, Paris, Haiti and more distant points, shipped back to the United States, and turned over to the War Assets Administration to be disposed of as surplus goods.

Their troubles were not yet over. The War Assets Administration, which was having difficulty getting rid of more conventional goods, wanted no part of pictures called "Bird Bath," "Donkey Engine," and "Bowery Follies." It took a rousing legal argument before the House Appropriations Committee to persuade the WAA that it had no choice in the matter. With great reluctance the WAA hired as evaluators two consultants from the Whitney Museum and the Museum of Modern Art who added to the confusion by declaring that some of the paintings, while they may have seemed like scrambled eggs to the President, were worth better than two thousand dollars each. This estimate conspicuously included the Kuniyoshi which had so irritated legislative sensibilities. The artists themselves, who had sold their work to the government at a special price, were angry not only at their maligners but at the prospect of their paintings being disposed of at bargain-basement rates. Their feelings were reinforced by the art critic of the New York *Times* who commented on the merit of their work at the time of the final exhibition just prior to the public sale:

... the overwhelming majority [of the paintings] merits attention and there are many items which indeed rank with the best of the painter's production. The sale thus presents a rare chance to bid for exceptional modern American paintings such as seldom come on the auction market. . . .

Noted in the catalogue . . . were the two Marin oils . . . ; of the three Max Webers, the glowing "Fruit and Wine"; . . . an extraordinarily evocative and poetic Baziotes; . . . Presto-

pino's warmly human "Trolley Car"; . . . Gropper's "Home"; . . .
Loren MacIver's bewitching "Blue Landscape"; . . . and Ben
Shahn's unforgettable social comment, "Hunger."[6]

The sale was gratifying. The pictures moved briskly and, to
the mild consternation of the "scrambled-egg" school, the government made a tidy profit on this abortive venture into the
fine arts.

The affair provides more than a curious and instructive passage in the relations between government and art. It reveals also
some of the myths and misconceptions still befogging public
attitudes toward the artist. It is easy to accuse him of being
ridiculous and incomprehensible when he goes off into the
untracked areas of cubism and abstractionism. Or to attack him
for being dissatisfied with America because he paints slums and
the poor. To be sure, he is at times obscure and incomprehensible, but what is unintelligible to one generation is often clear to
the next. The American painter has made his way slowly in the
esteem of his countrymen during the present century, and his
position is better than at its turn. But he continues to suffer from
the distortion with which culture in its multiple phases is still
viewed.

IV

Intellectuals and artists are not above distorting culture themselves. Writers have pitched in with well-aimed shafts at reason
and thought. Some have accepted the caricature of reason as the
enemy of feeling and consequently of life. Others have seized
on the vignette of the intellectual as a highbrow snob, from
whom they wish to dissociate themselves. Ernest Boyd and

---

6 Aline B. Louchheim in the New York *Times,* May 21, 1948.

H. L. Mencken in their time attacked professors as pedants and "cans of undigested knowledge." There are professors who attack quite as indiscriminately all writers who do not compose in the classical tradition or who deal with shocking subjects or, being embittered, protest too much and in language unsuited to the drawing room. The war between creative artists and critics is as old as recorded history, and shows no signs of abating. The quarrels between scientist and aesthete are as acrimonious if not as ancient, and have varied very little in content and not at all in tone since Arnold and Huxley had their famous dispute nearly a century ago.

Among the writers who believe that enmity must exist between thinking and feeling, none has been more articulate than E. E. Cummings. Beneath his eccentricities of grammar and punctuation, beneath his perverse, clever-child exhibitions of verbal obscurity, Cummings is a sensualist to whom sex is the breath beat of the universe, the sensations of the present quivering and ephemeral moment the end-all of experience. Any interruption, however induced, causes this moment to slip by and be forever lost, and so becomes the poet's deadly enemy. To this enemy and the faculties that induce it he addresses himself with hatred and contempt. Of these faculties the mind ranks highest since by its very nature it thrives on reflection and looks beyond the present to the onrushing future. To Cummings the brain is a frigid destroyer of experience:

> to think is the slippery contours of a vase inexpressibly
> fragile it is for the brain irrevocably frigid to touch a
> merest shape which however slenderly by it caressed
> will explode and spill the immediate imperceptible
> content[7]

---

[7] E. E. Cummings, *Collected Poems* (New York: Harcourt, Brace, 1938), poem 97.

One cannot both love and be wise. In a contest between the two, the poet chooses the first:

> since feeling is first
> who pays any attention
> to the syntax of things
> will never wholly kiss you;
>
> wholly to be a fool
> while Spring is in the world
>
> my blood approves,
> and kisses are a better fate
> than wisdom
> lady i swear by all flowers. Don't cry
> —the best gesture of my brain is less than
> your eyelids' flutter which says
>
> we are for each other: then
> laugh, leaning back in my arms
> for life's not a paragraph
>
> And death i think is no parenthesis[8]

Knowledge leads to negation, progress is only a grave:

> that you should ever think,may god forbid
> and(in his mercy)your true lover spare:
> for that way knowledge lies,the foetal grave
> called progress,and negation's dead undoom.
>
> I'd rather learn from one bird how to sing
> than teach ten thousand stars how not to dance[9]

---

8 *Ibid.*, poem 180.
9 *Ibid.*, poem 315.

So we are led to a flood of mindless feeling, bathed in sensuous fantasies, immersed in the sharp urgent ecstasy of the fleeting present. In his visions of fleshly delight Cummings contributes to the myth that thought renders existence juiceless and sterile. His anti-intellectualism is all reflex and instinct, hot recriminations and angry rejections, illustrating in a striking way the spasms of feeling-without-reflection which to him is living at its most intense. Despite the differences in form, there is little difference between his view of mind and matter and that of the movies and magazines.

Flashes of the same view are visible among other writers. One of Charles Jackson's documentary novels, *The Outer Edges,* contains this scornful sketch of the intellectual:

George Gundersen had only met three or four intellectuals at the most, but it seemed to him that he had never known one of them who did not seem to be talking to himself, or, which was the same thing, exclusively for the benefit of each other. The more intellectual they became the less communication they had with life and people. They revolved in increasingly smaller and smaller circles, without any real interest in anything, sustained only by a specialized vocabulary that was utterly incomprehensible to outsiders and little more than a standardized yet ever-changing ritual to themselves, not unlike the newest slang phrases of the slick advertising world that are dropped almost as soon as they become known and quickly replaced by others even newer.[10]

Here, too, the accent is on isolation from life, on cultism and incomprehensibility, on brainy human beings as bloodless thinking machines.

Reason and intellect have also been demeaned through the

---

[10] Charles Jackson, *The Outer Edges* (New York: Rinehart, 1948), p. 232.

glorification of blood, action and instinct. A chief literary exponent of this viewpoint was Sherwood Anderson. His characters feel a great deal and think hardly at all. They sense when things are right for them, or wrong, without any coherent notion of what or why. They are moved by the sudden, deeply lodged, unfathomable impulses that led Anderson himself to leave his post as manager of a paint factory in Ohio for the uncertain and obscure prospects of vagabondage, journalism and literature. His men and women fall in love because of vibrations set in motion between them, and out of it when the vibrations stop. Their souls, which move in rhythms and pulsations, yearn for other souls with a similar tempo. Borrowing from Ruskin and D. H. Lawrence, Anderson was convinced that the rhythm of the machine was out of key with the consciousness of men and, like Lawrence, he quested for the pulse of more primitive societies. The Negroes in his novel *Dark Laughter* are relaxed and free in a way that the tense straining whites are not. The whites are bundles of nerves: explosive, despondent, giving off a constant ominous crackling. Their world is all psychic sunlight and shadow, spurts of ecstasy and gloom. They have only the vaguest knowledge of why they feel as they do, of where they are going. Their surprise on their occasional moments of success partakes of the same bewilderment. They are engaged in a grim comedy of self-ignorance. Anderson's figures swarm with sensibility but they are singularly lacking in intelligence, and, without it, their stature as human beings shrinks to narrow proportions.

His work illustrates one main direction taken by those writers who flee from the rational and conscious mind, or seek to minimize it, whether under the influence of Freud or in revolt from the age of science and technology or while yearning for the static simplifications of primitivism where thought has no function and takes no root.

V

Ideas and learning, which are supposed to make men impotent, women sexless, and people in general mousy and withdrawn, have also been credited, in popular myths, with having the opposite effects. The man of ideas, in some configurations, is a dried-out, bookish, nearsighted stick, but in others he is seductive, dangerous and full of worldly temptations. The very title Professor acquired in nineteenth-century America overtones of rascality and cunning. Ross Lockridge, Jr., in his novel *Raintree County,* describes this association:

From the beginning Raintree County called him 'the Perfessor.' Johnny Shawnessy, some cuts above the other hicks . . . was careful always to preserve the first syllable pure, but the rest of the County said it perversely wrong; and even to Johnny this quaint distortion had an ideal fitness. For it was the same title that had been applied from time immemorial in the County to all the glib, fraudulent creatures who appeared at carnivals and festive anniversaries to sell hair tonic, quick success, and brand-new sexual potency to the common folk. Each of these egregious fakirs was known to his assistants and to the unschooled yokels as the Perfessor. It was a title of respect for an itinerant wizard who robbed the people by sheer power of language. Johnny had seen it happen a hundred times and never failed to enjoy the magnificently comic spectacle of a victory won by cunning from human hope and greed.[11]

His most potent shape has been the Devil, and the Devil, in nearly all versions, has been intellectually superior to God. The Serpent outwitted the Lord in the Garden of Eden, and took revenge for his fall from Heaven in Milton's *Paradise Lost* by corrupting Adam and Eve despite all God's efforts to the con-

---

[11] Ross Lockridge, Jr., *Raintree County* (Boston: Houghton Mifflin, 1948), pp. 147-8.

trary. As Mephistopheles, in the play by Marlowe, the poem by Goethe and the opera by Gounod, he has little trouble buying the soul of Faust and carrying it off to eternal damnation. The Devil is always a brilliant fellow, full of ideas and stratagems, ingenious and inventive, running rings around God in sheer intellect. God is ultimately triumphant because of his goodness, which in direct clashes proves mightier than the cunning of Lucifer. The struggle between them is posed in terms of the struggle between morality and brains, these two elements being conceived as not only separable but antagonistic. Theologically, braininess has acquired a distinct flavor of wickedness. Intellectual brilliance, at the very least, is something to be distrusted.

The clash of heaven and hell has its counterpart on earth, where the war between goodness and intellect has been as fiercely waged. Its symbols are everywhere in literature, in the struggle between the monstrously intelligent and wicked Iago and the good and stupid Othello, Edmund and Gloucester, Blifil and Tom Jones, Julien Sorel and the conventional world he assaults. The contest has found its way even into the pages of cowboy fiction. The popular horse operas of Max Brand deal frequently with the clashes between Barry Christian, the wicked but highly intellectual criminal, and Jim Silver, the essence of untiring virtue. Silver's strength and goodness invariably defeat Christian's wiliest stratagems, though the crook always survives to provide the impetus for another book.

The act of thinking carries with it not only the suggestion of villainy,[12] but also elements of riskiness and danger distinct from

---

[12] In the most recent film version of *The Three Musketeers,* Richelieu, the chief villain, says to Milady de Winter, his chief assistant: "We will defeat our enemies because we think and plan, whereas they are only creatures of impulse." Or words to that effect. At any rate, he allies himself with superior brains, whereas the heroic persons are only impulsively good. Needless to say, the impulsively good win out. Dumas himself did not arrange things so neatly. His D'Artagnan is brainy as well as agile. The Hollywood D'Artagnan is merely agile.

questions of morality. Thinking has nearly always got people into trouble. It has led them to doubt prevailing notions, to probe into unknown territory, or to challenge convictions long accepted as valid. One never knows where thinking is headed for or where it will wind up. It is therefore risky, dangerous and probably antisocial. Many of the martyrs of history, beginning with Socrates, were men dedicated to thinking regardless of consequences, who ran counter to the institutions of their society. The suspicion directed today against the use of brains has a long historical accumulation. Let us not analyze things too closely, we are told; what we find may not be altogether agreeable, it might make us dissatisfied, turn us into skeptics, radicals, heretics, atheists. At the very least, thinking is sure to make us restless, in itself an undesirable state since it is a prelude to agitation and worse.

Side by side with being a dull impractical fellow, the man of ideas is also presented as dangerous and intellectually seductive. In this second role wickedness and a rebellious spirit cling to him in about equal measure. Too much grubbing in musty books will turn him into a devil-ridden Faust. Too much monkeying with test tubes will create Frankenstein's monster. Too much speculative peering through a telescope will produce Galileo and all the trouble he gave the authorities of his day. Too much brainwork will transform the thinking man into either an absent-minded fogy or a community menace. As the first, he can be ignored; as the second, he must be suppressed. The recorded past and the active present chronicle the multitude of these ignorings and suppressions, and have nourished the widespread conviction that men who live too much with ideas are somehow not balanced or normal. The curious and contradictory variety of sins ascribed to them suggests the illogic of this conviction, and gives it a prominent place among the prevailing distortions of intellectual activity.

VI

High on the list of prevailing myths with regard to the intelligence is the belief that it breeds unhappiness. An advanced I.Q. is supposed to bring with it a greater capacity for boredom, a higher incidence of neurotic traits, an increased susceptibility to illness, and a lessened adjustability to the strains of modern living. A rash of magazine articles have devoted themselves to this theme, quoting heavily from psychological experiments of one sort or another which sought to demonstrate that people are better off without brains. An article by John E. Gibson in *Collier's,* significantly called "It's Smart to Be Stupid," characterized the lot. It begins on a note of easy finality:

Science has discovered that in many ways it's better to be stupid than to have plenty of stuff on the ball. In fact it would appear, in the light of the most recent findings, that a high I.Q. is a definite liability. . . .

If you're slightly weak in the brain box, you're likely to be happier and live longer. You'll recover from illness quicker, be able to get along with a lot less sleep, be less subject to boredom and insomnia—and you'll even be able to drive an automobile better.

The guy who moves his lips when he reads is better able to adjust to the stresses and strains of modern living than his brainier brother, psychologists have discovered.

It continues by asserting that individuals of high intelligence have more automobile accidents, develop a greater number of chronic ailments and are socially maladjusted. Which leads with irresistible logic to the conclusion that morons are better off than normal persons:

Dr. R. J. Reeves Kennedy, professor of sociology at Connecticut College, made a survey of hundreds of typical morons from various walks of life. Their I.Q.s ranged from 50 to 75. . . . Dr. Kennedy found that the morons were making just as much money, and adjusted themselves just as well to society as did nonmorons. And she found that the typical female moron was actually making *more money* than the normal women workers. . . . The survey showed that the typical moron has a congenial job, a good home and family; has a radio and telephone, reads the newspapers and magazines, and lists the movies as his favorite form of entertainment. The typical male moron is a semiskilled worker, and frequently earns *more* than slightly over $50 a week—the national average for industrial workers.[13]

This attitude—that being intelligent is undesirable—is widespread, and runs through many layers of American life. In politics men with disinterested ideas are generally regarded as a bit cracked; they are troublemakers who do not observe the rules of the game. Abstract thinking among politicians is enough to make faithful machine followers shudder, and violates one of the oldest and best-established taboos. In the Presidential campaign of 1952 the supporters of Adlai Stevenson feared that his speeches were too "brainy" and over the heads of the electorate, while his Republican opponents referred scornfully to him and his highly educated speech writers as "egg-heads." Independent and original thought is seldom rewarded in political life, and rare are the figures who hook them together into a working combination.[14]

Nor is ordinary, day-to-day living free of the feeling that thought somehow leads to misery. The antirational element present in the common saying "You'll go nuts if you think too much about it" is accepted as true without much scrutiny. Troubles will pass more quickly if they are not examined too closely, is the implication, as though examining them, reflecting

---

[13] *Collier's,* February 5, 1949.

[14] One is hard put to name such figures: Woodrow Wilson, Franklin Delano Roosevelt, Adlai Stevenson; and only Roosevelt, least intellectual of the three, was fully successful.

on them, will somehow aggravate them and prolong their existence.[15] The act of closing off a part of oneself from contact with experience, to expose only a minimal surface to the outside world, is regarded as a short road to happiness, or at least to the absence of pain. This shortening of the personality, this psychological shrinkage, becomes an inevitable result of the attack, open or covert, upon the brain and its reflective powers; and insofar as it renders the wholeness of man impossible, it becomes at the same time an attack upon the functioning of the democratic idea with its concern for the fulfillment of the whole self.

Another sign of this attitude toward the high I.Q. is what educators refer to as "the problem of the bright child," as though intelligence in itself is a problem. The principal of a junior high school, in addressing the parents of a group of superior children, remarked: "I feel sorry for you parents of bright children," and "There's a little girl in this school with an I.Q. of 162, poor thing. Yes, I say poor thing, because she's cut off from the rest of us." The implication was that the "rest of us," fortunately of only average intelligence, are normal, happy and well-balanced, while the superior child is a maladjusted freak.

The association of brains with neuroticism, eccentricity and queerness is in plain view elsewhere in the American scene. Though we are a mechanically curious, gadget-minded people, our attitude toward inventors is wonderfully perverse. Inventors are the real professionals of a mechanical society; one would expect them, of all people, to be regarded with respect, if not actual reverence. Yet few groups are more scorned. Until, that

---

15 On a literary level the same result emerges from the image of Hamlet "sicklied o'er by the pale cast of thought," as though Hamlet's tragedy consists of his thinking too much. His dilemma is cited as the familiar one of the intellectual, constantly forced to inactivity by the inhibiting drag of his intelligence.

is, their inventions succeed, at which time they become garlanded heroes instantly escorted to the hall of fame, where they are set up as exemplars for future generations of boys to envy and emulate. Before an invention is commercialized, however, the inventor must be prepared for calumny. He is a crank, crackpot, dabbler, nut; he is a fool slightly tilted toward the bughouse; he is an irresponsible loafer probably neglecting his wife and children; he just isn't right in the head. But the minute he hits the jack pot, these accusations are washed away and forgotten in a flood of acclaim. His eccentricity has been known all along to be a sign of genius. His impracticality has become vision; his neglect of loved ones concealed a desire to win for them a greater security; his indifference to criticism is no longer a mark of footlessness but of courage. So long as the inventor has only his brains, he will be labeled with contemptuous epithets, from harmless crank to raving lunatic. Only the successful marketing of his product can save him, and by then his brains are no longer relevant. From the days of Poor John Fitch and his early experiments with the steamboat on down to our own time American history swarms with rejected inventors, most of whom went scorned to their graves.

Even in juvenile books the ingenuities of invention are seldom encouraged for their own sake. The most famous boy inventor in our literature, Tom Swift, has a shrewd business head on his shoulders, and it is doubtful if he would have long survived without one. At an early stage of a career that extended through forty-odd volumes, he set up a corporation called the Tom Swift Enterprises, not only to prevent his inventions from falling into the hands of piratical promoters, but to provide his own activities with a constant supply of funds. These activities carry him on adventures to the far corners of the globe, with his current invention in tow. Through its use at the critical moment the villains are upended, and Tom returns to his home base with the invention proved and ready for mass manufacture. Enough varieties of bicycles, airplanes, automobiles, radar equipment, radio and searchlight devices and scores of other items have emerged from Tom's teeming brain to fill a mail-order catalogue, all of them ready for the merchandising process at the end. Without this process Tom Swift might have been the embodiment of the pure inventor, but he would have been less characteristic of the social scene, and in all probability much less popular.

To make absolutely sure that no intellectual taint clings to Tom, he is made handy with his fists, resourceful in physical difficulties, and courageous in tight spots. His activities as an inventor are always quickly siphoned off into melodrama, so that Tom will be in no danger of acquiring the pasty complexion and remote look of the laboratory experimenter. He has none of the moods commonly associated with the scientific recluse, being cheerful, frank, courteous, and quick to answer any call to action however muted. Nothing is permitted to interfere with the impression of manliness that he exudes and no pains are spared to make him an unimpeachable example of the ideal American boy: at home in the world of mechanics, an eye always cocked on the main chance, a sense for the concrete and practical so strong that he never wastes time or gets caught in blind alleys of pure theory or abstract research leading to no place in particular. His tie with brains is hedged in with numerous protective devices, themselves ingeniously arranged and elaborated, so that it becomes not a passionate relationship but a passing flirtation. Finally, he never works up an intellectual sweat. At the beginning of each book he emerges from the laboratory, his latest gadget already perfected, whatever problems or difficulties he encountered entirely behind him, and indeed never specified. The great drama of a new invention coming to birth, with all the obstacles that must be overcome, the false turnings retraced, the brave persistence put to a supreme test, is deliberately omitted. Tom lives in a world not of mental toil but of physical application, and is careful never to mix the two. Through the exercise of such care he avoids the neuroticism that is supposed to attend all but the mildest intellectual effort, and qualifies as an acceptable representative of that intensely material environment which he exploits on the juvenile level. He thereby enjoys the titillating attractions of thought without seriously risking its arduousness. Here lies the key to his easy popularity, suggesting at the same time the kind of inventor the public is prepared to embrace without reservation.

The laboratory, the inside of which Tom cannily avoids in the presence of his readers, has occupied a place almost equivalent to that of the classroom in American esteem. Important discoveries might occasionally emerge from it, but the men who labor there are pale bloodless shadows of the real thing. In general, the indoors has never been able to hold its own with the outdoors in the race for popularity in the New World. Since brainworkers, by the very nature of their trade, operate indoors almost exclusively, they have been looked on as people out of touch with reality, their life-giving sources somehow dried up. In *The Web and the Rock,* Thomas Wolfe demonstrated this feeling in one of his typical outbursts:

There are some people who have the quality of richness and joy in them and they communicate it to everything they touch. It is first of all a physical quality; then it is a quality of the spirit. With such people it makes no difference if they are rich or poor: they are really always rich because they have such wealth and vital power within them that they give everything interest, dignity, and a warm color. . . .

Those who have this quality are the young policemen sitting in shirt-sleeves in the all-night eating places, taxi drivers with black shirts, prize fighters, baseball players, and racing drivers, brave and gentle people; steel workers sitting astride a giddy spar, locomotive engineers and brakemen, lone hunters, trappers, most shy and secret people who live alone, whether in the wilderness or in a city room; in general, all people who deal with sensuous things, with what has taste, smell, hardness, softness, color, must be wrought or handled—the builders, the movers, the physical and active people, the creators.

The people who do not have this quality are the people who rustle papers, tap keys—the clerks, the stenographers, the college instructors, the people who eat lunch in drug stores, the countless millions who have lived meagerly in pallor and safety.[16]

Brainwork puts one out of touch with the sensuous and physical, thereby snapping off the connection between man and Nature. Little wonder that those who work with paper by artificial light, who concentrate on their minds and allow their bodies to atrophy through disuse, lose the co-ordination and balance potential to all men. They do not function in space. Space has been the dominant dimension of American history, and remains so today (though with diminishing force) despite the closing of the frontier with its intoxicating promise of free land. Time, memory, thought—the indoor dimensions—are just beginning to acquire meaning and prestige as a result in part of the overpowering dilemmas of the century, but they still play second fiddle to space, in its now industrialized but no less muscular context.

The laboratory scientist, no less than the inventor, is thought to be a "nut" when engaged on an inquiry whose usefulness and success are not immediately evident. The experiences of Martin Arrowsmith in Sinclair Lewis' famous novel are exact illustrations of the point. So long as Arrowsmith is willing to allow his medical investigations to be halted at any given stage, poured into bottles and marketed, he makes money and advances in the hierarchy of his profession. Whenever he refuses to interrupt a line of clinical inquiry before its final scientific resolution, he loses ground. These contests between money and truth, practice

---

16 Thomas Wolfe, *The Web and the Rock* (New York: Harper, 1939), pp. 377-79.

and theory, materialism and integrity, occupy the whole of the book. At last, in order to devote himself to his research, Arrowsmith is forced to give up all thoughts of professional advancement, the comforts of money and the warm glow of public approval, and withdraw to an isolated rural laboratory. He wins in a sense, but at a heavy cost which Lewis makes no effort to play down. He is at last willing to be jeered at by the successful practitioners, resigned to the prospect of appearing to most of his contemporaries as that most pitiable of specimens, the misguided idealistic crank.

The pressures of the second World War leading to the manufacture of the atom bomb catapulted the academic scientist into a national spotlight he had never before enjoyed. Let the scientist produce something of definite use, like a super war weapon or a sure cure for cancer, and his work becomes understandable and acceptable, with a corresponding rise in his status. But results must be immediate, visible and practical.

Yet even in his practical success with atomic energy he was treated as not quite responsible, as not wholly grown up. Frantic efforts were made by "practical" people to put the scientist under some sort of supervision, supervision by almost anybody being preferable to letting him continue on his own. First it was proposed that the physicists be controlled by the military men, whom nobody could accuse of not being realistic and down-to-earth. This ran up against the traditional aversion to turning over civilian affairs to the Army, and so was abandoned. Strong pressure was then exerted to turn atomic energy over to private business. The industrialists would surely see to it that the absent-minded, unpractical scientists did not endanger the nation's safety. In the end a government agency under civilian control was set up to handle the project.

It took the horrors of the atom bomb to shake the public loose from its old contempt for the pure scientist. But though his work received a new respect, he himself was considered—after the first shock wore off—as still somewhat unfit for the rough-and-tumble realities of everyday life. This was conspicuously true of the public attitude toward Einstein. Immediately after Hiroshima, his public statements received a wide hearing, but as time went on his social and political—that is, nonscientific—pronouncements were attended with diminishing interest. The feeling that scientists, at least outside their laboratories, were naïve and a bit softheaded was soon re-established.

The coupling of brainwork with emotional unbalance applies with particular force to women. The female intellectual, whether she be a schoolteacher, doctor, lawyer, or magazine editor, is notoriously the object of ridicule and pity in America. The old regressive belief that woman's place is in the home, where thinking is the least of her activities, underlies this attitude. In each instance the professional woman is supposed to pay a heavy emotional price for her career, her womanly side drying up in some way so that the role intended for her by Nature (benevolent and all-wise) is subverted. This is assumed to be self-evidently true of the schoolteacher, with her traditionally spinsterish attributes. In the popular view the female lawyer-doctor, if married, usually steps on the ego of her husband to the extent of either destroying him as a man or making their cohabitation intolerable. More often she is not married, wishing to pursue her career without distraction, which in time makes her severe, mannish, tailored in an unfeminine way. As a magazine editor (a favorite incarnation in movies and slick magazine stories), she may be flip, bright, sophisticated, but she is emotionally mixed up and her nerves are giving her trouble. A neat portrait of this stereotype appears in Moss Hart's musical, *Lady in the Dark*, where the heroine, an enameled and enormously successful editor, is as confused and immature as an early adolescent, fails to recognize her true love though he dangles prominently before her eyes, and has to be led out of her maze through a most complicated, psychoanalytic, dream-interpreting labyrinth. Here again the effect of brainwork is the breeding of nervous and destructive disorders.[17]

If the female intellectual is thought to be off key for one reason, the male of the species is regarded as equally off for another. In his appearance as artist or writer, bohemia still clings to his image. No matter how many instances of perfectly "normal" painters and composers there may be, leading perfectly uncolorful and unpicturesque existences, the impression persists of free love, explosive and irrational temperament and repudiation of the ordinary habits of society. The films, with their endemic impulse to jazz up everything they touch, have reinforced this impression. Every composer whose "life" has been done on the screen has had a raging temper, a rapt look on his face when playing or listening to music, and an excitable voice. Nor does the kind of music he composes make much difference. Beethoven, Gershwin and Jerome Kern possess the same qualities, in slightly altered combinations. Each in his movie version is distinctly not the type the movie-going American would care to have in his living room more than once.

The painter is also looked on as an unstable character, with overtones of those unwholesome figures Van Gogh and Gauguin. Moreover, there is something suspiciously foreign about him, more particularly something French since Paris is where all aspiring artists learn to paint, and France has long been considered the vortex of everything un-American in the realms of manners, morals and art. Since he deals in a medium which is often difficult to understand, it is all the easier to think of him as being out of normal focus.

The writer is better off in this respect than his fellow crafts-

---

[17] Nor does this popular imagining lack scientific supporters. From time to time tracts have appeared imploring women to return to the home. A most uncompromising example was *Modern Woman: The Lost Sex,* by Ferdinand Lundberg and Marynia F. Farnham, in which careers were attacked as the deadly enemies of the healthy, well-balanced woman, and the female argued back to the position she occupied in the Middle Ages.

men, not because of anything in himself, but because his medium is more comprehensible to the world at large. Since he can be read by almost everyone in an age of growing literacy, he appears less strange and eccentric. The market for his wares being larger, his chances for commercial success are brighter, which adds considerably to the respectability of his profession. Yet even he is a long way from enjoying the status of the doctor or engineer, not to speak of the businessman, and the core of the old prejudice that he too is not quite all there remains intact. No self-respecting parent would think of raising his child to be a writer. If American literature (or Hollywood) is any guide, no child has ever grown up to become one without a fierce battle with whoever was responsible for his upbringing. If he finally makes a living at it, it is in the face of the world's indifference. More likely he doesn't, in which case he becomes embittered, cynical, ill-natured, and ripe for the disturbances popularly associated with the arts. Or else he gives up the literary life and reverts to normal, becoming an insurance man, running an automobile agency, taking charge of Dad's business, or doing something equally respectable. He loses his feverish, wild-eyed look; his tousled hair is now properly combed; his rumpled clothes are properly pressed; he begins wearing ties and hats. The transformation of the agitated writer with his tortured visions and erratic conduct into the wholesome, well-balanced man harmonizing with the American scene is now complete.

All these distorted views reveal, from a variety of angles, the distrust with which the intellectual life is regarded in America. It is as though that life were held up to a cracked looking glass. The reflected images bear little resemblance to the reality, or at best are exaggerations of it. But so long as they are accepted as accurate, the creative and thinking man will continue to be looked on with suspicion and will function under a cloud.

Chapter III

Myths of Wealth and Poverty

I

PARADOXICALLY, WORSHIP OF MATERIAL SUC-
cess in America exists side by side with the feeling that wealth
is somehow corrupting. The pursuit of money has long been
regarded as incompatible with the quest for ideas and truth.
That the one often interferes with the other is self-evident, and
the conflict has appeared in a series of familiar alternatives. In
many a story and movie, the theme of the artist who must choose
between cultivating his muse while starving in a garret and
abandoning his integrity in order to paint shallow but lucrative
portraits, has been worked out with many variations. Equally
popular, as Sinclair Lewis demonstrated in *Arrowsmith*, has
been the situation of the doctor who must decide between a rich
fashionable practice and the economically unrewarding pursuit of scientific truth in an isolated laboratory. There is also
the writer who is torn between making a lot of money in Holly-

wood and living from hand to mouth in a miserable furnished room while writing the great American novel; apparently he can't do both.

The old adage about "selling one's soul for a mess of pottage" expresses the long-held conviction that wealth is often acquired at the expense of integrity. This belief has led to clichés that have gained wide currency and served to split Americans into hostile frames of mind. One is the notion that the rich man is *per se* greedy and wicked, has in every case made his money by exploiting the poor, and seeks only to make more of it at everybody's expense. This was a favorite tenet of the Populists and other agrarian reformers after the Civil War, and survives to this day in the widespread rural distrust of Wall Street. During campaigns political candidates talk warningly about "the interests" without subjecting them to close scrutiny, and it is doubtful that either the speakers or their listeners have any clear idea of who "the interests" are. The image of the skinflint banker, to observe the same attitude in another form, has long been popular in our literature and folklore and widely stereotyped in the movies.[1] During the hearings in October 1947 by the House Un-American Activities Committee, then investigating subversive influences in Hollywood, some of the witnesses claimed that this movie image was a Communist idea and hence un-American —a notion even more absurd than the literal application of the image itself. The image existed in the American imagination long before Lenin was even heard of—there are numerous traces of it in that peculiarly American phenomenon, Horatio

---

[1] The bankers themselves have always been sensitive to this unflattering public image and have tried whenever possible to alter it. The Manufacturers Trust Company publicized, in a special ceremony, the cancellation of a note to its millionth borrower. Said the overcome borrower: "Banking is a wonderful thing. A man can walk in and borrow money just on his name." Said the bank's vice-president: "This makes clear that modern banking is not ledger cards, but people." The New York *Times,* October 30, 1952.

Alger—and it bears about as much relationship to reality as its familiar corollary: that people are better off without money.

The distrust of the moneyed man is an old and deep-seated idea which goes back at least as far as the Bible.[2] The frontier was a fertile breeding ground for the feeling that a man of modest means was probably honest; the man who was well-heeled had no doubt acquired his money through skulduggery that ranged from gambling and bushwhacking to cattle rustling and claim jumping. The aesthetic analogue to the moral view of the rich man appeared in the 1920s, during the heyday of Greenwich Village: poverty and the artistic life were looked on as synonymous, while the pursuit of money was felt to blunt one's finer feelings and lead to bourgeois vulgarity. But not until the movies of the 1930s took it up, and in picture after picture showed the rich to be neurotic and unhappy largely as a concomitant of their wealth, did the notion become popularly formalized. Its formalization was officially acknowledged in the skillful and famous comedy by Moss Hart and George S. Kaufman, *You Can't Take It With You.* Here, the poor Sycamores are marvelously and richly happy, while the rich Kirbys are sterilely miserable. The antithesis between them results in a decisive victory of the first family over the second.

One of the most persistent propagators in our literature of both these attitudes toward money has been John Steinbeck. Some of his novels romanticize poverty; others assail it and the rich bosses who are blamed for its existence. The first type is illustrated by *Tortilla Flat,* where the troubles overtaking the indolent and happy *paisanos* begin when Danny acquires property and becomes a landlord. Until then everybody had been lying in the Monterey sunlight, bathed in a blissful and idyllic haze. The moment they become entangled in money matters their idyl

---

[2] ". . . it is easier for a camel to go through a needle's eye, than for a rich man to enter into the kingdom of God." Luke, 18:25.

is shattered, their happiness evaporates, they break up into quarreling groups, and menace one another in a variety of primitive ways. In the end Danny's house burns down, an act of symbolic immolation which pauperizes his comrades and with one stroke restores them to their former bliss.

Cannery Row extends the Rousseauistic paradise of *Tortilla Flat,* the same *paisanos* appearing shuffled in slightly different combinations but with the same conclusions emerging in the end. In *The Wayward Bus* the heroic central figure is the economically rootless, primitive man who breaks away from his attachments when they threaten to subdue his natural instincts. And in *The Pearl* Steinbeck confronts us with the story of a poor Indian couple who discover a pearl of fabulous size and because of it are involved in a maze of greed and crime. Not until they return the pearl to the sea do their misfortunes come to an end. This tale is grim where *Tortilla Flat* is tender, but though appearing in different emotional contexts, the approach to wealth is much the same. This approach, indeed, goes back to Steinbeck's first novel, *Cup of Gold,* which dealt with Sir Henry Morgan, the buccaneer, who decided at the peak of his fortune that power and money weren't everything, and retired to poverty and obscurity, a happier man.

II

Yet far more widespread than antipathy to the rich and idealization of the poor is the exactly contrary attitude of judging a man's worth by his income. Among the myths of wealth and poverty prevailing in America, this is the more familiar criterion. Poverty may be idyllic in the eyes of some, but in the eyes of most it is shameful. It is a mark of incompetence and a measuring cup by which the respect that an individual merits can be doled out. It has a comparative as well as an absolute meaning.

The shame attached to poverty accrues to the relative state of being less well off: having a house smaller than the next man's, clothes that are less expensive, or worldly possesions of any kind on a slighter scale. It is all right to have money without brains. To have brains without money, however, is to invite pity and contempt. Since, according to the myth, everyone tends to sink or rise to his own true level economically, money, it is felt, is an accurate gauge of a man's quality.

In a society which accepts this criterion as a yardstick, the position of those to whom the accumulation of property is not a primary aim is bound to be doubly difficult. To start with, the man with disinterested ends, with a passion for learning or teaching or scientific research or the creation of art or social work or any sort of reform, will find the going hard and the recognition meager. The situation is aggravated by the refusal of society to pay him adequately, and then holding him in contempt for not making money. As a result he is forced into making a difficult choice which is all the more painful because it is arbitrary and misconceived.

As Mencken puts it in his deflationary way, the choice is scarcely a free one:

Only an overwhelming natural impulse . . . can urge an American into the writing of fugues or epics. The pull is toward the investment securities business. That pull, yielded to, leads to high rewards. The successful business man among us . . . enjoys the public respect and adulation that elsewhere bathe only bishops and generals of artillery. He is treated with dignity in the newspapers, even when he appears in combat with his wife's lover. His opinion is sought upon all public questions, including the aesthetic. In the stews and wine-shops he receives the attention that, in old Vienna, used to be given to Beethoven. He enjoys an aristocratic immunity to most forms of judicial process. He wears the *légion d'honneur,* is an LL.D. of Yale, and is received cordially at the White House.

The literary gent, however worthy, scales no such heights under our *Kultur.* . . . If they happen to be genuine artists . . . they are as lonely as life insurance soliciters at a convention of Seventh Day Adventists. . . .[3]

This has been one of the tragedies of life in America: mind and money go together so seldom that it is hard to cultivate oneself and amass property simultaneously. A recurring theme in the novels of Henry James—*The Wings of the Dove* notably— was that one could not live decently without money and yet could not avoid corruption in the process of acquiring it. By corruption James meant a denial of one's integrity and a surrender of one's talent. No one can measure how much waste of human potentialities has resulted from the pressure of having to choose between the acquisitive and creative drives.

Gjon Mili, the cameraman, graduate of M.I.T. and author of twelve published scientific papers, was asked why he gave up scientific research in favor of photography. "I worked a whole year for Westinghouse's Research Department," he explained. "I abandoned research work not because I lost any faith in science, but because I discovered that in one afternoon of working with a camera I made more than Westinghouse paid me for a whole year."[4]

In his novel *Opus 21,* Philip Wylie protests angrily against a system that coddles trade and penalizes art:

Business is the lone God of our Congress. Let a man open a pie factory or begin to mold cement blocks and he becomes Privileged. His property is taxed as a sacred, eternal entity. His costs are deductible. Only the profit he pockets is thought of by our Congress as income; his every barrel of flour or bag of cement

---

3 H. L. Mencken, *Selected Prejudices* (New York: Knopf, 1927), pp. 120-1.

4 From the syndicated column by Leonard Lyons, New York *Post*, April 1, 1947.

is capital. But let a man create books or serials in his head and Congress sees him as a social inferior, a mere wage earner.

The accumulation of intellectual property for a book may require three-quarters of a life. Its sale, for a year or two, may be considerable. After that one book—or after two or three—an author may return to pittances. What he has written may become the mental and emotional capital of his countrymen, or of the world, for generations. Yet Congress does not deem it equal to pies or bricks and sometimes skims away in a year the whole capital of an author—as if it were but annual income. America bounteously provides for the makers of bricks and pies; it shortchanges book-makers and the winners of Nobel Prizes. Indeed, such is the unconscious hostility of the mob toward the fruits of intelligence that, not long ago, a group of representatives, commercial he-whores and contumelious morons, endeavored to do away with copyright altogether on the grounds that what a man thought and wrote down, or what he felt and painted, belonged free of charge to the whole people: noneconomic, since it was Art. To such men as these, only junk fabricators, gadgeteers, tram operators, pop bottlers and the like are entitled to the best profit for their contribution to life. History will note the fact when history writes how American avarice held in open contempt all culture and all thought, decerebrated itself and so died headless.[5]

Once money is set up as a criterion, our values automatically assume price tags. Fruitfulness and sterility are evaluated on a cash basis. Anything which produces money, whether by manufacturing a useless but salable gimcrack or persuading people to buy things they do not want or need or even, in some cases, should not have, is *per se* fruitful; activities which cannot be translated into money, such as reflection, meditation, the pursuit of creative impulses present in every person, one's self-realization as a human being, are considered sterile and unrewarding. College students wondering whether to major in history or Eng-

---

[5] Philip Wylie, *Opus 21* (New York: Rinehart, 1949), p. 13.

lish literature are often dissuaded by the question: what can you do with it when you get out? Does anyone want to write? It makes sense only if he aims at the jack pot. Would he enjoy teaching? There's more money in advertising. Careers, and indeed life experiences, are selected not on the basis of their personal satisfactions or social usefulness, but strictly in cash-register terms.

Our myths of wealth and poverty are often contradictory, but in actuality we prefer wealth even while glorifying the virtues of poverty. It may be the fashion to say that the rich are neurotic and unhappy. Bankers and millionaires may still be eyed suspiciously in the remoter rural areas where primitive Christianity remains strong. In Western farms and small towns Wall Street may continue to be a symbol of sin. But the attitude prevailing through most of America regards a low income as the badge of an inferior status, as the mark of shiftlessness, incompetence or failure.[6] Thoreau may be a great name in American literature but J. P. Morgan is a greater name in American life. The idea of doing anything for its own sake is regarded as idealistic folly, with the result that living tends to become narrowed into purely money-making channels, a tendency that only the stoutest souls, the most self-committed individualists are likely to resist. Since writers, teachers, artists run counter to the prevailing trend, and accumulate unimpressive amounts of worldly goods, the pressures and burdens upon them from public opinion increase correspondingly.

America's reputation for unfriendliness toward culture and the creative life springs in part from this attitude toward money and the economic discrimination against the noncommercial man.

---

[6] Except perhaps in times of external disaster, a great depression for example, when so many people from every social stratum are affected that the usual explanations of success and failure are temporarily suspended.

Chapter IV

The Artist:
Flight and Return

THE CREATIVE MAN IN AMERICA HAS OFTEN felt like a stranger in his own country. Its atmosphere has seemed hostile to the free and spontaneous expression of his ideas. The mechanical and commercial drives of American life have appeared to threaten the values for which he stood. The trend toward uniformity and away from individuality seemed to strip American civilization of the emotional richness and complexity which had always nurtured art. The artist felt that there was nothing here to write about and that even if there were, he would find no responsive audience among his own countrymen. Feeling like a fish out of water, he was often driven to leave his native shores and seek elsewhere the atmosphere, subject matter and encouragement which he felt were essential to his creative activities.

His exodus went into high gear after the Civil War. Before then the country was smaller and more homogeneous. The New England landscape blossomed with literary and intellectual groups. There were the Connecticut Wits and the Saturday Club. Great men had their circles and moved intimately in one another's company. This was the time of Emerson and the Transcendentalists, George Ticknor, William Ellery Channing and the Alcotts, famous Utopian experiments like Brook Farm —when even remorseless critics of American life like Thoreau found it possible to preserve their individuality while remaining at home.

With the end of the Civil War, the factory system which had so appalled Thoreau shot forward with tremendous strides, altering the face of the country, creating the Gilded Age with its new middle class given to ostentatious, vulgar and tasteless displays of wealth. The last frontiers were being conquered and began undermining the foundations of the New England synthesis by flooding the settled East with the raw energies and newly won fortunes of the rough, uncultured West. This change greatly complicated the position of writers, artists and men of ideas who felt themselves more and more cut off from the main channels of the new order. Herman Melville and Walt Whitman, after their early successes before the Civil War, spent the later decades of their lives in obscurity, silence and public neglect. Mark Twain, whose happiest days were as a boy in the simple rural society of the Mississippi Valley, was never able to accept with his whole self the later world consumed by gross money values. " . . . in his later years," remarked V. L. Parrington in *Main Currents in American Thought,* "an impassable gulf opened between Mark Twain and his generation. . . . He reveals its crudity, its want of knowledge, discipline, historical perspective; its intellectual incapacity to deal with the complexities of a world passing through the twin revolutions of industrialism and science. . . . The buoyant humorist of the seventies ripened into the bitter satirist of the nineties."[1]

---

[1] V. L. Parrington, *Main Currents in American Thought* (New York: Harcourt, Brace, 1930), Vol. III, pp. 88-89.

A whole generation of American writers and artists found this new America so discouraging to their creative lives that they fled it altogether. William Wetmore Story abandoned one career as a lawyer in Boston to pursue another as a sculptor in Rome. Stuart Merrill settled in Paris, became an ardent member of the Symbolist school of poetry and wrote all of his verse in French. James McNeill Whistler moved to London before launching his celebrated career as a painter. Henry Adams found nineteenth-century America so distasteful that he fled all the way back to the Middle Ages where, in the cathedrals of the twelfth century, he found a unity and design which he felt his contemporaries had lost. The most famous of this first generation of expatriates, Henry James, looked on his own country as a vast cultural desert, painfully lacking in traditions and standards of taste. He not only left America as a young man, to wander about western Europe while maintaining residence in England, but wound up in his old age by relinquishing his American citizenship altogether and becoming a Briton.

This aesthetic shrinkage from the rough contours of their native country made this whole group the targets of severe criticism. Somerset Maugham attacked James for turning his back on the thrilling spectacle of the geographic and economic conquest of his own land. Van Wyck Brooks, in his biography *The Pilgrimage of Henry James,* spoke of his retreat with equal disapproval. It was during this time and partly as a result of this withdrawal that the association of the intellectual life with foppishness and effeminate nonvirility sprang up, aggravated by the ruthlessness of frontier existence and the sudden markup in value of every kind of physical conquest.

By the turn of the century, the frontier phase had come to an end, the continental expansion of the country had reached its final limits, and there was a pause for stocktaking. The great industrialists were riding higher and wider than even in James's youth, making them visibly easier to blame for the ills of

society than a generation earlier. The literary figures made
a sharp about-face and rushed into the fray with as much
speed as their predecessors had retreated from it. Dreiser, Frank
Norris, Jack London, Upton Sinclair, Lincoln Steffens and the
rest of the new realists rolled up their sleeves and plunged into
an enthusiastic wrestling with the social evils of the time. An
odor of masculinity exuded from them as pungent and excessive
as the odor of femininity exuding from James and Adams. Cults
of the primitive he-man,[2] notably in Jack London, flourished
among them. Far from being daunted by the crudeness of industrial life, they were intoxicated by it, and with the zeal of all
early social reformers, proposed to reshape it to suit their idealistic ends. Though their writing was perhaps more effective as
sociology than as literature, they performed a greater feat in
public relations by halting, if not actually reversing, the "sissi-
fication" of the artist in the public mind.

Despite their efforts, however, the domination of American
life by purely commercial values went on relatively unimpeded
through the years of the first World War and the 1920s and
produced the second wave of expatriate artists, whom Gertrude
Stein called "the lost generation." Their immediate forerunners,
whose influence they fervently acknowledged, had taken up residence abroad because they found the European atmosphere less
provincial, more conducive to the free operation of mind and
art. Ezra Pound was born in Idaho, but became a kind of international cultural traveler, pollenizing and cross-fertilizing
dozens of poetic and artistic movements and coteries. He became so consumed with hatred for his own country that he wound
up his career during the second World War as a radio propa-

---

2 The heroine of one of Frank Norris's early novels, *Moran of the Lady Letty*,
is a kind of primitive he-woman. She is the skipper of a Pacific cargo vessel,
tough, aggressive, muscular, yet withal a woman. The characters of the fiction of
the early 1900s are all in excellent physical condition.

gandist for Mussolini, urging American troops to lay down their arms. Gertrude Stein transferred herself at an early age to France where she remained for the rest of her life, a catalytic center for the streams of young artists and writers who came under her influence. T. S. Eliot, born in Missouri and educated at Harvard, preferred the life of a bank clerk in England to that of a college professor in America and, like Henry James before him, became a British citizen, and based the bulk of his poetry and all of his plays on English themes and settings.

Their younger followers, "the lost generation" itself, were hard hit by the first World War. The war destroyed many of the old values and traditions, loosened others, and paved the way for the restless and rebellious anxieties of the 1920s. With the end of the war the United States passed into the feverish atmosphere of the boom, which the younger writers felt to be a latter-day equivalent of the Gilded Age that had embittered Twain and discouraged James. The country seemed once again so engrossed in money-making on a huge and accelerating scale that there appeared no room for art or thought or self-realization. Once again the artist felt deeply alienated from the life of his country. Malcolm Cowley, an active member of this new generation, described this alienation in *Exile's Return:*

All during the 1920s, many, and perhaps most, of the serious American writers felt like strangers in their own land. They were deeply attached to it, no matter what pretense they made of being indifferent and cosmopolitan, but they felt obscurely that it had rejected them. The country in those days was being managed by persons for whom they felt a professional hostility. It was the age when directors' meetings were more important than cabinet meetings and when the national destiny was being decided by middle-aged bankers and corporation executives. One saw their pictures week after week in the slick-paper magazines; they wore high collars and white-piped waistcoats beautifully tailored over little round paunches. Sometimes they assumed a commanding look, sometimes they tried to smile, but their eyes were like stones in their soft, gray, wrinkled cheeks.

These rulers of America, as they were called in magazine articles, showed little interest in books or ideas. . . .[3]

In addition to their sense of rejection, the lost generation found America barren of ideas, subjects, experiences worth dealing with. They were not only unstimulated but acutely bored by a society dominated by the Babbitts, Bible-belters and Booboisie that Sinclair Lewis and H. L. Mencken were presently to lampoon. Feeling rebuffed by their own country and gasping for creative air, they began frantically searching abroad for themes and sensations which they were unable to find at home. These they pursued with a recklessness and a sensual ardor altogether lacking in the activities of the Jamesian group. Ernest Hemingway, bellwether of the new exiles, displayed an extraordinary passion for boxing, bullfighting, big-game hunting and war. He sought in other countries and among primitive peoples a virility, a closeness to the intensities of life and death which seemed less vibrantly present in America. Other exiles, like E. E. Cummings, Henry Miller, Elliot Paul, Harold Stearns and Kay Boyle, traveled abroad or settled in foreign countries because they found their own stuffy, puritanical, crassly bourgeois, or stifling to the soul.

In this exodus, many settled in Paris which became a center of operations even for those who did not stay in one place but traveled restlessly through France, Spain, Africa. They found in Paris, as artists had found for centuries, their spiritual home. It was a city that had always swarmed with painters, writers, café philosophers, magazines expressing every shade of opinion. Wars and natural disasters appeared to make little difference.

---

[3] Malcolm Cowley, *Exile's Return* (New York: Viking, 1951), pp. 214-215.

The moment Paris was liberated and the Germans driven out of France in the last year of World War II, the country broke out into a familiar rash of movements, fresh philosophies of which the most widely publicized was Existentialism, new literary schools, and a great lively intellectual boiling.

What was endemic in France had obtained only irregularly in the United States. Our atmosphere had not been generally conducive to the flowering of the inner life. Our great cities had not fostered meeting places for the writers or salons for the artists. Sidewalk restaurants had not encouraged the fore-gathering of philosophers. An occasional Hotel Algonquin appeared to nourish Alexander Woollcott, F. P. A., and the genteel wits of a brief period; an occasional Mabel Dodge Luhan kept open house for apprentices and celebrities in the arts; localized centers of aesthetic activity like Taos, Woodstock, Provincetown, Bucks County, had sprung up but they were few and far between and tended to become quickly commercialized.

The exiles also found abroad public encouragement and social approval for what they were doing. Foreign artists, writers, educated men generally, may not have been paid any better than their American counterparts, but they enjoyed far more prestige. A professor at the Sorbonne or at any French *lycée* had a social position in the community considerably higher and more secure than the college professor in America. In pre-Hitler Germany the formally educated man was held so much in esteem that every civil servant, petty clerk, newspaperman, coveted the title Herr Doktor, which was carrying such respect to as snobbish an extreme as the converse American attitude. The contrast in its most acute form was expressed in the bitter comment of Henry Miller, himself an American expatriate writer of many years' standing: "America is no place for an artist. A corn-fed hog enjoys a better life than a creative writer."

Not all the artists in the 1920s left the country. Most of them stayed home. But many of those who remained behind expressed their sense of alienation in their writings about the American scene. Thomas Wolfe's early works were a frenzied record of this alienation. Hart Crane's poems struggled tortuously with the harsh contours of a world he was not quite able to master. Ring Lardner's short stories were savage records of his antipathy to the professional sports, lower-middle-class world in which he lived and moved. H. L. Mencken heaped an unending stream of ridicule on every aspect of American civilization. Willa Cather shrank from the era of industrialization symbolized by the repulsive and rapacious figure of Ivy Peters in *A Lost Lady,* an era which had swallowed the frontier she had idealized in *My Antonia.*

For every Robert Frost who was deeply attached to New England, for every Ellen Glasgow who grew with time more firmly embedded in her native Virginia, there were dozens who felt that they and their country were out of joint. There were more poets like Robinson Jeffers who, though remaining fixed in one place, repudiated the materialist civilization of their native land, than like Carl Sandburg or Archibald MacLeish who, in the tradition of Whitman, stressed the potentialities of American life. There were more playwrights like Eugene O'Neill who emphasized the horrors of the modern world than like Robert E. Sherwood who proclaimed the greatness of the democratic spirit. There were more novelists like F. Scott Fitzgerald who recoiled from the frenzies of the Jazz Age even while recording them, than like Joseph Hergesheimer who fitted snugly into the times. As for the short-story writers, the norm was set by Katherine Anne Porter, who described the agonies of sensitive characters in disharmony with their environment. The main literary weight was in the direction of dislocation and impasse, as though the soul of the American writer were moving one way and the soul of the country another.

The painters and composers were in their special ways worse off than the writers. American literature since the first World War had won its independence from Europe. American art and music were still struggling to win theirs, and though native craftsmen were in individual cases gaining recognition and financial support, the position of the average American artist, in the face of overwhelming competition from abroad, was still far from secure. Where the painter could once rely on the interested patronage of the native aristocracy, in recent American history he had no such reliance. Dixon Wecter summarized this change in his book *The Saga of American Society:*

Society's patronage of painting in the United States has been acquisitive rather than creative. It has consisted largely in the purchase of Old Masters painted under the more virile stimulus of Italian princes and Dutch merchants of the Renaissance, and Tudor, Stuart, or Bourbon kings . . . .

In Colonial times the art of portrait-painting was richly supported by Society, and many artists were welcomed at aristocratic tables. . . . Benjamin West, of lowly Quaker stock, gained by his art the friendship of Governor Hamilton of Pennsylvania. . . . Charles Willson Peale started his career in desperate poverty as apprentice to a saddler; when art brought him fame and fortune he married Elizabeth de Peyster of New York. Gilbert Stuart, son of a New England snuff-maker, gained the patronage of the Duke of Northumberland and upon returning to America spent his later days as an honored guest of John Jay and the New York smart set. Today such rapid mounting in the social world through art is less possible.

In review the self-justifications of society in America are none too impressive. It has bought Old Masters, but fed few living artists. Its tastes in music and opera have been both timid and grandiose, and its patronage of literature has been negligible.[4]

---

[4] Dixon Wecter, *The Saga of American Society* (New York: Scribner's, 1937), pp. 469, 470, 482.

The position of the composers was equally precarious. Despite the phenomenal spread of symphony orchestras throughout the country and the growth of public interest in music, it was still possible, as late as 1948, for Huntington Cairns to observe: "In the United States we are confronted with the apparent fact that not a single composer is able to subsist by his serious work."

Gian-Carlo Menotti, himself one of the most successful of the younger composers, in writing "A Plea for the Creative Artist" in the New York *Times,* commented:

It is my contention that the average American has little or no respect for the creative artist and is apt to consider him as an almost useless member of the community. The average American father is still dismayed at the thought that one of his sons may choose to become a composer, writer, or painter. He will consider any such pursuit a sign of "softness," an unmanly and, I venture to say, an un-American choice. . . . No wonder that the young American artist is perhaps the most neurotic in the world and for generations has sought in Europe his spiritual home.[5]

This clash between the "useless" and "useful" members of the community, this antagonism between the artist and the businessman, reached its maximum point of inflammation during the great boom, and began to recede only with the explosions that brought it to a shattering end. The stock-market crash and the depression blew many established ideas sky-high. The captains of industry were toppled from their exalted places by the national calamity for which they had no remedy, and lost their grip on public opinion. For the first time in nearly a century people began turning to other avenues and directions for solutions to the problems of life. The sufferings and difficulties through which the country passed during the depression inevitably made

[5] The New York *Times,* June 29, 1952.

it more self-conscious, more responsive to serious examination of its ideals, institutions and ways of living. The larger movements of the heart began to be as engrossing as the smaller movements of the pocketbook.

With the weakening of the hitherto dominant commercial values, the atmosphere of the country appeared more favorable and attractive to its writers and artists. The difficulty of the times lent the altered scene an emotional significance, a tragic importance it had seemed totally lacking in before. For these reasons, as well as the drying up of their funds, the expatriates came trooping back from their islands of exile in Europe and Africa and merged with the main streams of American life with a new sense of involvement and responsibility.

The '30s and '40s saw the expatriate impulse die out almost entirely and marked a new stage in the return of the artist to the native scene. He plunged deeply and even enthusiastically into American problems and themes. F. Scott Fitzgerald came back from Europe and, after a series of heartbreaking personal experiences, wound up in his last unfinished novel writing about that uniquely American phenomenon, Hollywood. Thomas Wolfe, who had devoted his first three novels to describing how lost the individual was in America, devoted his fourth and last to a passionate demonstration of how he was found again. Sinclair Lewis, who had made a great reputation satirizing the American small town, now devoted himself to discovering its virtues. A whole new indigenous literature sprang up in which American society was analyzed and imaginatively re-created from the ground up.

The expatriates had complained that there was nothing in America to write about. But now they and the younger writers were discovering in the country challenging themes coming from every level of life and demanding treatment. James T. Farrell found in the lower middle class of Chicago enough dramatic material to last him a lifetime. Carson McCullers, Tennessee Williams and Eudora Welty discovered in Mississippi and Louisiana an enormous variety of human types, psychological situations and disturbed states of mind. There was even a change of attitude toward business life and its meanings. The salesman, ridiculed in the '20s as a miserable flunky embodying the worst characteristics of the commercial world, was portrayed by Arthur Miller in a celebrated tragedy of the '40s as a sympathetic and intensely human figure to whom "attention must be paid."

The rediscovery of the American present was accompanied by an equal rediscovery of the past. Henry James had accused America of lacking traditions and even a history. But that history was now being re-created and presented to an interested and responsive public in immensely meaningful terms. Stephen Vincent Benét wrote a long series of short stories dealing with the characters of American folklore. A whole school of historical novelists arose, led by Kenneth Roberts and Margaret Mitchell, who retold the significant events of our history. And even William Faulkner, who had labored for so long reconstructing the legends of the South since the earliest days of the Mississippi wilderness, was being acclaimed at mid-century by a public that had neglected him for twenty-five years. There was a tremendous revival of interest in American ballads and folk songs, marked by the numerous collections of B. A. Botkin, Carl Sandburg, and the Lomaxes. The emergence of ballad singers like Burl Ives and even the increasing number of native-born singers beginning to appear with the Metropolitan Opera were further evidence of America's awakening interest in her own culture and recognition of her own native talent.

A hundred years ago Nathaniel Hawthorne wrote from abroad: "I had rather be a sojourner in any other country than return to my own. The United States are fit for many excellent purposes, but they are certainly not fit to live in." This bleak sentiment, having been tested in many a pattern of exile, has now almost vanished, to be replaced, not by its opposite, but by the feeling that the United States, for all its surviving coolness to the artist and his viewpoint, has created a challenging and stimulating society. If that society is not always encouraging to him, it has at last provided him with complex themes and the intense emotional experiences which have made contemporary American literature, music and art rich centers of Western expression. In this way the return of the artist after his long period of flight has narrowed the gap between the American people at large and the creators of their own culture.

Chapter V

Diluted Studies and Harassed Teachers

I

THE AMBIVALENCE OF THE AMERICAN WITH regard to his culture is sharply evident in his attitude toward education. There are two mutually exclusive traditions with regard to education in America. One claims that the individual cannot grow into a mature and self-governing person without a well-rounded general education, which therefore becomes vital to the proper functioning of a democratic society. The other claims that formal education, as distinct from purely vocational or technical training, is not only of little use in solving the problems of life but is often a handicap when grappling with them. This group tends to look on the humane or, as they often put it, the "impractical" studies as without real value and therefore a luxury which the school system can ill afford. A variant of this group are those who believe that a humanistic education has a great value but that only a few are capable of profiting from it, while the many, if they are to be educated at all, should be trained only for jobs.

One result of these conflicting viewpoints has been to obscure the relationship between education and life. The vocationalist camp has driven educators into questioning whether traditional academic education is of any real use. They have half accepted the idea that, somehow, students are not living but only preparing for life, waiting until it begins, as though the span from five to twenty is a period of passivity that becomes active only with the granting of the last diploma. The acceptance of this notion has meant the consequent acceptance of education as something not justified in itself, requiring justification in terms of conditions outside itself. One reason for the vast and ineffectively challenged spread of vocationalism, and the consequent retreat of philosophy and literature, has been this view of education as worthy of existence only in demonstrably practical and tangible terms. This has backfired curiously. Seymour E. Harris in a New York *Times* article, "Millions of B.A.'s But No Jobs," suggests the time may come when there will be far more graduates than can be absorbed in business and the professions. He then concludes:

. . . our traditional attitudes toward higher learning may need to be re-examined. We profess to believe in higher learning for its own sake. Yet we expect a college degree to pay cash dividends, to open up greater economic opportunities. Perhaps we overstress the vocational gains.

It may be that we should stop putting so much emphasis in our own minds on the monetary value of a college education and put more emphasis on the intangible social and cultural values to be derived from learning. The time may be coming when we will have to start accepting the idea that education is life, not merely a preparation for it. As John Dewey put it, "Living has its own intrinsic quality and the business of education is with that quality." In any case, the graduates of the next generation will have to find more and more justification for their college education on other than economic grounds.[1]

The original aim of public education in America, preparing the young for citizenship in a democratic community, has been replaced in many instances by the nondemocratic concept of training the human unit solely for a specific job in the economic machine. The full development of the individual personality, accepted by the eighteenth-century political theorists as the goal of a democratic society, has been reshuffled into the narrower channels of material usefulness so that the development of mechanical skills rather than the whole personality has become the program of the day. This constitutes a narrowing not only of the educational focus but also of the democratic view and is a blow against the total culture which a democracy, in the largest sense, can be expected to produce. The full life must necessarily include the acquisition of economic skills; but it has many other resources as well, and to neglect them is to distort the powers and potentialities of the individual man.

Resistance to simon-pure vocationalism has taken several forms. Some, however, have been misguided and based on errors almost as great as the errors resisted. The hundred Great Books program, sponsored by the University of Chicago and St. John's College of Annapolis, has been the most ambitious and sharply reasoned of these. Based on the fanatical purity of the medieval curriculum, it rejects with inquisitional fervor every trace of education for practical use in the four undergraduate years. It believes that college should develop the intellectual resources of the individual so that he may see and understand the forces behind the world as a whole. He will then be ready for citizenship; and the mechanical training of professional and graduate schools will be less likely to narrow his vision of life. There is

---

[1] The New York *Times*, January 2, 1949.

a fascinating logic to all this quite in keeping with the admiration of Aristotle and the medieval thinkers which is a constant overtone of the program. An exposition of this logic is to be found in Richard M. Weaver's *Ideas Have Consequences*. Mr. Weaver attacks with ruthless scorn democracy, equalitarianism, the bourgeoisie, the machine age, nominalism, trust in the senses, the abandonment of absolutes, the newspapers, materialism, even modern war so different from the discipline and chivalry of medieval war—indeed everything that has occurred since the fourteenth century. His horror of the public in the mass sense permeates his view of education:

Nothing is more certain than that whatever has to court public favor for its support will sooner or later be prostituted to utilitarian ends. The educational institutions of the United States afford a striking demonstration of this truth. Virtually without exception, liberal education, that is to say, education centered about ideas and ideals, has fared best in those institutions which draw their income from private sources. They have been able, despite limitations which donors have sought to lay upon them, to insist that education be not entirely a means of breadwinning. This means that they have been relatively free to promote pure knowledge and the training of the mind; they have afforded a last stand for "antisocial" studies like Latin and Greek. In state institutions, always at the mercy of elected bodies and of the public generally, and under obligation to show practical fruits for their expenditure of money, the movement toward specialism and vocationalism has been irresistible. They have never been able to say that they will do what they will with their own because their own is not private. It seems fair to say that the opposite of the private is the prostitute.[2]

These ideas rest on the false assumption that training for a job is somehow degrading, the enemy of the young mind in search of truth. This aversion to materialism is as great a dis-

---

[2] Richard M. Weaver, *Ideas Have Consequences* (Chicago: University of Chicago Press, 1948), pp. 136-7.

tortion as the aversion of the practically-minded to theories and abstractions. It, too, repudiates a whole vital area of life. The assignment of philosophical purity to one object and not another stems from the same premise that leads to first and second-class citizens, "superior" and "inferior" people, and divisionalism everywhere. Experience cannot be divided into arbitrary categories. In seeking to do so, both the neomedievalists of the Great Books curriculum and the utilitarians who sneer so readily at "impractical" education, move in separate vacuums where the sounds of life, in all their fullness, are only dimly heard.

Other attempts to hold back the flood of commercialism from the schools have been less spectacular and intense than the monastic theories of the University of Chicago, but they have at least avoided the error of repudiation. The bold experiments at small colleges like Antioch and Bennington have sought to combine theory and practice in a way that promised, on paper at least, to merge these hitherto conflicting elements. Their pattern of alternating periods of study in the classroom with intervals of work in shops, studios and factories, has been a brave effort at settling the long war between the pro- and anti-theorists in education. The effort, however, has not been contagious. It has shown no signs of spreading away from the limited confines of a few experimental colleges, and has been looked on more as a freakish by-water than a forceful current in the huge sea of educational ideas.

There has been a general unwillingness on both sides to come to terms. The defenders of the humanities and the classical-discipline subjects have tended to build walls around themselves, and regard with outraged hauteur all proposals of alteration in deference to the changing times. They have given up some bastions, Greek and Latin notably, with grudging reluctance, and have fought for the others with unreasoning literalism. Their chief weapon, around which their arguments have mainly revolved, has been the word *discipline.* Foreign languages and literatures have been offered not so much because they might enable the student to become better informed about other peoples, but because they discipline the spirit. The same is true of English and American literature. Philosophy has been urged less because it supplies an integrated view of the world than because it sharpens the power to think in a logically disciplined way. Mathematics is presented not as a background to nuclear physics or the material world at large but as the greatest of all mental disciplines. The world is in need of humane discipline, but this arid application of the term only reawakens memories of the Puritan state, where discipline was a harsh weapon to flog dissenters into line, and self-control was glorified to the point of heartless frigidity. Clinging to old slogans which they have stubbornly refused to redefine, some of the advocates of the old-line subjects have been losing touch with the public, the times, the new generation, and have withdrawn to islands increasingly removed from the main shore.

The vocationalists and pragmatists have been equally loath to make reasonable concessions. Flushed with support from the business and industrial community, made reckless by the large inroads they have effected in the schools since the first World War, they have spread their ideas with a disregard for the damage done to education dedicated to the whole life. Jacques Barzun has posed both the problem and its solution in his book *Teacher in America:*

Technique, technology, routine, does no harm when applied to inanimate matter; on the contrary, it saves time and work and makes possible mass production. The danger is in aping the machine with our brains, in thinking like an assembly line, fed from a storeroom of cheap interchangeable parts. Clearly we are all impressionable enough to become robots, so that industrial slavery is not only a fact of the body which we must prohibit, it is a state of mind which we must forestall. There is only one way, which is to pit intelligence against it, to make a dead set for qualitative work, to strengthen the Mark Twain and Whitman tradition against factuality, to make education the proudest feature in the American personality, instead of an alien minority trait. For the purpose, we must get into the habit of distinguishing citizens from mere inhabitants, true engineers from "mere" engineers, business men with ideas from the hard-headed impervious kind, and the college-*trained* person from the standardized alumnus.[3]

But the advocates of technical instruction have demanded more and more of the curriculum, insisted that nothing be taught which was not provably and substantially useful, and put on the defensive every subject that could not visibly pass this test. Under the appealing banner of "every student must be trained to earn a living," they have blanketed the high schools with commercial courses, as contrasted with the dwindling academic ones, and attempted to turn the colleges into vast feeding mills for the professions and industries.[4] In the new vocationalism the ideas of William James and John Dewey, originally intended to develop the individual fully by bringing him into closer harmony with his environment, have found their most vulgarized fruit. Nothing is to be left in the schools unless it passes the test of "Does it work immediately?" and "Is it needed in the workaday world?" Will the study of Latin or history make

---

3 Jacques Barzun, *Teacher in America* (Boston: Little, Brown, 1945), pp. 309-10.

4 Accompanying the spread of vocationalism has been the growth of big-time athletics that has proved such a headache to the colleges. William G. Craig, Dean of Students and member of the Athletic Council at Kansas State College, believes that "collegiate sports began to get out of hand at precisely the time when our schools shifted their major emphasis from liberal education to vocational or professional training . . . at that point education may have lost some of its excitement, some of its ability to engage the whole man, and . . . the sports craze is an effort to overcome a certain boredom in lives devoted too exclusively to making a living." Quoted in "Basketball Madness," by Kenneth S. Davis, the New York *Times,* March 1, 1953.

a girl a better housewife? Will reading Shakespeare make a boy a better engineer?

Vocationalism has established numerous outposts in our schools and one of the largest of these, labeled "Education," has acquired a particular importance. This new force, equipped with a jargon and a *mystique* all its own, has mushroomed in recent years. In nearly all colleges Departments of Education have been set up and in some institutions have become the largest and most powerful in the school. Elementary and high-school teachers must take a growing number of courses in Education as prerequisites for a teaching license. Afterward, they are required to enroll from time to time in what are euphemistically called refresher or alertness courses in Education in order to win professional advancement or financial increments.

The subject of Education consists mainly of vocational methodology, with a light smattering of philosophy and theory. Its courses stress method rather than content. It deals with *how* something should be taught instead of *what*. It equips students with techniques instead of ideas, and seeks to make them mechanically efficient rather than educated. Even the philosophy and psychology of education, "idea" subjects of the greatest importance, are in actual practice limited to their relevance to methodology. No one would deny the value to prospective teachers of learning the techniques of their craft. But craftsmanship should be a tool, not an aim. And when Education pretends to be a liberal-arts subject, when it turns the ancient art of pedagogy into a collection of methods made arid by their divorce from content, it advances still farther the process by which the schools are being mechanized.

The enthusiasts of the program for turning the schools into training grounds for our economic machine, are the busiest agents of anticulture, and they operate, ironically, within what should be one of the cultural centers of society. For this reason they are more effective than the open enemies of democratic education who proclaim their enmity to it on the basis of Plato's famous argument that only the very few are fit for leadership and hence worth educating. These open enemies, though chronic, are in a minority since they go against the grain of a primary American conviction. But their allies within the schools, who hold to the corollary conviction that the many, if exposed to education, should be exposed only to the mechanics of a given vocation, are by no means doomed to remain a minority. Their point of view has an obvious plausibility. The insistence on the useful appears to have the sanction of the honorable and characteristically American philosophy of pragmatism. When the vocational program appears under a cultural and humanistic guise, as in the Schools and Departments of Education, it assumes a surface resemblance to the liberal, noncommercial arts, deceiving to the casual eye. And the great accent of the century on industry and technology, on mechanics and mechanical training, has given this program a tremendous social sponsorship. The respect accorded the man of general education a century ago has been shifted to the technician, the applied scientist, the engineer, all of whom are favored darlings of the new curriculum. The context and dynamism of the times have made them the graduates for whose services the bidding is liveliest and most lucrative.

The growing espousal of the mechanically efficient man not in terms of the man but in terms of his mechanical efficiency is inimical to the interests of a democratic society. It threatens the concept of the wholeness and many-sidedness of the human personality, which is surely one of the centers of the democratic idea. Democracy requires carefully thought-out moral values, an understanding of history and the role of government, and a development of the responsibilities of citizenship. These are the unique concern of the humane studies. It was a common complaint against Germany and German education that it produced men who were wonderful economic instruments but naïve and hence subject to prejudice and error in every other walk of life. The same tendency is to be seen in different forms in the Soviet Union where emphasis on mechanical ability and political propaganda are intermingled to produce masses of productive but blindly obedient citizens.

Nothing of the sort has appeared in England or France; and even Mussolini's Italy, which went in heavily for obedience, made little pretense of turning the Italians into economically efficient robots. But in the United States, the humane tradition, devoted to the reasoning powers of the individual man, is being driven back. In 1952-3, ninety per cent of all the money invested by the government in the colleges and universities was earmarked for the physical sciences with only a fraction set aside for the humanities and none for the social sciences.[5] If this trend continues, the humane studies are in for a long siege, with even their minimum survival by no means assured.

In the lower grades this process has been abetted from another direction by the spread of Progressive Education, not as John Dewey originally conceived it but as applied by professional pedagogues. Dewey had thought of Progressive Education as the testing of the individual pupil's ideas and convictions in the crucible of actual experience. As a revolt against the nineteenth-century method of teaching by rote and memory where the student passively swallowed what was forced into him from the outside, Dewey made the child an active participant in his own education. But in the hands of his disciples in the school systems, Progressive Education rapidly degenerated into the very process, though in reverse, against which Dewey had revolted in the first place.

Where formerly the teacher was all-powerful and the student a passive agent, now the student became all-powerful and the

---

[5] Figures taken from the New York *Times,* December 7, 1952.

teacher reduced to a kind of moderator. Since the pupil was to learn nothing unless he learned it by himself, the teacher turned the learning process over to him bag and baggage, and the co-operative balance between the two was destroyed in the reverse direction. From the earliest age, the pupil was now to educate himself. Instruction from the instructor was kept to a minimum. The project method arose by which students went off on their own whether they knew where they were going or not. Classes were divided into committees which co-operated with one another in self-instruction while the teacher made frantic efforts to "integrate" their work. The result was a meaningless chaos considerably worse than the old-fashioned regime in which the teacher was absolute boss. In seeking to teach themselves subjects about which they knew nothing, pupils simply scooped out of encyclopedias information which they copied down mechanically and proceeded to bore one another in class with reports on subjects about which the other students knew nothing and cared less. The end result was that though theoretically the student learned to work with others, actually, as far as subject matter was concerned, he learned nothing at all.

The watering down of the American curriculum in the lower grades, which has been so marked since the first World War, is in large measure due to the sterile and self-defeating extreme to which Progressive Education has been pushed. This, too, like rampant vocationalism, has helped empty the schools of intellectual content. In trying to eliminate the faults of the old-line curriculum, the all-out advocates of Progressive Education undermined the curriculum altogether, and threw the baby out with the bath water. English, history, art, the social studies were no longer taught as such. They were "integrated" in a new subject called "core," a hash in which the individual subject lost its distinctive meaning and flavor. Grammar became an unpleasant word, which was supposed to make the small fry flinch.

It was called instead "language structure," and was hardly taught at all. Progressive Education developed a bad case of anti-intellectualism and turned its schools into formless masses of activity divorced from organized knowledge.

II

If the assault on the curriculum has grown increasingly sharp, the assault on the American teacher has been as intense, and of longer standing. The images in which he (and she) has appeared in our literature and mythology, from Ichabod Crane down, have been nearly all unflattering. As a male, he has been a stern taskmaster wielding a hickory stick with more vigor than justice; an absent-minded pedagogue fumbling with his glasses and constantly hoodwinked by his pupils who are always far more alert than he; or the inept figure unable to earn a living at any of the respectable masculine professions. He thus falls back on teaching as a last resort and is not much good at it either, illustrating George Bernard Shaw's epigram, "He who can, does. He who cannot, teaches." As a female, she has been the angular spinster in whom the warmth of life has long since chilled, who takes out her frustrations and vinegary bitterness upon her students; the pretty young schoolmarm who is just waiting to get married and will leave her class the moment that anticipated event rescues her from the fate of the first type; or the bluff battle-ax, efficient, aggressive, loud-voiced, and about as womanly as a two-ton truck. To offset these acid portraits, there has been but one relatively friendly image in the public mind: the timid, sweet-tempered schoolmistress who taught her pupils the right lessons of life so well that they all went out into the world, became brilliant successes and international celebrities, then returned to honor the lady, now old but still timid and sweet-tempered, at a

formidably resplendent banquet, at which they attributed all
their triumphs to her.

This was more or less the script of that tenderly typical motion
picture *Cheers for Miss Bishop,* intended as Hollywood's tribute
to the American schoolteacher. In it, Miss Bishop, unsung, un-
heralded, was personally responsible for molding the characters
of a United States senator, a Nobel Prize-winning scientist, an
internationally acclaimed social-settlement worker, and a small
herd of other figures scarcely less distinguished. This American
version of Mr. Chips, however, has not escaped the patronizing
flavor which the unpleasant conceptions of the teacher have in so
marked a degree. The Miss Bishops may be honored after they
have retired, but are singularly unhonored while at their jobs.
Gratitude and recognition in their case come late, and everyone
involved is faintly surprised that underneath their unpromising
exterior so much substance and resolution should reside. To the
very end, that withdrawing modesty, that soft-spoken gentleness
suggested by the helpless waving of the hands and fluttering of
the eyebrows, remain to accent what is after all a personality not
geared to material success and not generally admired in the social
sense, modesty and sweet temper being among the conspicuously
lost characteristics of the American temperament. Even the female Mr. Chips, then, American-style, is still a second-class
citizen to whom a certificate of first-class citizenship comes too
late for her to make much use of or fully enjoy.[6]

The Mr. Chipses of England suffer from no such patronizing
admixtures of feeling. In their older and more settled society

---

[6] There appeared late in 1948 an astonishing motion picture called *Apartment
for Peggy,* which also dealt with teachers and teaching. What made it astonishing was the affirmative way in which it approached the subject, regarding
teaching as more important than the pursuit of money, and necessary to the pre-
vention of war. Moreover, it presented teachers as alert and articulate human
beings deeply involved in the problems of society. For Hollywood, this was a
revolutionary exception.

they have the affection of the public when they are sweet-tempered, and its respect when stern. The English schoolteacher is poorly paid, as poorly if not worse than his American confrere, but he enjoys by way of compensation all the intangible values of social esteem, unflecked by pity or contempt. In this respect he is far better off than the teacher in America regardless of whatever economic differential may exist. The British attitude has prevailed generally in Western Europe, in France and Italy certainly, and in pre-Nazi Germany emphatically.[7] Among the countries of the Western world, the United States has the awkward distinction of being the only one to deny its teachers unquestioning approval on a par with other professional groups. Since the teacher is one of society's principal carriers of ideas, any damper imposed on his spirit or morale is a damper placed on the movement of ideas themselves.

Nor are the restrictions upon the teacher limited in the negative sense to a withholding of prestige. They are applied in other ways as conspicuous and inhibiting. A teacher's private life must be far more exemplary than that of the average citizen. He must observe the conventions of etiquette, behavior, the complicated routine of respectability, more rigidly than his fellows. As Benjamin Fine pointed out,[8] in the smaller towns this routine is marked by egregious bans on such details as cigarette smoking, cocktail drinking and late hours. Other surveys have revealed taboos in many areas on using lipstick, drinking beer, getting married or "keeping company" with young men. There have been instances of teachers discharged for attending dances held under perfectly respectable auspices.

Furthermore, the teacher is expected to participate in civic

---

[7] The fault in German education, as has been frequently pointed out, lay not in its social attitude toward teachers, which was admirable, but in its excessive, almost exclusive, emphasis on the technical, nonmoral sides of knowledge.

[8] In a series of articles on the nation's schools and colleges which appeared in the New York *Times* during February 1947.

functions after school hours and contribute financially far out of
proportion to his salary to the numerous charities which exist in
every community. He is expected to assume a smiling and bene-
ficent expression for a longer part of the day than almost anyone
else except a salesman or professional fund raiser, without the
monetary rewards that make their public faces somewhat easier
to assume and bear. All this becomes less true the larger the city
in which the teacher is stationed, obviously one reason why the
chronic shortage of teachers is most acute in the rural areas.

As if all these social blue laws invoked against him were not
sufficiently galling, the teacher is constantly being scrutinized by
censors and politicians. He must express no dissenting ideas nor
be associated with controversial movements. He must be cautious, often to the point of vacuity, about what he says outside
the classroom as well as in. Loyalty oaths are required of him
earlier and more frequently than of others, and his patriotism
is a subject of constant suspicion and frequent examination.
Legislative committees descend on him with the directness of
bears on a honeypot in search for unorthodox ideas. He is seldom
defended by school boards and administrators,[9] and can expect,
indeed, only disapproval, vilification, and in many cases outright
discharge. It is not surprising that a great many of his colleagues
have become, in these circumstances, timid creatures, afraid to
raise their voices even when moved to speak by genuine con-

---

9 James Bryant Conant is a notable exception. On retiring from the presidency of Harvard to become High Commissioner for Germany, he remarked: "If
there are members of the staff of any university who are in fact engaged in
subversive activities, I hope the Government will ferret them out and prosecute
them. But in so doing, I trust they will not create an atmosphere in which professors would be afraid to speak freely on public issues. . . . It would be a sad
day for the United States if the tradition of dissent were driven out of the universities. For it is the freedom to disagree, to quarrel with authority on intellectual matters, to think otherwise, that has made this nation what it is today. . . .
Our industrial society was pioneered by men who were dissenters, who challenged
orthodoxy in some field . . . successfully. The global struggle with communism
turns on this very point." The New York *Times,* January 26, 1953.

viction, and have withdrawn into the safe mechanical routine of their jobs with no deviation from the laws of conduct prescribed for them. Ernest Boyd's harsh comment about them back in the 1920s still applies:

Terrorized by economic fears and intellectual inhibitions, they have no independence. They are despised by the plain people because of their failure to make money; and to them are relegated all matters which are considered of slight moment, namely, learning and the arts. In these fields the pedants rule unchallenged, save when some irate railroad presidents discover in their teachings the heresy of radicalism.[10]

The image of the schoolteacher as an impractical fellow, cloistered in an ivory tower, with nothing important to say about the real affairs of life, has been created by society as a strait jacket into which he has been crowded and forced to remain. There are even some intellectuals who have contributed to this image. H. L. Mencken, for example, carried on a long war against professors. "Two-thirds of the professors in our colleges," he wrote on one occasion, "are simply cans full of undigested knowledge, mechanically acquired; they cannot utilize it; they cannot think."[11]

Still another irritant is the attitude of the American schoolboy, encouraged by generations of usage. Hostility between pupil and teacher is, of course, a universal phenomenon, but seldom in any society has this hostility been given such widespread approval as in our own. Playing hooky has been an ideal of boyhood for generations. In rural sections particularly, the notion that a boy has more to learn wandering through the fields, fishing, soaking up, however unsystematically, the phenomena of

---

[10] Ernest Boyd, "As an Irishman Sees it," in *Civilization in the United States,* ed. by Harold E. Stearns (New York: Harcourt, Brace, 1922), pp. 491-2.

[11] H. L. Mencken, *Selected Prejudices* (New York: Knopf, 1927), p. 113.

Nature, than attending his books, has long persisted. The growth of the big cities has curbed this feeling somewhat since there are no satisfactory alternatives to school attendance for the boy confined in an urban street, but the old tradition lives on sturdily. This has contributed to the paradox of compulsory public education and an intrenched aversion to it having a simultaneous growth, and the people for whom that education was designed being often those who care about it least.

The inferior social position of the teacher has been matched by his depressed economic condition. Notoriously underpaid, he belongs to a profession whose average salary as late as 1946 was lower than that of unskilled labor. After an inclusive survey in 1947 for the New York *Times,* Benjamin Fine concluded:

> A tremendous teacher shortage exists. The teaching profession no longer attracts the top young men and women of the community. They can get more money, easier working conditions, greater community respect and more freedom working for the Government, for private industry or for the neighborhood druggist.
> They can get more money driving a truck, collecting garbage or serving as a bartender than they can teaching. Everywhere teachers are regarded with pity or scorn; too often they are treated as second-class citizens.[12]

The flight from the profession after the second World War created an acute shortage of teachers which directed public attention to them. Salaries in some cases were raised, an awareness of the importance of the teacher, spurred in part by the ideological struggle with communism, began to spread. For the first time the public took a good hard look at its teachers and their tremendous importance to the community.

But concrete improvements were sporadic, and the situation of

---

12 The New York *Times,* February 10, 1947.

the American teacher remains far from encouraging. His small increases in salary, wrung from reluctant boards and legislatures after great effort, have long since been swallowed up by the rising cost of living. Attempts to curb his civil rights have been resisted, but not always effectively, and there is no assurance that these attempts will not continue in the face of future crises of one kind or another. In the schools the vocationalists have been steadily thinning out the curriculum in favor of technical courses while the defenders of the old traditions of cultivation of mind, the many-sided outlook and the whole man, have been retreating almost everywhere. The position of the teacher, social, political, economic, remains highly vulnerable. Despite occasional improvements he will never attain full recognition so long as bigger and better technology continues to be the chief aim of the country.

Though there has been much talk about democracy during the present period of crisis, and the need for a resurgence of the democratic spirit, it has not yet become translated into a refostering of those elements in education which look to the encouragement of democratic man. These elements actively exist, but they have been on the defensive for a long time. Yet their prospects are not unrelievedly bleak. On the surface the acquisition of material goods and more efficient and profitable techniques of production continue to be the exclusive goals of the American people; but to take these apparent goals for the totality would be profoundly erroneous. The recent war and its painful aftermath have aroused a realization that great social and political problems cannot be solved by wealth alone, that mind and spirit are involved as well. In our grappling with these problems the ideas and convictions of democracy must play a vital and decisive role. We are becoming conscious that the difficulties of life are more complicated than we had ever suspected and, moreover, that these difficulties are not going to turn over and play dead at the first sign of our national income heaving statistically into sight.

This realization has been an event of the first importance in the spiritual existence of the American people, creating bewilderment and a temporary disorientation, but inducing also a new humility, a pause for stocktaking, a consciousness of depths beneath the surface—all the classic stages of intellectual growth. In this growth lies a main hope for the resurgence of the humane values in the schools, and indeed everywhere in the country. The rounded human personality of the democratic dream clearly cannot be created until there is a general awareness that he has more than a surface and beneath it more than one side.

Chapter VI

The Public Life of the Intellectual

IN OUR TIME THE INTELLECTUAL IS TOLER-
ated in public life only in periods of distress, when conventional
solutions have failed and new ones are being sought with varying degrees of eagerness and desperation.

When the depression hit bottom in 1933, familiar attitudes
were so shaken from their moorings that it was possible for
Franklin D. Roosevelt, then beginning his first term, to import to
Washington a whole corps of professors of law, economics and
political science (chiefly from Harvard, Columbia, Cornell and
the University of Chicago) without anyone raising a cry of protest—at least not during the early months. When the banks re-
opened with their deposits insured, when men began returning
to work and the economic machine commenced functioning once
more, when hope and the feeling that the worst was over acquired a firm ascendancy over the gloom of the darkest depression years, the attacks upon the brain-trusters got under way.
So effective was this campaign that there was re-established

in the public mind something of the contempt for academicians and theoreticians that had prevailed during periods of prosperity. The brain-trusters, gradually squeezed out of Washington, straggled back to their respective campuses, and the later Roosevelt administrations, particularly after the outbreak of the war in Europe, enlisted the services of few of them.

The end of the war, however, brought with it a new crisis, the propaganda war between the Soviet Union and the United States, in which the services of the intellectuals were once again solicited—and this time by the very business community which had hitherto regarded them with alternating suspicion and dislike. Russell Porter, in an article in the New York *Times* suggestively entitled "New Ratings Given to Intellectuals," wrote: "The Committee for Economic Development last week announced the election of a woman, a churchman and two college presidents to its board of trustees. This was regarded as highly significant of the growing importance being attached by responsible business leaders to cooperation with intellectual groups for mutual survival of American free enterprise, free labor, free government and intellectual freedom in a world increasingly menaced by the totalitarian crusade of Communism."[1]

Before the Civil War men of learning had played a considerable role in public affairs without any crystallized sentiment against them. This may have been due in part to the illiteracy that prevailed among large sections of the population, with the consequent premium placed on the political services of those who had been formally educated. In the early Puritan settlements the ministers also were the leaders of the community, and for a long time the fusion of intellectual and political leadership persisted. Hamilton and Jefferson, theoreticians and men of ideas, were characteristic examples of eighteenth-century leadership, a lead-

---

[1] The New York *Times*, October 26, 1947.

ership that persisted well into the nineteenth. The Adams family, stretching through consecutive generations, provided the most glittering illustrations of influential figures combining theory and practice. Abigail, the wife of the second President, was a writer. Her son, John Quincy Adams, the sixth President, pursued literary occupations all during his political career. His son, Charles Francis Adams, was Lincoln's Ambassador to England during the Civil War. He, in turn, had three sons who continued the tradition of fusing thought and action. Charles Francis Adams, Jr., was a lawyer, railroad magnate and historical writer. Brooks Adams wrote two trenchant and celebrated historical analyses, *The Law of Civilization and Decay* and *The Theory of Social Revolutions.* A third son, Henry Adams, was the author of the famous *Education of Henry Adams,* a great political and historical memoir based in part on its author's experiences in the diplomatic service.

Besides the Adamses there were other literary and intellectual figures who combined literature and public service. Washington Irving was Minister to Spain. Nathaniel Hawthorne was for four years American consul at Liverpool. The rolls of the early nineteenth century are crowded with the names of men who merged both professions: William Austin, George Bancroft, Rufus Choate, Caleb Cushing, Alexander and Edward Everett, James Russell Lowell, and a galaxy of others. What they did was considered the rule rather than the exception, not something freakish at which to wonder or look askance.

A respect for learning was not confined to the formally educated. In *The Flowering of New England,* Van Wyck Brooks describes the factory girls of Lowell, Massachusetts:

There were joint-stock pianos in their boarding-houses; the walls of the mills were covered with their poems; they subscribed to the British reviews; they had classes in German; they all seemed to know *Paradise Lost* by heart and talked about Wordsworth, Coleridge and Macaulay in the intervals of changing bobbins on the looms.[2]

And the public in general:

. . . most of the writers of the coming age were actively encouraged by their fathers and mothers, for whom the career of letters seemed as normal as that of the pulpit or public affairs. Not even in Catholic countries, where almost every peasant family aspired to produce a priest, was there a keener wish, in the poorest household, that a brilliant son might have "advantages" and follow the line of his intellectual interests.[3]

After the Civil War, however, this fusion of theory and practice began to break up. The vast growth of industrialism brought with it a great imbalance in favor of practicality and purely material values. The spread of compulsory education made formal education less rare, and by increasing supply decreased the indispensability of educated men. The gap between the educated man and the average man shrank until the former no longer enjoyed the advantage of being uniquely literate. Swarms of hard-handed practical men produced by frontier life and by the rise of the new industries, fought their way to the surface and began controlling the movement of the country, pushing the professors back to the universities, the writers back to their studies, and shaking the offices of government loose from the grip of what Henry Adams called the eighteenth-century man. Adams himself, ironically observing this process during the last half of the nineteenth century, felt himself forced out of public service by what he regarded as the vulgarity of the new mechanical age. It was the spread of this traditionless materialism which oper-

_____

2 Van Wyck Brooks, *The Flowering of New England* (New York: Dutton, 1936), pp. 176-7.
3 *Ibid.*, p. 112.

ated so powerfully in persuading the young Henry James to take refuge in the tradition-packed societies of Western Europe. Everywhere, fastidious, sensitive intellectuals were shrinking from contact with the new tough order of things that lay so plainly under the genteel surface of the Gilded Age, to borrow Mark Twain's epithet, and retreating to the backwaters of American life.[4]

By 1900 poets were no longer being summoned to diplomatic posts; historians were no longer being invited to become cabinet ministers. It was considered something of a political miracle when Woodrow Wilson, a college professor, became governor of New Jersey shortly after the turn of the century, and even more of a miracle when, in 1912, he was elected President of the United States, the first intellectual to reach the White House since John Quincy Adams. Our Presidents since 1920 have reverted to more familiar type.

The emergency years of President Roosevelt's first administration brought a brief resurgence of men of ideas in public office. F. D. R. himself was not a conspicuously intellectual man. The upstate New York country gentry from which he sprang, his close friends and intimate associates until he ran for the Presidency, were not writers or scientists or professors or theologians, but rather gentleman farmers, lawyers and naval men. The early circumstances of his life had not brought men of ideas his way, but he was to prove receptive to them when the time came. In 1931 and 1932, as his campaign for the Democratic nomination got under way, the pressures of the worsening depression were beginning to loosen the habits and familiar thinking of the country, opening the way for new methods and solutions. The loss of confidence in the bankers and business-

---

[4] Or were being devoured by the new order, a process described by William Faulkner in his novels dealing with the Snopes family, and by Lillian Hellman in her plays *The Little Foxes* and *Another Part of the Forest.*

men, who seemed not only responsible for the depression but unable to find a way out of it, created a vacuum in the public mind, into which new types of men could enter and be accepted.

Columbia professors like Raymond Moley and Rexford Tugwell became Roosevelt's associates side by side with professional politicians like James Farley. Liaison between the government and the universities, severed by the Civil War, was momentarily re-established, and the President was for a time surrounded by men far more interested in the theories of economics and political science than he. For a brief period the bankers and businessmen fell back or waited in the anterooms, hat in hand, for the New Deal to get the stalled economic machine into motion again. In time the public was to witness the remarkable spectacle in twentieth-century America of a professional poet, Archibald MacLeish, becoming Assistant Secretary of State, a successful playwright, Robert E. Sherwood, becoming one of the President's principal speech drafters, a professor of law, Thurman W. Arnold, who was an acute student of the theory of capitalism,[5] becoming an Assistant Attorney General, and a social worker, Harry Hopkins, evolving into the President's closest and most intimate adviser.

This transfusion of intellectual energy into the political bloodstream had a corollary in another of the manifold pulmotor operations of the New Deal: the subsidizing of the artist by government funds. This was arranged by the WPA, which set up subdivisions for the several branches of the arts: the Federal Writers' Project, the Federal Theater, the Federal Artists' Project and others. While state funds had been available for artists in France and England at various times (the poet laureate of England is an employee of the Crown), and sinecures for American writers had been available in the nineteenth century (Haw-

---

[5] His book *The Folklore of Capitalism* was a provocative study of our economic myths and their effects on our thinking and behavior.

thorne in the Customs House), nothing so formally institutional and inclusive as the WPA had been witnessed on the American scene.

The Soviet Union had subsidized its artists since the Revolution in 1917, but the profound difference between the Soviet and American form of subsidy was characteristic of a profound difference between the two countries: the Soviet artist had to write, paint or compose propaganda for the regime; the American was free to do as he pleased. He did not have to write lyric poems in praise of Roosevelt or concertos glorifying democracy or murals showing the signers of the Declaration of Independence in heroic attitudes. There were no strings attached. Though there were many who cried that government support of the unemployed artist was un-American, the contract set up by the WPA was in the best democratic tradition. It served not only to keep several thousand artists from the miseries of unemployment, but enriched the cultural life of the country in many ways. Post offices, hitherto barren, bloomed with murals; audiences which had never before been able to afford admission to theaters and symphony concerts, were seeing plays put on by the Federal Theater and hearing music performed by WPA symphony orchestras; libraries were enriched by numerous almanacs, sometimes erroneous but often exploring new byways of folklore and state history, compiled by the writers' projects. A good many men were kept alive during a critical period, and given a chance to exercise their talents in the public good.

The opposition to the projects was furious. The conservative wings of both major parties were against them as they were against all legislation which assumed direct government responsibility for the jobless. Their sense of outrage at the sight of artists supported by public funds was peculiarly intense. In a vague way they suspected artists of being radicals, disseminators of "advanced" ideas and somehow against the respectable middle-class home. They were bohemians or Communists, or both; and at the very least, were motivated by impulses quite different from those guiding normal men. Conservative newspapers during the era of the WPA blossomed out with cartoons depicting unskilled laborers raking leaves ("boondoggling" was the word used to describe this loafing process) at government expense. But their highest anger was reserved for "long-haired aesthetes" being maintained and encouraged at the taxpayers' expense.

Their attitude reflected that of many Americans, particularly in the small towns and rural areas, who felt that the artist lacked the qualities which had made America great. He had neither brawn nor physical energy. He was not noticeably acquisitive. He had no conspicuous desire to "get ahead in the world" or "make something of himself." He was not usually a church-goer. Moreover, there was something foreign about him. One could see him living in sin on the Left Bank, tippling absinthe and other immoral concoctions at sidewalk cafés, spouting bombast or lapsing into moody un-American silences, and doing any number of other unwholesome things. That a person of this wicked and blasphemous sort should be supported by the hard-earned money of respectable taxpayers was monstrous, was intolerable.

The artists' projects came after the WPA as a whole had been established, and were liquidated sooner. The special antagonism they aroused stemmed from feelings deeply grounded in American life. The projects ran counter not simply to the conviction that free men should rely on themselves and not accept support from the government, but to the feeling that art itself was somehow frivolous and illicit. The powerful opposition raised almost from the start to the creative activities sponsored by the WPA was a part of the general opposition to the pump-priming of the

Roosevelt administration, but it was also a perfectly spontaneous, instinctive reaction to art itself.

Yet the very appearance of the projects was a cultural and political wonder, a first-hand indication of the forces making for a new outlook on the arts, a new acceptance of them. The ancient conflict between trade and art, the practical and the theoretical, the distrust of culture and its encouragement, which had been for so long heavily weighted on the side of the first, was for one brief and exciting time equalized. The significant point was not how much or how little the projects accomplished, how efficient or inefficient they were in handling the funds allocated to them, but their being established at all.

No account of the public life of the intellectual in America would be complete without reference to Adlai E. Stevenson, whose Presidential campaign in 1952 was notable for its devotion to reasoned principle. Though he was defeated, more than twenty-seven million people voted for him and he was acclaimed on all sides as a man who had brought something new to the political scene. The very fact that a man of his quality should have been drafted by a major political party was in itself a remarkable testimonial to the growing recognition of the importance of reason and reflection in public affairs. This recognition pointed to the narrowing of the gap that has so long existed between political action and the resources of the mind. It is the fusion between the practical politician and the man of ideas which produces the statesman. And it is the statesman— as distinct from the politician—whose sustained appearance will symbolize the political maturity of the country.

Part II

Diverging Movements in Our Popular Culture

Chapter VII

Oceans of Print

IN THE LARGE AND DIVERGENT PATTERN OF American culture the newspapers and magazines play a conspicuous role. Here, too, we see the contrasting sides in our national life. There are papers and periodicals which water down ideas and events to an elementary level, and appeal to fears and prejudices rather than reason. Through the use of prose capsules, pictures as a substitute for print, tabloid sensationalism and diversions such as comics, horoscopes and advice to the lovelorn, they encourage the reader not to think, and provide him with easy replacements for a process which he requires, to start with, no great encouragement to avoid. There are also newspapers and magazines which treat their readers as intelligent and grown-up human beings and supply them, more or less objectively, with the material necessary for them to arrive at their own independent judgments.

One test of an enlightened newspaper is the extent to which it assembles facts and how fairly it presents them to the reader. Many newspapers slant the news one way or another. Some editorialize openly or covertly outside the editorial page itself. The worst slanting is done by the two extremes: sections of the Hearst and tabloid press, with their shrill invective and vindictive commentary, at the extreme right, and the Communist press, with its infantile clichés and blatant falsifications, at the extreme left. To the tabloids might be added the Chicago *Tribune* and the Washington *Times-Herald,* conspicuous for their intensely one-sided political passions. Their belligerent language and tone do not exactly induce clarity of thought and scarcely encourage the reader to draw his own conclusions.

A leading example of the tabloid newspaper is the New York *Daily News,* with the largest circulation in the United States. The *News* has developed an editorial style marvelously suited to communicate to its more than two million daily readers (and over four million Sunday) the most complicated issues in a trenchant, slangy English that takes hold of even the most casual peruser. Admiration of this technique—and it is a great technique—does not obscure the ultimate effect. The *News,* stridently dogmatic on every subject, never for a moment doubts its own wisdom, never for an instant relaxes its tone of aggressive certitude. The world's thorniest problems are solved in its inner sanctum before appearing in print; once in print, it takes a hardy reader indeed to outface the bold stare of these solutions. No method of journalism has been more perfected than this; none is less suited to a society which depends on the voluntary exercise of individual reflection. The process by which the *News* influences the free movement of thought is made all the more effective by its artful make-up. A daily horoscope, one Hollywood and two New York gossip columns, a short story, serial, a crossword puzzle, pages of pictures, racy coverage of sports and as much scandal as space and censorship permit, constitute an irresistible appeal to nearly every interest, dream and superstition of a mass audience.

The best American newspapers avoid the omniscient tone of

the belligerent press. Their convictions might be no less strong, but these convictions usually appear in a style that seeks to persuade rather than shout down. Our society has produced not only the New York *Daily News* but also the New York *Times,* not only the Hearst newspapers but also the Washington *Post* and the Atlanta *Constitution,* not only the sensation-mongering tabloids but also the St. Louis *Post-Dispatch,* the New York *Herald Tribune,* and the *Christian Science Monitor* which lives up admirably to its unique motto, "to injure no man but to bless all mankind." These newspapers are conspicuous for their exhaustive news coverage, their balanced presentation of events and their sharp definition of leading issues. In addition to supplying the reader with the relevant facts, they encourage him to draw his own inferences from them. To the degree that a newspaper does this, to that degree it is a constructive force in the culture of the nation and is discharging its responsibilities to the literate public.

The successful performance of these functions depends in large measure on how freely the press can operate. One of our proudest boasts has been the freedom of our press. In this we take a legitimate pride. Our newspapers are often partial but there has been little evidence of venality or corruption. Unlike sections of the Continental press, American newspapers are not for blatant hire. They are not open to purchase by political parties or by special groups wishing to turn them into out-and-out propaganda sheets. Nor is our press a channel of propaganda for the Government. We have no "official" newspapers, no *Pravdas* or *Izvestias* laying down the line for a sullenly obedient public. In fact we have no government censorship at all. Our papers are free to criticize the government without fear of retaliation. There is no minister of press or propaganda to choke off an unfriendly newspaper by cutting off its supply of newsprint. And the very phrase "freedom of the press," guaranteed by the Constitution, symbolizes one of our most jealously guarded rights.

But there are factors which operate against freedom and

variety of the press in the broadest sense. One of these is the trend toward chain ownership. "By 1900," wrote Frank Luther Mott in his comprehensive survey *American Journalism,* "eight chains could be listed, controlling twenty-seven papers and perhaps ten per cent of daily circulation. By 1910 there were a dozen chains; and the number of papers had doubled. . . . In the next decade . . . many new chains were established; and the number of papers doubled again. But it was in the . . . twenties that the number of chains reached about sixty and the number of dailies owned by them passed 300, carrying over one third of the total daily circulation of the country. . . . In the Sunday field, chain papers furnished about half of the total circulation."[1] Linking newspapers into chains has the same unhealthy effect as monopolies elsewhere, concentrating the publication of news in too few hands and reducing the number of editorial viewpoints.

We not only have fewer newspapers, as a result of chain ownership and consolidation, but they are growing more and more alike. The rise of the press associations—the Associated Press, the United Press, the International News Service—and the spread of nationally syndicated columns, features, comics, have greatly hastened this uniformity. We have already entered the age of the "canned" editorial, prepared at a central source and sold like packaged goods to papers all over the country. Agencies like the Newspaper Enterprise Association have sprung up, supplying standardized editorial opinions which are printed in widely scattered areas often without critical examination of their contents. Rare is the newspaper like the Louisville *Courier-Journal,* which not only stands for individuality of editorial judgment but encourages on its editorial page open disagreement among members of its own staff.

Our newspapers have been drifting steadily toward sameness,

---

[1] Frank Luther Mott, *American Journalism* (New York: Macmillan, 1941), p. 648.

with their contents, viewpoints and even their formats becoming less varied. A basic reason is the hedging-in of the whole newspaper business by staggering problems of finance. The day when a man of small means could start a paper with a few thousand dollars has long since passed. Ten or fifteen million dollars is now required to start a metropolitan daily. Furthermore, the tremendous expense of maintaining a corps of national and foreign correspondents has made newspapers growingly dependent on central news-gathering agencies which themselves have become major capital undertakings. The result is an inevitable tendency to favor the viewpoint of corporate wealth while treating the interests of organized labor with scant sympathy if not outright unfriendliness. We can claim rightly that our press is free, but with the major reservation that the launching of fresh enterprises and hence new ideas has become very difficult. Free competition in the laissez-faire sense is as restricted here as it is elsewhere in the American economy.

In the largest cities papers expressing several points of view do exist; but the smaller cities, with limited resources, have found it increasingly difficult to maintain more than one. In a survey of local monopoly in the daily newspaper business for the *Yale Law Journal* of June 1952, John G. Simon found that more than eighty per cent of all cities with local dailies have only one paper, and many cities with more than one have two or more owned by the same publisher. Mr. Simon discovered that single publishers served nearly half of all cities with more than 100,000 people, and that the total number of daily papers declined by one fourth between 1909 and 1950. A huge metropolis like New York City may have a wide range of newspapers, giving its readers a wide area of choice. But this is decidedly restricted in the smaller cities where the few existing papers tend to be exclusively conservative and liberals generally lack editorial support.

Newspapers in America suffer from other occupational short-comings. They yield all too often to the pressure of advertisers —who provide from one half to three fourths of a newspaper's income—whose opinions they treat with gingerly respect. As Quincy Howe put it in *The News and How to Understand It:* "Bearing in mind the importance of advertising revenue, you obviously cannot expect the average American newspaper to de-nounce the largest department store in town as a fire hazard or a sweatshop."[2] American newspapers have displayed a singular lack of ardor in the interests of reform and a carelessness toward individual reputations that is combined with hypersensitivity to any criticism of themselves.[3] Our press has remained unrespon-sive to public opinion. "I do not know of a single case," remarked Oswald Garrison Villard in his book *The Disappearing Daily,* "in which public opinion has compelled any radical alteration in the mental attitudes and policies of a daily journal."[4] Villard also claimed that the accuracy and objectivity of American jour-nalism have deteriorated in the past hundred years. Though the newspapers have trumpeted the sacredness of a free press in their editorial columns, they have not been, in the opinion of Morris Ernst, stout allies in the legal battle for it. "The papers, as far as I know," he commented acidly, "practically never aided in all the battles for a free press. . . . I have tried close to a hundred cases in the last two decades involving free press. I know of only one real contribution made by the press . . . the really great brief presented through the *Chicago Tribune* attorneys in defense of Near in the great case of Near against Minnesota."[5]

---

[2] Quincy Howe, *The News and How to Understand It* (New York: Simon and Schuster, 1940), p. 39.

[3] The sharp-tongued, crabbedly honest Harold L. Ickes documented these short-comings in considerable detail in his study of the newspapers, *America's House of Lords.*

[4] Oswald Garrison Villard, *The Disappearing Daily* (New York: Knopf, 1944), p. 26.

[5] Harold L. Ickes, *America's House of Lords* (New York: Harcourt, Brace, 1939), p. 131n.

In an age when mass communications play a large role in American life, the newspapers have a great influence on public opinion. They are private enterprises to be sure, but like the utilities they have a responsibility to the public which they cannot discharge by sponsoring one-sided viewpoints nor justify by claiming that, being privately owned, they can be as partial as they choose. In theory the press itself agrees with this. Rule three of the seven ethical rules adopted in 1923 by the American Society of Newspaper Editors reads as follows: "Freedom from all obligations except that of fidelity to the public interest is vital. Promotion of any interest contrary to the general welfare, for whatever reason, is not compatible with honest journalism." In actual practice promotion of the general welfare has not always been paramount.

The potent influence of the press has not, however, been an insuperable handicap to the free maintenance of personal conviction on the public's part. This has been eloquently indicated by five of the last six Presidential elections, where in each instance the candidate heavily favored by the press lost. And even in the campaign of 1952, when the bulk of the newspapers supported the winning candidate, they did so far more heavily than did the electorate. According to a survey conducted by *Editor & Publisher,* 67 per cent of the newspapers polled supported General Eisenhower while only 14 per cent supported Governor Stevenson,[6] as against 55 per cent and 45 per cent in the actual returns. Still more one-sided were the circulation figures. The papers backing the Republican candidate had a total of forty million as against five million for the Democrat. While Eisenhower had newspaper support in every state, there were nine states in which Stevenson had no editorial backing at all.[7]

This gap between press and public can be closed only by providing a journalistic voice for all the divergent groups in

---

[6] As reported in the New York *Times,* October 31, 1952.
[7] *Ibid.*

the country, so that our press will speak for and to the whole nation, instead of catering to limited viewpoints. The functioning of our newspapers will then equal in quality their amazing physical techniques. In the meanwhile the very act of assembling news with the remarkable completeness and speed displayed by the American press plays a part in the maturing of the reader that is too often ignored or taken for granted. The supplying of facts, the presenting of information, the retailing of events as they occur provide the raw material by which men may form their own judgments and arrive at their own opinions of the world. Without this material the struggle against ignorance is greatly hampered. In this respect American journalism has been successful, communicating the affairs of the planet with great efficiency while retaining its free status among the newspapers of the world.

II

What is true of the newspapers applies to the magazines as well. Indeed the relationship between them is analogous to the relationship between radio and the movies, so frequently similar are their problems and effects. Though the primary aim of the newspaper is to inform, while the magazine seeks both to inform and entertain, each goes about the execution of these aims in much the same ways and arrives at the same limited cultural denominator.

Magazine editors, unlike radio and film producers, do not feel that they are producing a deficient product for a public whose taste is low, whose mental resources are slight and whose craving for simplification is endless. The producers say the public is lazy, tired, if not actually weak-minded as well. Magazine editors generally deny this and take their products seriously, even

at their thinnest level. With few exceptions the editors assume
a serious responsibility toward their readers and view them not
cynically but earnestly. Conceiving themselves as agents of the
public good, they will crusade at times for worthy causes. The
Woman's Home Companion, by way of illustration, has been
engaged for some years in spreading word about venereal dis-
ease, the sad plight of alcoholics, the inadequacy of children's
institutions, the brutal practices prevailing in insane asylums,
and similar matters having to do with social welfare.

This editorial attitude, however, has not yet made the average
mass-circulation magazine any more grown-up than the average
film. The editors' estimate of their readers' intelligence, however sincerely arrived at, is no higher than in the other mass
media. Magazine fiction, which is mostly light, takes a roseate
view of life. There are periodicals which supply as much sex
and scandal as the censors will allow. Others, to satisfy the
strong vicarious craving for violence, show as much horror as can
be found, everything from photographs of dead soldiers im-
paled on barbed wire to automobile accidents with brains and
entrails identified by careful arrows and X's, the more realistic
the better. Still others, convinced that the public cannot digest
excessive quantities of prose and print, feed it pictures, boldface
captions, cartoons, snapshot versions of the news and eye-catching "art work." All this without cynicism and in a spirit of
faithful adherence to popular demand.

There is obviously enough truth in their analysis to have established the fortunes of numerous magazines. The public does
crave easy cures and shortcut solutions; people are lustful and
have a taste for violence. Pictures are fascinating and escapist
fiction is a drug that few can resist. The success of popular
periodicals from *True Story* to *Life* is founded on a shrewd appraisal of the exploitable attributes in human nature. But as in
the case of the movies, the approach is one-sided. Lust, violence

and a flight from reality are not the only appeals to which the reader responds. He is interested also in an adult presentation of reality, in fresh approaches to the problems of living, and in forms of literary relaxation that are not relentlessly formulized and banal. There are, to be sure, magazines that do stimulate these interests, like *The New Yorker, Harper's Magazine* and *The Atlantic Monthly.* Among thoughtful magazines with particularized points of view, there are *Fortune,* devoted to a lively and intelligent conservatism, the *New Republic,* maintaining in difficult times a zealously liberal viewpoint, and the *Nation,* which in recent years has veered toward the extreme left—on down to the little magazines with their specialized aesthetic and political programs. Yet the circulation of all these runs only to the thousands, that of their competitors among the pulps and slicks to the millions, with the ratio of advertising revenues between them even more heavily weighted. On an immediate, short-term basis there is far more money to be made pursuing the line of stock fiction, lavish pictures and sentimental inspirationalism than any other. An investment in the reflective powers of the public can conceivably pay off but only in the long run, and our economy is scarcely geared to the long run. We are enamored of the fast pay-off, the quick knockout, and are impatient with endurance hauls requiring patience and stamina. As the launching of a new magazine becomes progressively more difficult and expensive, the pressure to show an immediate profit increases, as do the odds against publications that will prove lucrative only in the speculative future.

Like the newspaper publishers, magazine editors must be hardheaded businessmen in order to survive. Nor is it their primary function to raise the cultural standards of the public at whatever cost to themselves. Yet the loss of the long-range audience and the appeal to the lowest rather than the highest potential of the reader restrict not only the maturation of the magazine-reading public but the markets of the magazines as well. In purely economic terms the loss of any prospective audience is serious to the producer. The raising of editorial sights, with a view to attracting the more intelligent reader without loss of "entertainment" value, would widen the market and improve taste simultaneously. Profit and intelligence are no more mutually exclusive here than they are elsewhere. The record of the magazines in this respect has been depressing.

The subjects with which their articles deal are, with rare exceptions, treated superficially, and their fiction bears about the same relationship to the actual life of their readers as do soap operas on the radio or most movies. They carry a weight slighter than their numbers, circulation and total talent would lead the observer to expect. In this sense, they are like the newspapers. Like the newspapers too, they freely acknowledge the welfare of the public to be one of their basic concerns. But by failing to deal with emotion authentically and in an adult way they miss, as the movies do, the great opportunity of becoming an essential part of the nation's inner experience.

Yet the magazines, whatever their intentions or failures, have been turned out with a polish that no other country has been able to equal and that has been identified the world over as one of America's unique accomplishments. Striking examples of this surface quality are the slicks, with their smooth paper and elaborate formats. Their attractively packaged contents stretch thinly over a wide assortment of subjects sandwiched between mountains of insistent advertisements. Their editors have become conscious in recent years of a growing hunger for information on the part of the public, and so have slowly increased the amount of space devoted to reportage and commentary. *Collier's* and *The Saturday Evening Post* have printed memoirs by prominent political figures. Slicks directed to women, led by the *Ladies' Home Journal* and the *Woman's Home Companion,* have crusaded against such evils as unsanitary conditions in restaurants and discrimination against illegitimate children. This in addition to familiar material, now considerably expanded, on cooking, clothes, infant care and other phases of domesticity. In recent years *Seventeen,* a slick for teen-agers, has entered the field, striven, not without success, to address youngsters in a mildly serious way about their problems and experiences, and decorated its fiction with illustrations by celebrated American painters.

But however the slicks may respond to the times in their factual items, their fiction remains uniformly static. The formula story —with its stock types, cute twists and turns of plot that themselves sink into formulas almost as fast as they are invented, and saccharine endings, all wrapped around the more obvious types of romantic gratification—is one of the least digestible and certainly least adult phases of popular magazine literature. The stories are nearly always the same. They unwind endlessly the routines of boy-meets-girl, and wife and husband rediscovering each other after an estranged interlude. Or they propel mechanical heroes through standardized adventures in various settings and through detective serials, where the final triumph of right is achieved without damage to the virtuous. A close reader will detect minor variations in quality. If one uses the stories in *The Saturday Evening Post* as a norm, the stories in *Collier's* will seem a shade brisker, those in *Cosmopolitan* a degree less bound by conventional reserves, in *Good Housekeeping* constructed more solidly, in the women's magazines several shades more sweet, roseate and sentimental. But virtually all of them have a substance that is fatiguingly threadbare and an insight into the lives of their characters that is monotonously shallow.

There is one group of slicks which is an exception to this and which does have fiction and articles considerably more serious and adult. It is, oddly enough, the fashion magazines, whose main purpose is not to entertain their readers with editorial content but to keep men and women of various income groups informed about what to wear. This is particularly true of *Harper's Bazaar* and *Mademoiselle.* Their stories avoid the cut-and-dried formulas so insistently present elsewhere. Their feature articles often deal intelligently with the leading social and cultural issues of the day. This high-level quality, however, does not carry over into the major portion of their contents. These are devoted, on varying notes of gushing whimsicality and romantic idealization, to a fantastically exaggerated emphasis on an exclusively physical attractiveness, as though this were all that made life meaningful. If women readers were to take this emphasis literally they would have to devote the bulk of their time, energy and money to acquiring the same lacquered, mindless surface as that illustrated by the models whose waxlike doll faces stare out from the glossy pages. It is indeed a challenging job of exploration to find the editorial matter at all, buried as it is beneath the deluge of fashion articles and lush advertisements.

The men's fashion magazines, headed by *Esquire,* maintain about the same ratio between a small amount of top-quality editorial content and a heavy mass of fashion and specifically male diversions. Their cartoons are for the most part risqué, the humor almost entirely parlor-car. In the pages of *Esquire* we find the bold, dominant male whose aim in life is to enjoy the company of as many attractive girls as possible while avoiding the trap of marriage. Bachelorhood, sleek, elegant, man-about-town-ish and without emotional responsibilities, is the ideal to which most of the ads, features and even some of the articles lead. The war between the sexes in its crudest form is nowhere more evident than in the shiny, self-assured pages of the men's fashion magazines. They advance ideas and promulgate ingenuities with great energy, but purely on the level of sex, clothes, food and sport narrowed to the range of the ultrafashionable.

What the slicks do on smooth paper, the pulp magazines do

on rough. Their audiences are on the whole less demanding, their illustrations cheap line drawings instead of expensive art work, their advertisements cruder and chiefly addressed to lower income groups. But they, too, cater to the needs of their readers for vicarious love and adventure. This they supply without pretension. Pulp stories emphasize plot at the expense of character, and sacrifice everything to the needs of swiftly paced action in every genre: Westerns, weird and supernatural tales, detective stories, sport, science and adventure. The one exception to this is the love pulp which has an interminable amount of emotional dialogue and, despite the somewhat titillating captions on its front cover, little action. Pulp writing is at times surprisingly good—many early stories by Dashiell Hammett and Raymond Chandler appeared in the pulps—but it is more often lurid and jejune. Pulp stories, like those in the slicks, deal in escapist fantasies, rigidly observe the conventions of proper moral behavior,[8] and bear no more relationship to present reality than do some of the weird tales of interplanetary travel they narrate in so florid a key. More violent than the slicks and less suavely mannered, addressed to a less intelligent audience, the pulps are miracles of sustained mindlessness, relaxing but empty of meaning in the same swift passage of incident piled helter-skelter on incident.

Yet they are miracles of interest and sophistication when compared with those peculiar occupants of the demimonde between pulp and slick, the confession magazines. *True Story, True Romances, True Confessions* indicate that "truth" is what these magazines are after. The truth is nearly always an "autobiographical" account of a broken or postponed romance, usually narrated by a young woman in a crude homespun style. A typical confession has the girl living in a small town where her widowed

---

8 Codes of ethics and sex are the same in *Dime Detective* (now selling for fifteen cents) as in *McCall's.*

father has a steady but not lucrative job as superintendent of the local ice plant. She is in love with the post-office clerk, a steady, loyal young man, whom her father does not want her to marry because this would remove from the house the person who has ministered to his wants since his wife died. Our heroine is hung up between her father (she had promised her dying mother to take care of him) and her young man. She remains in this somewhat soggy dilemma through most of her account, mooning, solemn and very very good. Just as the impasse threatens to last forever, divine intervention in the form of an attractive widow drives up to the ice plant (why she does is not quite clear; she is plainly not the type who fetches and carries her own ice), takes one look at Father and falls aggressively in love. He is quite willing to be had, but demurs for his daughter's sake. This paves the way for the big scene between the lady and our sacrificing heroine. The widow, prepared to do combat, discovers that the girl is longing to marry too and looks on her prospective stepmother as a liberator. The story ends with the dull chime of lower-middle-class wedding bells. The style of the whole piece is of a contrived semiliteracy that, far from lending authenticity to plot and characters, exaggerates their tedious cipherdom. Designed for love-starved women, stressing routine and familiar settings in order that the process of reader identification may be the more intimate, maintaining rigid moral standards, the confession magazine functions on a dead level of emotional blankness. It supplies its audience with pacifiers that from start to finish are synthetic substitutes for the real thing, manufactured in job lots with no art, little taste, and contents that approximate a spiritual and literary zero.

Livelier than the confession magazines and appealing to a larger and more varied group of readers, are the comics, which swept the country during the 1940s with astonishing speed and, despite the growing storm of protest over their more lurid features, show no signs of slackening popularity. They are in essence picture pulps for children (though they have a miscellaneous adult audience as well), combining the story line of the regular pulps with the techniques of the comic strips. There are detective comics, Westerns, action and adventure comics of all kinds. Superman and Captain Marvel are the comic equivalents of the weird and supernatural pulps. Walt Disney, Roy Rogers, Gene Autry, Dale Evans, have invaded the comic field from the movies; The Lone Ranger and *A Date with Judy* have done the same from radio. The mass-advertising, chain-publishing features governing the pulps govern the comics also, as do standards of taste and techniques of narration. The comics stress superduper action, made more vivid by pictures, with just enough loose continuity to keep the attention from one colored page to another. They, too, satisfy in rapid abundance the longing for escape which has swelled so hugely in a world where reality has become progressively harder to endure. They, too, accept the general code of morality prevailing elsewhere in the pulp scene, avoiding overt references to sex, punishing criminals and arranging for hero and heroine to prevail.

Yet, as in the crime movies which end with the formal capture of the criminal, the comics accent the crime itself so dramatically that it often becomes exceedingly attractive to the juvenile imagination. This has been one basis of parental and community protest against the comics which, as in the case of organized pressure against the films, has induced comic-book publishers to begin censoring themselves. Despite the isolated instances of children killing or torturing one another under the possible influence of comics, it is doubtful whether criminal tendencies are aroused by them, any more than gangsters were manufactured among the young spectators of the gangster movies when these crowded the screens in the 1930s. The late Jimmy Walker once remarked that no girl was ever corrupted by a book. The remark is applicable to youngsters. Comics may be trash. They are certainly appalling substitutes for good juvenile literature. They simplify their contents and deaden thought as much as the standard pulps and confessions do. They have even invaded the field of serious literature by reducing the classics to comic proportions, so that it is not impossible for a whole generation to appear which has not read Scott, Stevenson, Shakespeare, Melville and the rest, but only comic-book versions of them. In many ways they narrow the tastes and interests of their readers by a constant substitution of melodrama for reality. These are serious enough matters to charge them with. To accuse them, however, of instigating crime, upsetting emotional stability and creating psychic disorders is to exaggerate their influence. As with most other magazines, their effect is more restrictive than creative. If they fail to stimulate the mind, it is because they leave it strictly alone, not because they are engaged in a concerted effort to destroy it.

With all these oceans of print flooding out of the presses, how can the busy American, in the increasing tempo of his life, keep abreast of the news and ideas of the day? To meet this need, our technical ingenuity once more rose to the occasion, and produced the digest magazine. Instead of each reader inefficiently wading through the huge mass of newspapers and periodicals trying to find out what is going on in the world, the digest editors do it for him. They select what in their opinion are the most significant news items and articles and present them in condensed or even capsuled form.

There are digests in every field: news, science, religion, fiction, general information. There even appeared a publication called *Quick,* announcing itself as "a news digest of news digests," which moved Clifton Fadiman to remark gloomily, "One can easily imagine a digest of *Quick (Quicker)* and finally one of *Quicker (Quickest).* From *Quickest* to the non-reading of the news seems a logical next step. . . . "⁹ In its successful effort to save the reader time, the digest magazine frequently eliminates the necessity for thought. In our frantic national rush we tend to move away from such time-consuming activities as reading and thinking. The digests, with their strong editorial judgments, tell us not only what to read but also what to think, and by so doing reduce our capacity and, in the long run, our willingness to do our own thinking.

The giant among the digest magazines is *The Reader's Digest*. Many among its millions of readers regard it as the fount of all information and moral wisdom. The *Digest* deals with almost every problem in life and offers a ready and cheerful solution. It serves as a bedside almanac for all ills: alcoholism, melancholia, physical ailments from the common cold to cancer, all kinds of business and labor problems, marriage dilemmas, spiritual and political confusion. Toward these and other difficulties common to mankind, it maintains an unwavering optimism based on the firm conviction that perseverance, sufficient faith and the right advice will carry the sufferer to triumph over every ill. The magazine encourages perseverance, preaches faith, and supplies benevolent advice with so much energy and documentation that only the most stubborn skeptic can resist it. Its stories of individual crises, its air of irresistible uplift, its breezy tackling of the thorniest issues, interlaced with condensations of the more vivid magazine articles of the month, the latest jokes and epigrams, and an abridged reprint of the timeliest book of the moment, comprise a package which retails for a quarter and can't be beat. Its ethics, values and idioms are exactly those of Main Street. As such, it is a miracle of uncanny anticipation, and has hardly ever ventured an opinion or taken a stand which has not been approved or at least not strongly op-

---

⁹ *Time*, August 15, 1949.

posed by the vast majority of its readers. If any magazine can be said to exert a direct influence over the habits and modes of thought of its audience, it is *The Reader's Digest*. Hence its unique and fantastic position, not simply in terms of circulation figures, which are astronomic, but as a force which is almost on the verge of becoming an institution.

Yet its every aim and act are directed, as Montaigne put it, to furnishing its readers' minds, not forging them. It covers an enormous amount of ground and discharges flying masses of predigested facts and conclusions. Its readers need not pause for reflection; that has been done for them. The *Digest* has strong political views, and like most American magazines espouses a pronounced conservatism. The old-fashioned business virtues seldom fail to work it into a lather of enthusiasm, while government-regulation and assistance schemes of almost any kind seldom fail to throw it into a rage. Its policies on every subject are whooped up in tones that are unshakably certain, in an atmosphere so unshakably sentimental that it bathes the reader in a warm glow of good fellowship.

It projects and epitomizes the vein of sentimental optimism which is one of the main threads of the American tradition with the superb craftsmanship typical of the American manufactured product. So carefully wrought are its stresses on conventional morality, its air of hearty friendliness, its embracing of the accepted civic virtues and the prevailing myths of the free-enterprise system (which, as so many economists and industrialists have informed us, has not been free for a long while), that it might serve as house organ for such characteristic booster societies as the Elks, Kiwanis, Rotarians, Oddfellows, Shriners and the American Legion. It reflects neither the best nor the worst in American life, but catches and holds to the last nuance the superficial thinking, strong feeling and boundless energy of the middle levels.

Like *The Reader's Digest,* the two outstanding news digests, *Time* and *Newsweek,* have emphatic editorial viewpoints. The opinions of their editors color and direct their accounts of the political events of the day. By stretching their range to include not only news, but art, music, movies, theater, literature, they supply their readers with ready-made opinions and judgments about the very experiences in which they should be most encouraged, from the point of view of discrimination and taste, to react for themselves. Written for a more sophisticated audience than *The Reader's Digest,* they address their public in a highly literate way. *Time* in particular has become famous for its special style and has even developed a distinct vocabulary of its own. Both are interesting examples of how a lucid and intelligent style can be used to reduce the activity of the intelligence itself.

Another short cut for the American who is "too busy to read" is supplied by the picture magazines. A picture can show in five seconds what it might take as long as five minutes to read. Or as one editor put it, one picture is worth a thousand words. Like the punchy paragraph of the digest, the eye-catching photograph gives the reader a quick flash contact with the world.[10]

The largest of the picture magazines is *Life,* where the photography is so finely developed as to become almost a new medium in the reader's comprehension of the news. Here, too, one is impressed by the extent and ingenuity of the resources at the disposal of the editors, and the incommensurate results achieved by them.[11] They have at hand an extraordinary instru-

---

[10] Fred Allen, the radio wit, took a jaundiced view of this visual trend: "Everything is for the eye these days—'Life,' 'Look,' the picture business. Nothing is for the mind. The next generation will have eyeballs as big as cantaloupes and no brain at all." Quoted in John Crosby's book *Out of the Blue* (New York: Simon and Schuster, 1952), p. 33.

[11] This disproportion is not confined to magazines. It governs other aspects of American life. In politics, for example, our industrial and military power far exceeds our ability to disseminate democratic or libertarian ideas elsewhere in the world.

ment for gathering and projecting the events of the day, and use it with very great skill. They are also moved by a desire to educate, which they discharge indifferently. They have in addition an editorial policy which, as with the digest magazines, is markedly one-sided. These three goals—to report, educate and editorialize—do not hang together in a cohesive pattern, but go off loosely on separate tangents so that *Life* reads like three magazines as often as it does like one. This diffuseness and triangularity dilute its character and weaken its potential impact. Without perceptibly checking its success as entertainment, they reduce its influence and make the reading of the magazine vaguely unsatisfactory, for all its photographic charms and hard-hitting prose.

The average content of any given issue of *Life* is a jumble of heterogeneous elements. Magnificent (and horrible) pictures of children starving to death in the streets of China and India appear side by side with accounts of the great Renaissance paintings, followed by the latest cancer experiments on the white rat or perhaps a highly personal sketch of the deeds of some American industrial leader or a snapshot résumé of the most promising young American novelists of the year or a survey of Atlantic migratory birds. There is hardly a subject too specialized in range to escape its attention. Religion and philosophy, even in their more esoteric phases, have been examined. Literature, the films, the stage, the arts down to the smallest out-of-the-way crafts are reviewed at periodic intervals. Botany, zoology, medicine, the latest cults and fads, fan dancers, murderers, traffic accidents in their most gruesome forms, are scrutinized if not microscopically, at least with an eye on their melodramatic aspects. The effect of all this is an aimless hodgepodge.

Interlaced are *Life's* editorial ideas, which are not confined to the editorial page but run through the numerous political articles dealing with the great affairs of the hour. These ideas are inspired by Henry Luce's vision of the American century. *Life* argues that we are destined to take control of the great trade routes and flow into the power vacuums because we are the world's most dynamic and technologically advanced power. To protect and guarantee this position, the magazine calls for efficiency, in government, the armed forces, foreign policy. Efficiency appears far more often in its pages than democracy and affects its policy on leading issues. *Life* seems less concerned with whether a democratic society is morally superior to a dictatorship than whether it is technologically superior. Its editorials are hence crowded with calls for operational skill which, if vigorously practiced at home and abroad, will secure the future. The stress throughout is less on ethics than on streamlined power.

The magazine is technically beautiful and ingenious, but peppered with buckshot effects, assertive and partisan in its political views, and full of curtain-raising inquiries into many fields which do not, somehow, hang together. Here again is a characteristic American enterprise: a cultural commodity lavishly produced, full of sensuous and physical attractions, but lacking in penetration and organic unity. In the end it sacrifices the solid and meaningful to the merely plausible or spectacular.

From the magazine mass of America there rise certain periodicals that address themselves directly to the adult intelligence and have been remarkably successful. One of the more striking of these is *The New Yorker,* carrying off week after week small miracles of unanalyzable humor even when it has nothing much to say or is occupied with objects scarcely worth attention. Its chief features are the packaging of its contents in a uniquely witty, peculiarly brilliant style, and its persistently ironic attitude toward the world. Even serious correspondence on political or military subjects and the solid contributions by such diverse persons as Rebecca West and Lewis Mumford, generally have a knifelike edge. At its best the magazine combines sophistication, urbanity, literate and cultivated intelligence, and a rhetoric so deft that nearly everything in range sparkles responsively.

But since unrelenting wit can develop a tediousness of its own, *The New Yorker* has its dull issues where its heavy artillery fires away at minuscule targets, and the reader longs for a change of pace. Though occasionally dealing with affirmative ideas, most of the magazine is devoted to laughing at events and people who have in some way become subjects for ridicule. To expose stuffed shirts, fools, and fanatics from all camps, is certainly valuable. But *The New Yorker,* having created every week a vacuum from which folly has been ejected, seldom provides anything with which to fill it. It has been said with justice that the critics employed by the magazine are more at home with bad plays, movies and books than with good ones because attack provides more scope for wit than does praise.[12] This points up *The New Yorker's* narrowness of range, a narrowness deliberately cultivated and perhaps, from the point of view of maintaining its particular style, wisely so.[13] But after the weaknesses have been identified and the fools demolished, what then? In this critical interlude from no to yes, from what should not be to what should, from the irrational to the rational, we discover that *The New Yorker* has been left behind. Or rather has stayed behind of its own volition. The wittiest and most urbanely intelligent periodical in the United States is in the end a brilliant monument to negativism and creates effects no more durable than the absurdities of the hour.

---

[12] When H. Allen Smith read the magazine's review of his book *Larks in the Popcorn,* he rushed home in excitement. "This is terrific," he shouted to Mrs. Smith, waving a copy of the magazine. "Terrific. I got a so-so review in *The New Yorker."* Related by Leonard Lyons in the New York *Post,* December 9, 1948.

[13] In this sense it resembles the style of George Meredith, full of dazzling epigrams and an occasionally wearying intellectuality, in which warmth and sentiment are kept under careful control. *The New Yorker,* indeed, seems to have been born from the pages of Meredith's *An Essay on Comedy.*

But the support it gives the intelligence is not to be underestimated. By respecting the maturity of its readers and never pandering or writing down to them, it promotes belief, in however limited a sphere, in the capacities of the rational mind. It lends the thinking man an air of worldliness and presents him without the stuffiness and vague impracticality which often blur the public's image of him. Finally, and by no means least effectively, it endows him with humor, a rare thing indeed for the intellectual, generally eyed as a heavy fellow given to polysyllables and pedantry.

Humor indeed has become a vanishing item in magazine circles, *The New Yorker* being the only large periodical in the country with humor as a major editorial aim. Recalling the days when humor magazines, the early *Life, Judge, Ballyhoo, College Humor,* flourished, one wonders whether the hard times, wars and crises of the past generation can claim among their victims the American capacity for laughter. *The New Yorker* is a vivid survivor of what was once an abundant field. Its preservation of laughter as an element in the vast scene of print ranks with its considerable services to the intellectual man and to the long tradition of cultivated comment.

There are other intelligent and stimulating American periodicals, but these address smaller audiences. There is *Fortune,* which is a superb recorder of the doings of Big Business with occasional excursions into politics and the arts when these bear on the large commercial interests. Its research is conspicuously thorough and objective, its writing on a thoughtful plane. The same is true of the liberal weeklies and of those periodicals known in the trade as the quality magazines, whose very name suggests their character and caliber. The liberal weeklies, which include publications like the *New Republic* and *Commonweal,* have faithful but small audiences and have had to be almost constantly subsidized. Their fault, if fault it be, is not that their point of view is unpopular, but that they are too exclusively thoughtful. Most readers also require entertainment or relaxation of their magazines; thoughtfulness alone is not enough. The liberal weeklies have never been entertaining and their partisanship, except for brief periods, has been waged in very quiet tones. But whatever the number of their readers, they have seldom yielded to the temptation to sensationalize or water down their contents for the sake of increasing their subscription lists.

The quality magazines, whether published weekly like *The Saturday Review,* monthly like *Harper's* and *The Atlantic,* or quarterly like *The American Scholar* and *The Yale Review,* cover the whole range of human experience in a consistently mature and literate manner. They keep alive, often under great difficulties, the civilized and humane traditions of our country. Their editorial focus is balanced rather than one-sided, and is aimed, not at handing the reader ready-made opinions, but rather at providing the materials by which he can arrive at independent judgments of his own.

At the bottom of the circulation picture are the "little magazines" headed by *Partisan Review,* many of which, like *The Antioch Review, The Kenyon Quarterly* and *Accent,* are centered on college campuses, and attract on the whole purely intellectual audiences. But though their readers are few and specialized, it would be a mistake to assume that their influence is nil. Their services to creative literature alone have been extraordinary. James Playsted Wood, in his study *Magazines in the United States,* noted the following:

In 1946 three investigators who looked thoroughly into the little magazines came to the conclusion that these unsung periodicals had discovered and sponsored about 80 per cent of the important novelists, poets, and critics who began to write after 1912, and that they not only introduced but also remained the basic magazines to publish 95 per cent of the poets of this period.[14]

The little magazines demonstrate that one cannot always judge the impact of a publication by the mere quantitative number of its readers. This is often forgotten by those who too quickly judge the cultural level of the nation simply by the mass-circulation magazines.

The immense variety of periodicals, large and small, catering to every conceivable taste and functioning on all levels of literacy and complexity, belies simple and stereotyped classification of our national reading habits. The fact is that American culture is so rich and complex that it provides fare for every kind of reader. Aside from the large groupings already noted, there are numerous special-purpose magazines: house organs; trade publications such as *Women's Wear* and *Iron Age*; journals devoted to health, science, history, music, art, scholarship; magazines designed for every age group from *Baby Talk* to *Geriatrics;* publications expressing every religious viewpoint. Even our hobos have their literary outlet in *The Hobo News.*

All this should keep us from arriving at the too-easy conclusion that our periodical literature is addressed to a single mass audience—and not a very bright one at that. To be sure, many of our magazines address themselves to readers who may be able to read but are not yet truly literate. But the continuous existence of magazines devoted to the literate reader not only suggests the many-sidedness of our life but keeps alive the possibilities of developing a more mature and thoughtful citizenry.

III

Among the more recent developments within the machinery of print are the pocket-sized books and the book clubs. Pocket-

14 James Playsted Wood, *Magazines in the United States* (New York: Ronald Press, 1949), p. 274.

sized books had appeared in America at various times in the nineteenth century, usually ballooning out spectacularly, then folding under economic and legal pressures. In their modern phase the pocket-sized books began as twenty-five-cent reprints designed to reach those millions of readers who were unwilling or unable to buy books at the regular price. The retail outlets were originally train depots, bus stations and drugstores where the reader could pick up something to read easily and cheaply to kill time on trips or over a lunch counter. But so rapidly did their growth mushroom that in 1952 alone more than 257,000,-000 books, worth $65,000,000, were sold, and they had spread into bookstores, department stores, candy stores, subway stands, newspaper kiosks, and indeed wherever there was a small space to squeeze them into. They also moved into the field of original publishing, offering even relatively unknown writers large advances for original manuscripts, though so far most of their efforts in this direction have been of inferior quality.

The impact of the cheap reprints upon the reading public has been very powerful. By turning books into inexpensively packaged commodities, they have certainly encouraged the book-reading habit in countless thousands of people. But what kind of reading habits? To this vital question two diametrically opposite answers have been advanced. One takes a dim view of the paper-backed books, and argues that most of the items have been in the realm of sub-literature, advertised on the level of elementary biology. This, it has been claimed, has resulted in flooding the country with great quantities of bad books that can only depress standards of taste. Since the cheap reprints compete mainly with magazines selling at roughly the same price, especially the pulps, their appeal has been to the lowest instincts of the public. Hence the enormous quantities of material, luridly displayed, dealing with sex and violence. Moreover, the distributing apparatus of this new book industry places great pressure upon it to play up the sensational at the expense of the meaningful. Competing for limited space on display racks with eye-catching magazines and with one another, dependent on wholesalers and retailers who look on their goods as so much merchandise to be packaged and unloaded, operating under terrific competitive conditions geared to high turnover and narrow profit margins, the paper-back publishers, no matter how well-intentioned, are caught in the vise of their own mechanism and must rely essentially on the mass production of literary items cheap in content as well as in price. The most charitable view that can be taken of their operations, argue the unfriendly critics, is that if they have not debauched public taste, they have assuredly not improved it. At best, the role of the paper-bound books is analogous to that of the chain supermarket in the life of the food shopper: providing a less expensive product without noticeably changing its quality or radically altering eating habits.

The opposing view concedes that in their early years the paper-bound books fed on an almost exclusive diet of mysteries, Westerns and sexy novels with front-cover illustrations devoted entirely to beautiful, half-naked young women. But the percentage of these items dropped steadily and more substantial literary fare began to make its way into the pocket-sized market. David Dempsey described this change:

Although sin, seduction and statutory rape are still the tested ingredients of a goodly part of the year's fiction crop, there has been a noticeable increase in the number of classics published. Out of 1952's 1,000 new titles, at least a hundred can be classed as established works of literature. The range is considerable, from "The Confessions of St. Augustine" to Machiavelli's "The Prince." Pocket Books, in its new Cardinal Editions, has made available seventeen vintage novels. Out of sixty-six titles released in the United States this year by Penguin Books, the English firm, it is notable that the best seller was Nevil Coghill's new "translation" of Chaucer's "Canterbury Tales."[15]

15 The New York *Times,* December 28, 1952.

Furthermore, wholesalers and retailers are slowly being educated to a consciousness of books as books rather than commodities; and methods of distribution in the midst of the competitive jungle of limited space and quick sales are gradually improving. The strong showing of serious books, while perhaps not of best-seller proportions, guarantees a growing place in the profit picture for more substantial literature, with many reprint publishers convinced that with the market for the assembly-line product close to saturation, the future advances of their industry lie in gratifying the tastes of more serious readers. Finally, if nothing more has been done than to supply millions of students in high schools and colleges with texts of the literary classics and the acknowledged masterpieces in many fields of learning, the pocket-sized books have made a constructive and indelible impact on our time.

Amid these conflicting approaches, certain facts seem clear. The paper-bound-book publishers have uncovered, to the surprise of some of them, a vast and unappeased hunger in America for serious and challenging books. In many instances the good books have outsold the routine products. An examination of reprint lists reveals an astonishing and increasing number of superior items, with the leading houses putting out special lines under separate signatures devoted entirely to books of solid content and high merit. There are even signs that the industry as a whole, as it emerges from its frantic early stage, is beginning to get away from its stress on salaciousness and sadism, partly because of public outcries, partly from a growing sense of where its own ultimate best interests lie.

In the light of the earlier flash appearances and disappearances of paper-bound books in America, it is hard to say with confidence that they are now here to stay. Yet a continuation of their present trend opens the way for the staggering prospect of good reading being easily accessible and purchasable by millions of people. If this should one day happen, the pocket-sized book may turn out to be the maker of a true cultural revolution instead of what it seemed to be at the start, the gimmick in a clever merchandising process.

The book club, like the paper-back reprint, is also essentially a marketing operation. It is concerned not with the publication but with the selection and distribution of those already published books which it believes will appeal to its particular clientele. The book club brings various kinds of literature to readers whose tastes are often already formed and who subscribe because of the physical conveniences and advantages, which include free premium books, selections at lower than retail prices, and deliveries made directly to the subscriber's home.

Much has been said and written about the bad effects of the book clubs on readers, writers and publishers, and hence on American culture in general. Writers are said to be corrupted because, tempted by the high fees, they turn out the kind of stereotyped product taken by some clubs, instead of following their own inward and original bent. The same criticism has been leveled at Hollywood which is supposed to have a similarly debasing effect on the serious writer with a great novel somewhere in his system. This whole line of reasoning, however, is too pat. One may claim with equal logic that writers willing to commercialize their talent will not wait on book-club fees and movie contracts to do so, but will seek out some other form of commercialization.[16] And if none exists, it is not likely that they will then sit down, for want of something more lucrative to do, and turn out great literature. No potentially great historical novelist has been kept from his grand design by the prospect of

---

16 When Ernest Hemingway was asked to comment on how much the big money of slicks, Hollywood, radio, etc., has taken writers away from serious personal themes, his caustic reply was: "Most whores usually find their vocations." *Time*, August 4, 1947.

writing a book-club or movie choice according to a hackneyed
formula of lavish décor, syrupy love affairs and swashbuckling
swordplay. It is more reasonable to suppose that left to his own
devices the commercial writer would be unlikely to produce anything much more original or artistic.

However, it would be foolish to deny that the book clubs exert
some pressure upon the serious writer, not only by holding before him the tantalizing prospect of a coup that might make him
financially independent, but by controlling the flow of reading
matter to large numbers of readers. Yet no proof has appeared
that at their worst the clubs have done more than intensify a
condition already in existence, or that writers are unlikely to
retain their integrity in this instance after resisting all the other
worldly temptations of life in America.

The effect on readers drawn to the clubs is much the same.
Books, like films, when addressed to a mass audience, are supposed to sink to the lowest level of content and style—this has
been regarded for a long time by the large producers and dis-
tributors of the popular arts, and by many critics, as an immut-
able law of culture. Yet the experience of the book clubs, like
that of the pocket-sized books, suggests the contrary. Henry
Seidel Canby, chairman of the Board of Judges of the Book-of-
the-Month Club, noted the many occasions when that organization's mass reading audience responded more enthusiastically
to superior selections than to cut-and-dried choices.[17] Though
the obviously poor items selected by the clubs somehow attract
more attention than the good ones, many of the choices have
been of high quality, with the editors of the larger clubs making
serious efforts to choose books as good of their kind as possible.

The literate reader to whom books are accessible tends to
read what he already has a taste for, just as he attends movies

---

[17] Henry Seidel Canby, "How The Book-Of-The-Month Club Began," *The
Atlantic Monthly,* May 1947.

and listens to radio programs which suit him. His interests might be elevated were the items thrown his way of consistently better quality, but it is scarcely likely that his standards would be destroyed altogether by the mediocrity of books distributed on a mass basis. For the reader living in less populated areas, to whom books are not easily accessible, the clubs have on the whole made available literature which strikes a respectable average in literary quality.

The impact of the clubs on the publishing industry itself was disturbing at the start when it was felt that they would put publishers and bookstores out of business altogether by their development of a superior selling mechanism.[18] In time this fear vanished, to be succeeded by other unsettling effects. Some publishers, for example, have been so tempted by the large returns that their lists have at times been slanted with one eye on the clubs and the other on Hollywood, with the result that worth-while but not immediately profitable manuscripts are rejected all too often. The clubs have also reinforced the trend in the publishing industry that was initiated by the great rise in printing costs. The impulse to publish "prestige" books is considerably weakened when rising costs force up the number of copies which must be sold to break even. And why struggle altogether with a serious but nonlucrative book when a club selection—or movie sale or paper-back reprint contract—will reap huge profits without any extra effort or expense?[19] But

---

[18] The same jitters affected publishing at various other times, with the appearance of the automobile, movies, television, the cheap reprints; jitters which in turn have proven equally unfounded.

[19] This in fact is a central dilemma of the publishing industry. According to Henry Seidel Canby, the rejection of good books "has become a threat to the true function of book publishing and a challenge to literate society. . . . These books that will die aborning," he said, "often have proved . . . to be the most important . . . for education, information and general enlightenment. . . . In the long run, the book trade lives by good books and not by ephemeral and synthetic best sellers, which on analysis will usually be found to owe their existence to good books of which they are popularizations or adulterations." The New York *Times*, February 6, 1947.

these effects have been neither as lasting nor as widespread as
they may have seemed at the start; and most publishers have
learned to accept and live with the clubs without any fundamental alteration in their own outlook.

The selections of the book clubs cover a wide range. The
Literary Guild concentrates on a mixed diet of historical, romantic and occasionally realistic fiction, the Book Find Club on
works of serious literary or social significance. The Book-of-the-
Month Club has no genre preferences, but roams all over the
field, picking weighty books and trivial ones in a successful attempt at supplying the varied entertainment required by its several hundred thousand subscribers. There are many smaller
organizations catering to more specialized tastes in travel, history, science and religion, some trashy, others conspicuously high-
minded. The book clubs in their totality, large and small, light
and heavy, have remained mechanically adroit devices to give
readers, particularly in out-of-the-way places with no book stores
and few libraries, the kind of reading matter to which they
seem most likely to respond. As this response has indicated an
improving rather than a declining standard of literary interest,
the clubs have done everything in their power to cement the
preference, not because they conceive themselves to be agents of
cultural improvement, but for the most hardheaded business
reasons. Here, too, profit and a maturing culture, far from
being antipathetic, have found common ground.

The book clubs and paper-bound books, in their highly developed marketing operations, have been loose aggregates of
mechanical and cultural elements. Yet their primary object is
practical convenience, not stimulation of mind or spirit, and
thus far their mechanical ingenuity has exceeded their cultural
achievement. The disproportion is less marked with them—as
it is indeed with the book-publishing industry to which they
belong—than with our newspapers and magazines as a group.
Here, the spread between craftsmanship and mature content

is considerably greater. In this sense our popular publications are a peculiarly American growth, and assume a natural place in that current of American industrial energy that has provided us with more physical comforts than have accrued to any nation in recorded history. Only an intellectual snob would make this statement invidiously. But it dramatizes the paradox of a society so full of technically perfected instruments that depend on literacy for their existence, so little concerned with the cultivation and spread of literateness.

This paradox is the central fact emerging from an inquiry into the world of popular print.

Chapter VIII

Three Arts that Beat as One

THE REVOLUTION IN OUR POPULAR ARTS which began at the turn of the century created three remarkably effective techniques of communication. They came at uncannily regular twenty-year intervals and have followed, with equal uncanniness, virtually identical careers. The first of these, the movies, was followed a generation later by radio. A generation after that, these two, as Clifton Fadiman put it, copulated and produced television.[1]

Each began with a tremendous initial outburst of enthusiasm, excitement, aliveness, experimentation. There was the thrill of working with a new medium, exploring its possibilities, taking off in new and unexpected directions. The amazing technical development of the instrument was matched at the start by a spontaneous generation of creative ideas. There came an early point, however, in the history of each when, with the success of the first formats and programs, the creative outburst began to

---

[1] Clifton Fadiman, "The Decline of Attention," *The Saturday Review,* August 6, 1949.

slacken, while the physical perfecting of the medium continued unimpeded. The successful early formulas hardened into road blocks which tended to bar the free flow of new ideas. As these media grew into big businesses, with tremendous capital investments, they channeled their efforts along the lines of assured success and became progressively less inclined to revitalize their thinking and experimenting along fresh paths. Soon the early ardor began to cool, the cultural quality began to thin out and the general level of entertainment sank to the lowest common denominator. While still physically in their extreme youth, these media settled into cautious, unadventurous middle age.

Lee De Forest, whose invention of the Audion tube helped make radio as we know it possible, lamented the results:

What have you gentlemen done with my child? He was conceived as a potent instrumentality for culture, fine music, the uplifting of America's mass intelligence.

You have debased this child, you have sent him out on the street in rags of ragtime, tatters of jive and boogie-woogie, to collect money from all and sundry for hubba hubba and audio jitterbug. You have made of him a laughingstock to intelligence. . . . Soap opera without end or sense floods each household daily. . . . Murder mysteries rule the waves by night and children are rendered psychopathic by your bedtime stories. This child of mine, now thirty years in age, has been resolutely kept to the average intelligence of thirteen years. Its national intelligence is maintained moronic, as though you and your sponsors believe the majority of listeners have only moron minds. . . .[2]

Fortune also observed bluntly:

. . . it is obviously a fact . . . that a very large part of America's radio fare (most soap operas, quiz programs, audi-

---

[2] "The Revolt against Radio," *Fortune*, March 1947.

ence-participation shows, gag-comedy acts, juke-music sessions, commercial announcements) would affect any person of modest discrimination somewhere in the range between complete indifference and acute illness.[3]

Television, just beginning to emerge from its formative stage, shows alarming signs of following in the footsteps of its disappointing parents. John Crosby, the New York *Herald Tribune's* radio and television columnist, feels that

Just as did radio, television is losing—or may already have irrevocably lost—the support of the most intelligent level of the American community, the most influential body of opinion in the country. . . . In five years TV has earned for itself a popular contempt which it took radio twenty years to win. . . .

Television is breaking the hearts of its own most able and imaginative creators—those who got into TV early, those who saw it as the greatest mass communications medium ever devised. It's only five years old, . . . but already a new idea is treated with the utmost suspicion.[4]

Jack Gould, radio and television critic of the New York *Times,* who has been passionately eager for the success of television, commented despairingly:

Let's face it: television is getting pretty bad. The high hopes for video which were held by so many are vanishing before our eyes. The medium is heading hell-bent for the rut of innocuity, mediocrity and sameness that made a drab if blatant jukebox of radio. The success of TV is proving a hollow and disheartening jest: television apparently can't stand prosperity.

Remember the proud words, many of them emanating from this corner, of how television represented a vital new form of electronic theatre that augured an exciting and challenging new

---

[3] *Ibid.*

[4] New York *Herald Tribune,* September 19, 1951.

cultural era? Or how the imperishable wonders of a vibrant and articulate stage would be spread to the far corners of the land?

Look at the television giant this season. Morning, noon and night the channels are cluttered with eye-wearying monstrosities called "films for television," half-hour aberrations that in story and acting would make an erstwhile Hollywood producer of "B" pictures shake his head in dismay. Is this the destiny of television: a cut-rate nickelodeon?[5]

Movie producers blame the low grade of their products on the public. They claim to be only the sensitive barometers of public taste. "So long," said Dudley Nichols, the Hollywood producer, "as the people demand witless entertainment and adolescent films and stay away in flocks when an adult film is presented, they will continue to get them."[6] Or, if moviegoers are not downright imbecilic, they are, at the very best, highly uncritical. Bosley Crowther, film critic of the New York *Times,* quotes the movie makers on the subject of historical films: "The motion-picture people have a slickly disarming way of excusing their frequent and deliberate distortions of historical fact. They say, quite frankly and bluntly, that they are phoney but that the public doesn't mind—and that so long as their thimble-rigged productions bring in the customers, who are you to bawl?"[7]

Among the producers themselves, only an occasional dissenting voice is heard. Joseph Mankiewicz, for example, believes that no picture is too good or adult for its audience. In his opinion the argument that an audience is not grown-up enough is "the producers' cheap alibi."[8] Few of his colleagues, however, seem to agree with him.

---

5 The New York *Times,* October 19, 1952.
6 As quoted by Bosley Crowther in the New York *Times,* November 23, 1947.
7 The New York *Times,* October 12, 1947.
8 As quoted in a *Collier's* article, "All about Joe," by Frank S. Nugent, March 24, 1951.

When the producers are not actually insulting the intelligence of the public, they are busy reminding us that they are, after all, in business. Their chief concern is to make money, not to improve the cultural status of the country. James Rowland Angell, former president of Yale, after working for the National Broadcasting Company as public-service counselor, concluded: "I have met a great many owners and managers of American broadcasting stations in my time and found them fine, upstanding businessmen, but I have infrequently met any whose concern for the public service they were rendering could be mentioned in the same breath with their interest in making money."[9]

There are certain phrases that make Hollywood producers jump: prestige pictures, "think-pieces," artistic integrity. To their minds these are synonymous with financial losses, highbrow impractical idealism, arty experimentation and bankruptcy. Producers are generally addicted to the philosophy of the quick return. Since most movie companies are financed by banks, considerations not instantly and visibly connected with money-making—art and emotional maturity, for example—are often hastily and contemptuously brushed aside. Herbert J. Yates, president of Republic Pictures, was asked by James S. Barstow, Jr., correspondent for the New York *Herald Tribune,* if he did not think that Republic's story formulas produced flat, one-dimensional pictures, and whether the studio would follow a growing trend toward making films with the emphasis on artistic integrity. His reply was emphatic. "We don't give a damn for artistic integrity," he said. "We are not concerned with 'prestige' pictures."[10]

The whole attitude was reduced to its naked simplicity in the following conversation from Budd Schulberg's novel about Hollywood, *What Makes Sammy Run?:*

9 "The Revolt against Radio," *Fortune,* March 1947.
10 New York *Herald Tribune,* October 26, 1947.

"What we need is more men out here who think of pictures as a commodity like any other—and forget this prestige business."

"That's exactly what I've been saying," Sammy jumped in. "After all, pictures are shipped out in cans. We're in the canning business. Our job is to find some way of making sure that every shipment will make a profit."[11]

In radio and television, since financial communication with the audience is indirect, it is the sponsor and his sales figures that call the tune. Programs, no matter how appealing they may be, have only a precarious existence unless underwritten by a sponsor, who requires an immediate increase in the sale of his product. On the assumption that the larger the audience, the greater the potential market, measuring techniques such as the Hooper ratings have been devised to test the popularity of individual programs. These have acquired a fantastic prestige and exercise a tyrannical pressure on programs and performers alike that serves to reduce their quality still further.

Another repressive element in the growth of our popular arts is censorship. Their economic structure makes them almost neurotically sensitive to boycotts and threats of boycotts, Congressional investigations, protests voiced by any well-organized group, the passions and prejudices of any section of the population. A political inquiry into Hollywood has immediate consequences in the film industry. The effects of the House Un-American Activities Committee's investigation were typical. Gladwin Hill of the New York *Times* summarized them:

Not only will anyone with pronounced left-wing leanings have difficulty getting a job of any consequence at the studios from now on but, one important executive hazarded privately, the prevailing attitude . . . will stifle for several years hence the

---

11 Budd Schulberg, *What Makes Sammy Run?* (New York: Random House, 1941), p. 273.

production of films containing any "social significance" lest they may be considered "red."

This may appear extreme and regrettable, but Hollywood's attitude is that it is better to be safe than sorry, especially when being safe costs nothing. Why handle a touchy subject when you are always reasonably sure of getting your money back with a harmless, if meaningless, musical?[12]

The late Mark Hellinger remarked shortly before his death: "Hollywood is gutless. You can't make an honest, forceful picture here. Hollywood is the whipping boy for all kinds of pressure groups, and the movie industry does not stand up to them." Hollywood reacts quiveringly to outcries of every kind: from religious groups like the Legion of Decency, which represents 24,000,000 Catholics, the Southern Baptist Convention with 6,000,000 members, and the Protestant Motion Picture Council; from organizations such as the American Legion and the WCTU, the Master Plumbers of America and the National Association of Women Lawyers; from a dozen other sources, many of them fantastic.[13] One reason for its clinging to vapid themes and surface treatments is that these are least calculated to arouse the ire of anyone. For every *Gentlemen's Agreement* and *Crossfire,* in which anti-Semitism is honestly dealt with, there are dozens of films totally innocent of content. For every *Fury* and *The Ox-Bow Incident* that treats lynching with candor, there are scores of stale boy-meets-girl romances, tired comedies of bohemianism and pastry sophistication, musical extravaganzas, all of whose expensive sets cannot hide their thinness.

The fear of censorship or any sort of social disapproval has been even more intense in radio and television than in Holly-

---

12 The New York *Times,* November 30, 1947.

13 These assorted facts and statistics, together with the comment by Mark Hellinger, are taken from Ezra Goodman's article "Are the Movies a Menace?" *Coronet,* July 1948.

wood. Nowhere was this more powerfully revealed than in the hold exercised by the magazine *Red Channels*. Edited by two former FBI agents and privately financed, it had often only to name an actor as having or having had "dangerous" political opinions or associations to make his employers regard him as a liability. The sponsors, whether they believed the accusation or not, wished to avoid "trouble" and "controversy" and not much more was needed to make them drop the actor in question. All this came not from an accredited government agency designed to screen employees on critical projects, but from a little private publication without official standing of any kind.

When these media are not reacting to censorship from the outside, they are busy censoring themselves. Radio and television scripts are inspected almost microscopically and anything even remotely offensive or controversial is carefully weeded out. In the movies the voluntary do's and don'ts imposed by the Production Code form one of the most rigid and proscriptive phenomena in the whole history of the arts. The Code governs plot, dialogue and characterization down to the last detail; it insists on upholding the prevailing taboos of the country together with its most persistent myths. The movies always punish sin, prove that crime does not pay after displaying it in the most attractive light, demonstrate that prostitutes really have hearts of gold, reward virtue in some visible way, and insist that the everyday speech of the average American, even truck drivers, prize fighters and G.I.'s, is aseptic, listless and unprofane. American English, so famous for its pungency and raciness as H. L. Mencken has demonstrated in *The American Language,* emerges through the purifiers of the screen limp, bloodless and underdone, a pale counterfeit of the real thing.

The frequent banality of the popular arts also stems from their natural inclination to follow the lines of least resistance. Like many Americans, the producers are not at home with ideas and prefer to deal with the smooth surface of life rather than its complex interior. Left to their own devices, considerations of money aside, they find the lavishly displayed musical, the soap opera, the light romance, the simplified historical film in an epic frame and the Western and gangster shows much easier to manufacture than programs that come to grips with the problems and passions of recognizable human beings. The one-dimensional character may be less interesting than the three-dimensional, but he is certainly easier to fabricate. He is easier to manipulate too, offers much less resistance to the requirements of plot, and can be batted out by the scriptwriters in jig time. The depths of the mind, like deep water, are enough to give one pause. Why take the plunge unless one absolutely has to? Everybody's natural tendency to do what is least difficult, other conditions being equal, is lucidly illustrated in the reluctance of our popular arts to depart from their hackneyed formulas and lush surface view of life.

Because our entertainment industries have become geared to quick financial returns, subject to pressure from every kind of lobby, hagridden by censorship, and run by men who have frequently assumed that the public is stupid and must be pap-fed, their products have congealed into flaccid stereotypes. Hollywood has produced some remarkable films since *The Birth of a Nation* and the early successes of Charlie Chaplin, but these have been swamped by a deluge of cream-puff romances, flimsy musicals and historical "epics" in the synthetic style of De Mille. These types of out-and-out escape pictures have proved highly profitable and so they have been manufactured on a mass-production basis. In his book *The Mature Mind,* H. A. Overstreet analyzed their appeal to both producer and audience:

What Hollywood discovered . . . was that the sure-fire way to attract people . . . is to give them compensatory illusions.

Motion pictures became the big business through which unsatisfied men, women, and adolescents in unprecedented numbers were granted a daydream fulfillment of their hopes. The motion picture did not aim to make these unsatisfied people go forth and take positive action to solve their own problems. It aimed to give them a dream that was in itself so thrilling in comparison with reality that they would return, and return again, for further hours of dreaming. So fixed has this money-making formula become that even novels and dramas of stature and integrity come out of the movie-mill something other than they were: they come out revised to fit the daydreams of the unsatisfied immature.[14]

Wading through the flood of bad movies to get to the occasional good one has always been a harrowing experience.

Formulas in radio have been much the same. The swarm of soap operas with their dim world of germless purity, the brassy giveaway shows, the interminable crooning and the endless commercials, have been a heavy price to pay for the rare moments of adult humor as practiced by Henry Morgan and Fred Allen, the occasional personality like Bing Crosby with his graceful and unaffected charm, and the periods of good music.

This freezing into safe and commercially successful formulas shows signs of becoming permanent in television too. The first decade of this hybrid combination of radio and film has repeated the early history of its predecessors. The television screens are assaulted daily with the same high proportion of raucous crime programs, sterilized soap operas, hackneyed Westerns and an apparently endless number of vulgarized and insipid variety shows. Punctuating this darkness at infrequent intervals are one or two outstanding comedians like Sid Caesar and Groucho Marx, an occasionally well-produced play and opera, a spectacu-

---

14 H. A. Overstreet, *The Mature Mind* (New York: Norton, 1949), pp. 220-21.

lar political event like the Kefauver Crime Inquiry, and a few discussion programs devoted to ideas, but the ratio of these to the total output is as depressingly low as in the older arts of radio and film. Imaginative programs like *Kukla, Fran, and Ollie* are shortened for lack of sufficiently profitable sponsorship.[15] Thus even the established good things on television have a way of being diminished by their makers if, in the intense competitive scramble, they cannot be readily converted into cash on the barrelhead.

Its higher costs have put television even more at the mercy of sponsors than radio, and its greater sensuous appeal has made it a more flourishing arena for the commercial, that deadliest of sights and sounds over the air waves. By assaulting the eye as well as the ear, television commercials appear the more ubiquitous, and on many programs compete drastically with and at times bite deeply into the "entertainment" portions. The organized and powerful opposition to educational television stems from the fact that this would cut into available time without cash returns, and create a more or less permanent enclave beyond the reach of the commercial. Nothing is more calculated to depress most producers and all advertising agencies.

Critics of our popular arts, surveying these formulized products, have accused them of conveying a distorted image of life in America. But they miss the fact that our mass media reflect with special accuracy many of the convictions of our intensely middle-class nation: its acquisitiveness and sentimentality, its queer mixture of high-mindedness and cynicism.

The devotion to middle-class attitudes and ideals supplies a key not only to the content of popular programs but to the psy-

---

15 The NBC vice-president in charge of the famous puppet show added insult to injury. "One obvious consideration," he said, "has been to give the public less of the thing they want so much, to sharpen their anticipation for the next night's appearance." The New York *Times,* December 9, 1951.

chology of their producers. The middle class in every country
has always glorified comfort, security and conformity once it
has reached a stable position. It has instinctively opposed
threats of change as endangering its investments and established
modes of living. The accumulation of visible property has been
one of its prime objectives, accompanied by a strong impulse to
avoid the harsher facts of life in sex, personal relations and the
social order. At home in the realm of physical and material
things, it has always been ill at ease in the presence of abstract
ideas and philosophical principles; its artistic and imaginative
expressions have usually been swathed in layers of cotton batting
to mute the sharp impact of reality. In public affairs, as Arthur
M. Schlesinger, Jr., demonstrated in *The Vital Center,* it has as
its aim the preservation of short-term profits at almost any cost,
which tends to make it cautious, quick to compromise on larger
issues and unwilling to take a firm stand on anything other
than this immediate interest.

But the middle class is also energetic and socially fluid. It encourages ingenuity, fosters the practical talents and tends to
keep the doors of worldly opportunity open to persons of initia-
tive and will. While not heroic, perhaps, in terms of philosophic adventure, it is sturdily attached to the solid facts of the
material universe, and has been responsible for the great
achievements of science and the vast expansion of industry. In
America it has largely absorbed the old landed gentry, and its
ideals have so thoroughly permeated the working class that of
all Western countries the United States has witnessed the smallest growth of native socialism and communism.

Our popular arts have faithfully reflected this bourgeois
spirit. They have glorified physical comforts and luxuries, suggested the advantages of conformity (how many young heroes
in the movies have rebelled against convention, only to be
convinced at the end that it's the best way after all), and used

the happy ending as a device to indicate that all is basically right with the world. They have romanticized and glamorized sex and personal relations so that these appear in an agreeable haze. They have willingly submitted to moral censorship by both their own trade associations and organized religious groups, and have accepted unwillingly, though no less submissively, the large number of state and municipal censorship boards. Censorship has not eliminated sex but, in forcing a surreptitious treatment of it, has made it only more suggestive, titillating and, in the eyes of many observers, obscene. A frank avowal of the sexual drive and its consequences is banned on both movie and television screen, but the bosoms of attractive young women may be daringly exposed and sniggering innuendoes may crowd the script. This attitude is entirely characteristic of the middle class, which will enact a Prohibition statute and proceed at once to violate it, and will pay pious lip service to matrimony and flout it in clandestine ways. Yet middle-class energy and vitality are also prominent in the popular arts, together with a constant technical experimentation which has made them known throughout the world for their astonishing virtuosity. They may not say very much, but they say it extraordinarily well.

Where these arts err most grievously is in what they fail to say about America. While reflecting some impulses in the national character, they take no account of others. Americans, like other peoples, have a variety of interests and a multitude of impulses, all of which search for expression. They seek relaxation and escape, but they also want to know what life is all about. They wish to lose themselves in musical comedies and hardboiled action thrillers, but they also have an insatiable curiosity about other human beings and how they behave. They have a natural urge to laugh, yet the urge to weep is strong too. There are times when they are diverted by obviously synthetic versions of the past, but the passion for authentic history is viable too and so they are deeply moved by a movie like *Abe Lincoln in Illinois*. They will digest cardboard lovers and papier-mâché heroes by the carload because it requires no effort, yet nothing excites them so much as characters who are recognizable and realistically drawn human beings. People are frivolous, but they are also serious. They have juvenile moments but mature ones too, and cannot be boxed up into simple categories or treated as abstractions.

To human beings with their complex needs, the producers have brought only a limited understanding. On the level of simplified entertainment and relaxation, they have attempted to satisfy the requirements in great abundance. Year in, year out, the musicals, the soap operas, the crime programs, the smart lightweight comedies, have been ground out with ever-increasing richness of technical detail. They have addressed themselves to the important functions of providing escape, relaxation, effortless soothing of tired nerves. To sneer at their efforts in these directions is to deny a tremendous aspect of human nature itself: its need to be temporarily freed of tension and responsibility, without which the maintenance of psychic health, difficult enough at any time, becomes almost impossible. The great achievement of the mass media, in which they can take a legitimate pride, lies in their catering to this aspect of man with all the great physical powers at their command. No industries that persuade fifty to eighty million Americans to buy tickets at movie box offices every week and purchase twenty million television sets, not to mention the countless numbers of radios, can do so without satisfying some profound need in human nature itself.

Yet even in the matter of entertainment they have consistently aimed at the lowest and most juvenile forms. They have seldom supplied higher and more adult levels of entertainment which would attract the vast grown-up audience that is searching for relaxation, but is repelled by the drivel that pours out of sound-track and amplifier. Gilbert Seldes, in an *Atlantic Monthly* article "How Dense is the Mass?", describes the effects of this on the movies:

> ... the movies have not provided the kind of entertainment that the average adult feels he must have. The people who stay away from the movies are not a lunatic fringe of intellectuals; they are the people who used to go regularly, they are average grownups no longer satisfied by the infantile myths of the movies. In their astounding miscalculation of the audience, studio executives not only recognized no difference between children and adults: they thought of maturity as a purely intellectual quality. Neither the movie-makers nor their bankers are peculiarly sensitive to the varieties of human experience; they keep thinking of the mass man and seem not to know that regardless of intellectual level the texture of a man's life is more intricately woven in the years when he is finding his place in the world, starting a family, going to war, buying a house. . . .
> What needs to be done in the movies is relatively simple: make pictures for grownups. This does not mean, as Hollywood pretends, grim, slow-paced European films. The mature mind takes satisfaction in comedy, too, and in farce.[16]

It is no wonder that two thirds of all those who purchase movie tickets are under thirty years of age,[17] and that the films are rapidly becoming a pastime for children and teen-agers. What is surprising is their persistent neglect of the adult audience, especially when the occasional mature entertainment films have often been box-office successes. Pictures like *The Maltese Falcon, Treasure of the Sierra Madre, Letter to Three Wives, All About Eve* and *High Noon* were pure entertainment with-

---

[16] *The Atlantic Monthly*, November 1948.
[17] From *The Hollywood Picture*, a CBS Documentary, broadcast November 3, 1948.

out any of the intellectual elements of the "think-piece" that so scare producers, and drew large and responsive audiences. Instead of profiting from these examples and tapping the purchasing power of this great market now slipping out of their hands, the film makers—and their counterparts in radio and television— have continued to cling to their preoccupation with the juvenile and the banal.

If the producers have brought only a limited understanding to the need for entertainment, to the other needs of human nature they have brought hardly any understanding at all. They have tended to look on an interest in reality with cool indifference, when not actually regarding it with blank astonishment. The number of pictures and programs, comic or tragic, dealing with solid themes has been small indeed. One recalls a somber masterpiece of politics and psychology like *The Informer* and an infrequent satire on political bossism like Preston Sturges' *The Great McGinty*. On radio and television, there have been discussions of literature and philosophy like *Invitation to Learning* and the witty radio essays of Gilbert Highet, informative programs like the *Johns Hopkins Science Review* and *You Are There,* lively forums on contemporary issues and books such as *Town Meeting of the Air* and *The Author Meets the Critics,* original and spectacular operas like Gian-Carlo Menotti's *Amahl and the Night Visitors* and Benjamin Britten's *Billy Budd.* Notable novels such as *The Grapes of Wrath,* plays like *The Little Foxes* and *A Streetcar Named Desire,* have been transcribed to the screen with no loss of their original power. But the total number has been small. Not so small as might be gathered from Paul Muni's cynical remark that out of the three hundred movies made annually, three or four are bound to come out well no matter how hard one tried to make them like the rest. But in the total ratio, lamentably few.

So long as the feeling persists that good programs spell bad business, the quality of our popular arts is not likely to advance.

The tug-of-war between artist and businessman, writer and sponsor, which has resulted in so much frustration to one and so much hostility to new ideas in the other, must be resolved not only in the interests of both but, even more, of the public as a whole. Budd Schulberg describes this conflict as it takes place in Hollywood:

A good businessman . . . aims to please as many people as possible while minimizing risk and standardizing production. The aim of the good artist, on the other hand, is exactly the opposite. He turns his back on every formula, keeps breaking new ground, risks everything, and whether he succeeds or fails, prepares to risk again. When the definitive history of Hollywood's first fifty years is written, . . . it will concern itself with this still unresolved struggle between the business machine and those men and women of talent who failed to check their personal integrity and artistic conscience at the gate when they came in.[18]

In radio and television this antagonism has been equally sharp. The unwillingness of sponsors and broadcasters to take risks and constantly invigorate their medium is excused on grounds of practicality. Yet by an irony we have observed before, this kind of practicality, this sacrifice of long-range planning for short-range returns, this sacrifice of mature ideas and emotions for the sake of what one critic has called "a batch of synthetic popularity ratings," proves ultimately to be the most impractical of policies. Jack Gould, in a brilliant commentary on the state of television, demonstrates the folly of this shortsightedness:

To be content with the "products" of television as they stand now, merely because their acceptance by the public is beyond doubt, is to follow the most perilous course open to broadcasters

---

[18] Budd Schulberg, "Movies in America: After Fifty Years," *The Atlantic Monthly,* November 1947.

and sponsors. It can only lead to one end: a constant shrinkage of the base upon which the whole medium rests.

If only in economic self-defense, the sponsors and broadcasters must now embark on a program of research and experimentation in television programming. This goal is not altruistic or intellectual; it is eminently practical. By constantly broadening and stimulating the public taste, the sponsors are widening the billboards upon which in future years they can paste their advertisements. . . .

How is this to be done, asks the business man? . . . In television the answer is the . . . writers, actors, directors and producers who have devoted a lifetime to learning their specialized crafts. For heaven's sake let them do their jobs as they know they should be done.

Give the writers the chance to write what is in their hearts and consciences and give them the chance to say it in their own way. What do writers know of the problems of vice presidents in charge of sales; what do vice presidents in charge of sales know of the problems of writers?[19]

In our popular arts, as in so many other aspects of our national life, the conflict between impulses pulling against one another has only damaged and retarded their growth. The contending groups animated by these impulses must recognize the natural harmony that can exist between them and work together toward their common goals. Signs of this co-operation are by no means absent. The debut, in 1952, of a ninety-minute television program *Omnibus* was an augury of this advance. Initiated by the Ford Foundation, this program was announced as "frankly experimental," offering the viewer "a vaudeville show of the arts and skills of man," aiming "to elevate TV's level of taste, yet attract a mass audience." A significant feature of the program was its absolute freedom from sponsor control. The sponsors—of which there were no lack—bought time on it without having anything to say about the contents.

---

19 The New York *Times,* October 19, 1952.

This was also a unique feature of the precedent-shattering contract between dramatist Robert E. Sherwood and the National Broadcasting Company which called for the playwright to prepare nine original plays for television. Though the plays will be commercially sponsored, the writer was expressly relieved of any requirement to confer with sponsors or advertising agencies. This, explained Mr. Sherwood, would serve the best interests of both the creative artist and the advertiser:

When you are dealing with sponsors and advertising agencies, you are dealing with people whose primary interest is not what you write in television. Their primary interest is in selling their product. We want to do the best possible work . . . and, having done that, let the sponsor come along.

Separation of the theatrical and advertising functions of television should lead to improved programming that would be advantageous to the sponsor.[20]

Mr. Sherwood, who had written many movie scripts, noted that the "failure of Hollywood executives to establish a direct business relationship with the writer and recognize the importance of his independence, thwarted the cultural growth of the motion picture industry for many years."

Developments such as these, together with the setting aside by the Federal Communications Commission of channels for educational television and the persistent survival, however limited, of adult films and broadcasting programs, represent the most encouraging prospect for the future of our popular arts. Once they overcome their distrust of their own potential maturity, they will emerge from the arrested adolescence which has shackled them so far.

---

[20] As reported by Jack Gould in the New York *Times,* November 24, 1952.

Chapter IX

Folklore of the American Hero

T HE DISTORTIONS OF THE WHOLE MAN PRES-
ent in our national life have been reflected in our heroes. The accent has been on muscle over mind, instinct instead of brain,
impulsiveness at the expense of reflectiveness, producing a series
of exaggeratedly one-sided, immature personalities. The idealized
American male has leaned strongly in the direction of brawn
and egotism. Rugged individualism has been his dominant
motif. As he appears in our folklore and fiction, he has been
more a creature of driving will power than of intelligence and
imagination. He has tended to be cocky, boastful and aggressive, and has seldom been projected into situations requiring
anything more from him than a physical response.

This character made his debut in the folk tales of the frontier.
Paul Bunyan was a legendary lumberjack of superhuman
strength who, accompanied by his gigantic helper, Babe the
Blue Ox, wandered through the logging camps of the Midwest
and Northwest. He made the Rocky Mountains, scooped out
the Mississippi River and carved the Grand Canyon while relaxing from his professional labors among the lumberjacks. His

counterpart in the southern camps was a figure almost equally gargantuan named Tony Beaver. Paul Bunyan's chief competitor was Pecos Bill, legendary cowboy hero of the Southwest, whose supporters claimed that it was he who excavated the Grand Canyon and dug out the Rio Grande. The Negroes had their legendary hero too, in John Henry, a steel driller, who pitted himself against a steam drill. In the contest between "de flesh ag'in de steam," John Henry won, but in the process burst a blood vessel and died.

Frontier effusion was not limited to imaginary characters. Prodigies of valor were attributed also to Buffalo Bill, Davy Crockett, Kit Carson, and Wild Bill Hickok, to horses, dogs and frogs, to individual men threatened by flood, stampedes, Indians and wild animals. The tall tale, inflated, grotesque, bragging, flourished like tumbleweed on every frontier west of the Alleghenies, shaping its size to the vastness of the landscape from which it sprang. The arrogance it illustrated had a naïveté in keeping with the new country, and was a kind of imaginative reaction to the breathtaking opportunities, grandeur and dangers of the West. A boast, however vainglorious, made a man feel better in the face of a rude, overbearing Nature, filled with savages and mystery. It was whistling to keep his courage up, a brave attempt to equalize the odds or even weight them a bit in his own favor. As such, frontier humor at bottom did not take itself seriously and recognized itself for what it was: the equivalent of a stiff drink before venturing into the storm. It was in the essentially lighthearted tradition of Munchausen, Cyrano and other energetic purveyors of comic braggadocio.

In its last stages frontier egotism hardened into a mold less good-humored and more overbearing. The he-man arose, equipped with a full set of muscles and instincts which, as Jack London would have it, enabled him not simply to survive but to master the rigors of life in Alaska and the Pacific Islands, those

last American frontiers. London became the chief apostle of the
he-man cult, which appeared also in the work of Frank Norris
and Theodore Dreiser shortly after the turn of the century, and
bobbed up in the creation of Tarzan, the epic American figure
who has served for almost fifty years as the juvenile symbol of
virility in a primitive environment. London's heroes flex their
biceps, beat their chests, speak in booming masculine voices,
and zealously observe the law of club and fang. This law, to
which they react unconsciously, governs the tough raw world
in which they live, whether they are men or animals. There is
indeed no real distinction in London's eyes between men and
animals, both being species struggling for existence in the grim
evolutionary universe of Darwin. Buck, the canine hero of
The Call of the Wild, faces the same problems and reacts exactly
as would a man in his position:

This first theft marked Buck as fit to survive in the hostile
Northland environment. It marked his adaptability, his capacity
to adjust himself to changing conditions, the lack of which
would have meant swift and terrible death. It marked, further,
the decay or going to pieces of his moral nature, a vain thing and
a handicap in the ruthless struggle for existence. It was all well
enough in the Southland, under the law of love and fellowship,
to respect private property and personal feelings; but in the
Northland, under the law of club and fang, whoso took such
things into account was a fool. . . . [1]

His adaptability, moreover, had nothing to do with intelligence. It was instinctive:

Not that Buck reasoned it out. He was fit, that was all,
and unconsciously he accommodated himself to the new mode
of life. . . . And not only did he learn by experience, but

---

[1] Jack London, *The Call of the Wild* (New York: Grosset & Dunlap, 1915),
pp. 53-4.

instincts long dead became alive again. The domesticated generations fell from him. In vague ways he remembered back to the youth of the breed, to the time the wild dogs ranged in packs through the primeval forest and killed their meat as they ran it down. . . . In this manner had fought forgotten ancestors. They quickened the old life within him, and the old tricks which they had stamped into the heredity of the breed were his tricks. They came to him without effort or discovery, as though they had been his always.[2]

London took this farrago of Darwinism, literary Bernarr MacFaddenism, Nietzscheanism (contempt for moral law which is regarded as a weak sentimental plaything for the flabbily civilized, made flabbier by Christianity), and the glorified nonrational unconscious, and wrapped it up into the gaudiest package of primitive romanticism in American literature:

There is an ecstasy that marks the summit of life, and beyond which life cannot rise. And such is the paradox of living, this ecstasy comes when one is most alive, and it comes as a complete forgetfulness that one is alive. This ecstasy, this forgetfulness of living, comes to the artist, caught up and out of himself in a sheet of flame; it comes to the soldier, war-mad on a stricken field and refusing quarter; and it came to Buck, leading the pack, sounding the old wolf-cry, straining after the food that was alive and that fled swiftly before him through the moonlight. He was sounding the deeps of his nature, and of the parts of his nature that were deeper than he, going back into the womb of Time. He was mastered by the sheer surging of life, the tidal wave of being, the perfect joy of each separate muscle, joint, and sinew in that it was everything that was not death, that it was aglow and rampant, expressing itself in movement, flying exultantly under the stars and over the face of dead matter that did not move.[3]

---

[2] *Ibid.*, pp. 54, 56.
[3] *Ibid.*, p. 83.

With this eloquence, in animated verbal technicolor, the worship of muscles and blood reached a climax. Buck, bestriding the farthest reaches of Alaska like a canine colossus, proceeded to spawn a whole line of male body beautifuls from Tarzan to Superman, though none quite equaled him as a triumphant piece of biology conquering a raw, red-meat environment.

London, dipped in pastels and muted to a juvenile market, was the catalyst for that fabulous folklore superman, Tarzan of the Apes. Tarzan represents the supreme triumph of behaviorist psychology. Left adrift in darkest Africa while still a baby, he is suckled by a female gorilla, grows up with the tribe, and responds perfectly to the demands of an exacting environment. He makes friends with Tantor the elephant and declares eternal war on Numa the lion. He acquires the skills and sense-sharpness of animals while retaining the superior flexibility and shrewdness of man. This combination makes him supreme in the jungle, and the terrifying "Ah-oó-ah" scream which he emits while standing on the slain body of a foe is enough to send shivers down the spines of the most ferocious beasts. His creator, Edgar Rice Burroughs, doesn't exactly stand in his way. At a strategic point in Tarzan's youth he deposits a knife in the underbrush where the boy will be sure to find it. With this knife, which Tarzan instinctively knows how to wield (he is not the son of Lord Greystoke, an English big-game hunter, for nothing), he becomes pretty much the uncontested boss of Central Africa, all the more awe-inspiring because he is so furless and pale of skin. Moreover, he is happy, free of tensions and neuroses, admirably adapted to his world. None of the anxieties that afflict civilized men disturb him, probably one of the many reasons for his popularity with Western readers and movie-goers.

His one potential difficulty might have been occupational

boredom, but here again the author comes to the rescue. Two volumes suffice to get him reared and engaged in miscellaneous combat with a variety of savages and animals. At the point where Tarzan is threatened with nothing to do, the jungle suddenly becomes populated with ant men, evil leopard women, men from Mars (Burroughs borrowed as freely from H. G. Wells as he did from Jack London), and European expeditions, each headed by a grade-B villain, in search of ivory or gold. It takes Tarzan a book apiece to dispose of these menaces to the security of his continent, just in time to be informed by one of the visiting Englishmen of the title and inheritance waiting for him back home. At first he is indifferent, but he falls in love with a beautiful young Englishwoman called Jane who understands him perfectly. For her sake he returns to England, becomes Lord Greystoke, masters English, begets a son, and is all the while secretly miserable. Here the theme that man is unsuited to civilization and like all other animal species is better off in primitive surroundings, is sounded once again, this time with a bell-like simplicity that a child could understand.

Back he goes to Africa, encouraged by his understanding wife. As a concession to his dual existence, he builds an ornate Western mansion in a clearing, but spends practically all his time in the jungle communing with his animal friends. There he remains permanently stationed, engaged in new adventures that differ little from the old, playing and replaying his supercharged role with little sign of fatigue.

The films took him over with one significant change: they made him even more primitive than he was in print, and indeed never had him leave the jungle at all. Thus the movie Tarzan understands little English and speaks even less despite the fact that he has been living for years with an educated English girl. This is presented as a quaint deficiency on his part, but it is also made quite plain that his mind is not up to it. His mind is indeed conspicuous by its absence or, if existent, is totally obscured by his oversized physique and its washboard array of rippling muscles. The film Tarzan is simplified beyond his literary prototype partly as a concession to countless moviegoing kiddies, and partly because of the general movie tendency to strip everything down to bare essentials. The jungle world of the primitive superman requires the predominance of muscle over mind and instinct over intellect. Tarzan fulfills these requirements as much as Buck and the earlier frontier giants. Like them, he remains undefeated in a ruthlessly primitive environment, a triumph of sheer naked brawn and naked instinct.

Another of London's latter-day progeny is an even more spectacular example of the man who makes himself king of the physical universe. Dubbed Superman without frills and with exquisite accuracy, he forced his way into our folklore through the comic strips and radio where his magnificently proportioned body and flying red cape have been familiar fixtures since the late 1930s. Superman has two types of adventure: skirmishes on other planets and jousts with criminals on earth. His activities on the side of law and order are less interesting than the others since their conclusions are foregone. Since he is virtually immortal and can move about in defiance of gravity, the advantage he enjoys over mortal crooks is formidable. It also makes the odds so uneven that suspense is reduced to the vanishing point. With Superman around, one can only wonder that there is any crime at all. Indeed, during the war, his sponsors were embarrassed by the insistent demand of some of his young audience that he proceed to Berlin pronto, drop bombs on Hitler and his associates, and bring hostilities to a quick end.

His experiences in space are more in keeping with his capacities. Himself a native of the planet Crypton which blew up one day leaving him sailing through the ether as the lone survivor, he is perfectly at home in the solar system. He is called on from time to time to save other planets from destruction because of changes in the gaseous structure of their atmosphere or because of scientific experiments that have got out of hand. With his embarkation cry "Up! Up! And *away-y-y-y!*" he traverses some millions of miles in a few minutes flat and lands without a bump on the ailing planet, where he faces creatures similarly endowed with supernatural powers. He is captured, dragged through underground passageways, witnesses strange religious rites, swims across molten subterranean lakes, intrigues with beautiful princesses laden with dazzling jewels and, at the end, like the cosmic impresario that he is, organizes the work of mass rescue with the aplomb of a ringmaster. In these exotic circumstances, bastard Jules Verne though they are, Superman meets worthy opposition and his superb physical equipment is brought to a proper test.

As with Tarzan, his actions proceed from his corpuscles, more highly charged than the corpuscles of ordinary men. He never asks "why?" or "how?" but "where?" Space is the dimension in which he operates, and into it thought never ventures. Not that Superman is anti-intellectual. He is only anti-crook. Thinking does not occur to him, is not necessary for the success of his enterprises, and would probably slow up their tempo. The person who sets out to discredit the mind is at least aware of and involved with it. Superman is sublimely indifferent, a condition in some ways more devastating than outright repudiation. He is, like Tarzan and most other factitiously primitive figures, a symbol of pure motor action, whose profound attraction lies in that very fact. To create personages who are free of the responsibilities of mind and have conquered the terrors of Nature is to provide a measure of release for oneself. Primitivism thrives in the bosom of every scientific and mechanical age, and has seldom been so strong or produced so many imaginative symbols as in our own time.

Superman heads the list of a whole group of comic-book characters more or less like himself. These include such well-known figures as Captain Marvel, Captain Marvel Jr., Batman, Mighty Mouse, Super Mouse and Kid Eternity. Perhaps the most famous comic-strip variant of primitivism is Al Capp's Li'l Abner. Li'l Abner, living in a stone-age village called Dogpatch, is all muscle and no brain. Boulders bounce off his skull without visible effect. His favorite exclamation is the half-strangled guttural sound *gulp!* With the aid of his shrewdly intuitive mother, however, he manages to foil the plots of big-city slickers and backwoods bad 'uns while himself fleeing the advances of beautiful young women who find his well-proportioned body irresistible. He combines good nature, stupidity, brawn and a flair for incredible feats of physical strength. He stems in a straight line from Superman, Tarzan, Buck, all the way back to Paul Bunyan.

When the geographical frontier came to an end and was replaced by the industrial frontier, another type of hero emerged. Egotism and the drive for power, the qualities necessary for success in the new technological jungle, replaced the physical strength and biological instinct that had been essential for survival in the primitive jungle. Frank Cowperwood, central figure of three of Theodore Dreiser's novels, was the first version of this new man, operating in the upper echelons of American finance during the 1870s and '80s.

The morality which London's dog had to shed before becoming a success in Nature's wilderness was also shed by Dreiser's Frank Cowperwood before becoming a success in man's. Dreiser's conception of the world was identical with London's. The dominance of the strong seemed to him the essential fact about American society, and there was no real difference between an unscrupulous and determined tycoon smashing competitors on his way to industrial supremacy and an unscrupulous and de-

termined dog killing his rivals on his way to leadership of the
wolf pack. The famous incident of the lobster and the squid
symbolizes this "eat or be eaten" view of the universe. When
Frank was a young boy in Philadelphia, he observed in a store-
window tank a lobster pursuing a squid, seizing it, and devour-
ing it slowly. The scene made an unforgettable impression on
him. It suggested in miniature the exact nature of life among all
species, and he resolved to act accordingly. He would be the
lobster and other people the squid. In the trilogy dealing with
his financial and sexual adventures, he proceeded to devour his
prey at a rapid rate in Philadelphia, Chicago and London, each
change of venue leading to an expanded theater of operations.
Whether carrying on political and economic jugglery on a high
scale, making love to a succession of attractive women, or
assembling vast collections of art, Cowperwood is a symbol of
consecrated egotism, acknowledging no law but his own need
for survival and thirst for power. He is an intelligent man
but his intelligence serves the interests of a carnivorous and
destructive aggrandizement. As such, it is a subverted faculty,
dangerous in the extreme and open to the accusations which have
been launched against it.

Cowperwood, like Jack London's Buck, was presented with admiration. London cheered Buck on enthusiastically, and Dreiser
was smitten with his hero's triumphant technique, for Cowperwood emerged a likeable figure despite his prolific thieveries
and lecheries. Elsewhere in his fiction Dreiser veered away
from power worship to consider the effects of a society run by
Cowperwoods upon its numerous victims, the Jenny Gerhardts,
Clyde Griffiths and others, and it is indeed in this aspect that
he is most remembered. But London remained steadfast to the
cult of muscular and ruthless primitivism, his pirating Sea Wolf
standing as the human equivalent of his Alaskan hound, both
predatory figures in the evolutionary jungle.

While Cowperwood was operating on the top layers of American business life, the heroes of Horatio Alger, Jr., were making their way through the lower. Tom the bootblack, Andy Grant, frugal Frank and other protagonists from celebrated tales like *Luck and Pluck, Sink or Swim, Bound to Rise, From Rags to Riches,* began life with empty pockets and nothing to recommend them but their tenacity, thrift, and an uncompromising instinct to succeed. They invariably succeeded. They rescued rich men's daughters from difficult situations, returned missing purses to their owners, resisted all manner of temptation dangled before them by a variety of villains and, in the end, received their reward in the form of handsome jobs, lucrative investments, or outright partnerships. The great adventure was to start with nothing and end with a pot of gold. If a young man had enough drive and stick-to-it-iveness, there was no limit to the fortune he could amass, and though the fortunes won by the Horatio Alger heroes were hardly to be compared with those of Andrew Carnegie, John D. Rockefeller or Frank Cowperwood, they were vast in terms of the modest dimensions and simple psychology through which their stories moved. In these mythical tales a whole series of small-sized, commercially oriented supermen emerged, within the fantasy reach of millions of boys from the farms and small towns of America.

The first great period of industrial expansion between the Civil War and the first World War came to its close a generation after the ending of the physical frontier. As it ended, there arose an inevitable nostalgia for those free and easy days when individual men could pit their strength against the resistant world and emerge triumphant. With the twentieth century rapidly closing in on people, restricting their freedom of movement and their sense of being able to do what they wished, there grew a longing for earlier times when a man could maneuver easily and place his stamp on life. The depth of this longing could be measured in the extraordinary vogue of historical romances and cowboy sagas that appeared in the 1920s and '30s.

Both had one element in common: the portraiture of characters in an earlier age who were free agents. The less possible free action seemed in the present, the more demonstrations of it from the past were welcomed. What prodigies of free will were performed by the swashbuckling hero without whom Washington could not have won the Revolutionary War and with whom Napoleon almost averted Waterloo! This hero defeated the best-laid plans of Bonnie Prince Charlie, and paved the way for Richard the Lion-Hearted to win his spectacular (if indecisive) victories in the Holy Land. Though history made little or no mention of this ubiquitous dynamo, he was real enough on the black-and-white page of a novel, and became even more so on a technicolor screen. He performed prodigies of valor, defeated formidable coalitions organized against himself or his cause, and made vital decisions which he proceeded to implement in the teeth of circumstances that would have discouraged any ordinary man. The delightful and magnetic thing about his environment was its pliability. It resisted just enough to generate a plausible risk, yet in the end assumed the shape required. The inevitable conflict between the individual and his environment invariably concluded with the satisfying triumph of the individual. In this triumph lay the sweet kernel of enchantment which lured the American reader searching for a way out of his own situation, where his environment was losing its pliability with alarming speed. The more the world pressed in upon one, the more necessary became that recall of a past where, so the romancers insisted, the world could be pressed back.

Nor did sex affect the issue. Women were blessed with the same resoluteness as men, and in many significant instances moved heaven and earth as efficiently. Heading the parade was

Scarlett O'Hara, who managed three husbands, survived the siege of Atlanta, rebuilt her ruined plantation, and performed numerous other feats of boldness while a civilization was collapsing about her. And all this less than a century ago, in the very midst of a bloody and calamitous war more terrible in many ways than any the nation has since endured.

The same rampant free will that operated in the costume, cloak-and-dagger drama dominated the Western. Costume aside, there was little difference between them. Dress the cowboy in knee breeches and powdered wig, remove his gun, strap a sword to his side and keep him on the same horse—he will blend without difficulty into any romance from the sixteenth century through the nineteenth. His tongue may have to be loosened a bit, otherwise he remains intact. Morally and philosophically, insofar as virtue and freedom of action are concerned, he can move from one genre to the other, in book and film, without significant alteration. The essence of *Forever Amber* and *Streets of Laredo*, *The Black Rose* and *Colorado Territory*, *The Three Musketeers* and *Red River*, the one book by Margaret Mitchell and the fifty by William MacLeod Raine, was identical; and their popularity sprang from the decline of confidence experienced by millions of readers living in an age of perpetual crisis.

The cowboy hero with steel-blue or slate-gray eyes, two-fisted and two-gunned, as fast on the draw with his left hand as with his right, fought his way through packs of enemies and never allowed the bruising he received en route to daunt his spirit or check his purpose. The villain enjoyed a similar freedom. He too cleared away formidable obstacles until the climactic duel in which he and the hero faced each other at point-blank range while the universe, in suspension, held its breath. Here again, sharply and simply put, was the lost reality: destiny held tightly in one's hand. This was the attraction in every horse opera, from those turned out skillfully by Ernest Haycox and Luke Short to the stalest hodgepodge whipped up in the pulp magazines.

The hero and the plot in which he came encased were long on action and short on gray matter, and gained very little in credibility since Zane Grey's time shortly after the start of the century. The hero said little, thought less, but was given to sudden outbursts of violent and effective physical activity. In chapter one he is a young cowboy, dust-stained, travel-worn, riding up to a large ranch looking for a job. If the scene is Texas, he has come from Montana, where he got into a shooting scrape, killed a man, and is now wanted by the law. If the scene is Montana, he has just come from Texas, where the same things happened. Colorado and Nevada, Idaho and New Mexico, Arizona and Wyoming, are other set geographical tandems. It is plain enough, without anything being said, that the shooting was a matter of self-defense, and that this would be made clear eventually. The trail-weary cowboy asks for a job, gets it, catches a glimpse of the ranch owner's daughter (or niece, or perhaps herself the boss—her father was mysteriously shot a year or two before), and makes the acquaintance of the foreman. He takes an instant dislike to this last character, hard on the heels of his falling instantly in love with the first.

The triangle now physically and emotionally complete, the story plunges into high gear. Chapters two, three and four set the scene: the ranch has been plagued by a gang of rustlers the identity of whose leader remains unknown. The foreman, engaged to the girl, suggests that the unknown cowboy is perhaps the man, so for the first half of the book the girl and the foreman are ranged against the cowboy. Midway, the triangle shifts and there is an exchange of partners. The girl's suspicions are aroused by a few little incidents involving her fiancé, which consume chapters five and six, and at the start of chapter seven she has slid over to the side of the cowboy. It is still two against one, but the foreman (who the inexperienced reader now realizes is the rustler chief; the experienced reader knew it from the start) is now the one. Two chapters are consumed in skirmishing between the realigned forces. The foreman has skipped off to his hide-out in the hills and is preparing his grand coup, nothing less than the embezzlement of the whole herd. To pave the way he kidnaps the heroine in chapter ten, using her as bait to draw off the hero who comes in hot pursuit. Chapter twelve witnesses the crashing denouement: the two lovers trapped by the rustler crew. The cowboy picks off the besiegers with deadly accuracy while suffering only minor flesh wounds himself. But their ammunition is running low, and when it runs out they will be overwhelmed.

We are now down to chapter thirteen and it is time for the *deus ex machina*. Three cartridges from the end of the hero's arsenal, whoops are heard from the horizon and in due course the rescue party from the home ranch sweeps into sight scattering the rustlers to the four winds. If the Western has a military background, the rescue party is announced by bugles and appears in the shape of the U. S. Cavalry from a near-by military fort. The foreman in the meanwhile has made his escape, making it necessary for chapter fourteen to be devoted to the pursuit by the cowboy, and the final gun duel with its calculable end. Chapter fifteen winds up loose ends, and is climaxed by the cowboy's declaration of love. This in itself is a supreme example of bathos. Though long on action, he is short on words, and his emotions, throbbing since he first laid eyes on the heroine, have not yet found expression. The moment, however, has come, and he can no longer avoid it. On the last page, riding with his lady toward a beautiful sunset, his heart choked with feelings that have long since outrun his vocabulary, he finally makes a supreme effort. His voice trembling slightly with strain, his passions at the flood, he manages to utter what is surely one of the immortal declarations of American literature: "I guess I kinda like ya, gal."

With that the tale comes to an end. Over the well-worn grooves of its plot thousands of similar, if not identical sagas have journeyed. On the stage of the Western all the trappings of determinism were removed, and the way cleared for the absolute sway of the individual will. Underneath the corn, the pubescent romantics, the incessantly infantile action, the unwavering routine, this fact was as visible and dominant as in the tragedies of Corneille, consciously devoted as they were to the study of will.

The literary and cinematic version of the Wild Westerner was as different from the reality as imagination and the needs of popular psychology could make him. Rustlers were not always caught; they frequently founded cattle empires on the foundation of early thefts. The cowboy lost his gun duel with the bad man as often as he won. The "wicked" railroad gained its right of way more often than not. The war between cattlemen and sheepmen was not always concluded, as the books would have it, in favor of the sheep. The dirt, the grinding labor of frontier life are conspicuously absent from cowboy fiction. Yet our tribal memories of that life, nourished less by the actuality than the fantasy,[4] center around its heroism, masculinity, physical freedom, virtues which seem all the more desirable during the present period of individual shrinkage in the face of a menacing world. As for the operations of free will, they certainly had more scope then, or at least people believed they had. The cowboy hero symptomized, symbolized and summed up these operations in a sublimely pure and elementary form.

---

[4] To the point where Westerners, according to Bernard DeVoto, began to adopt the myths, mores and even the drawl commemorated in cowboy fiction. Here is an instance of literature imposing itself on life with a vengeance.

The spectacle of the individual triumphing over the world has had its contemporary equivalents as well. Side by side with the heroes of costumed history and the sagebrush frontier, there flourished those more modern but no less extravagantly admired figures, the gangster and the cynical tough guy. The American gangster has been a unique member of his species. Robin Hood, after all, subscribed to the best traditions of Anglo-Saxon fair play and had a social conscience besides. The romantic desperado indigenous to Latin countries had something of the adventurous in him, following banditry almost for its own colorful sake. The American gangster, by contrast, was a cold, hardheaded businessman to whom killing was just another method of doing business (just as to Clausewitz war was just another method of conducting diplomacy). In sentimental moments he was portrayed as a slum product driven to crime by poverty and bad living conditions, and so not really to blame for what he did. But once grown up, he became a ruthless character out for the big money who permitted nothing to stand in the way of his getting it. During his heyday in the '20s and '30s, his exploits thrilled the country and supplied the plots for a series of sensational films starring James Cagney and Edward G. Robinson.[5] Al Capone was by way of being, if not exactly a hero, at least an object of as much awe as accrued to any great captain of industry, and John Dillinger, the last of the buccaneering school of gangsters, left a good many newspaper readers wishing that he could have continued his spectacular career yet a while longer, so dramatically satisfying did they find it.

In however perverted a way, the gangster was a rugged individualist, living off the enterprise of others according to

---

[5] The gangster movies were supposed to have influenced juveniles into becoming delinquents but in all probability succeeded far more in supplying adults with vicarious excitement.

rules enforced by himself, enforced so ruthlessly that his personal role in the process of plunder was aggrandized. Like the robber baron of an earlier age, he stood out sharply from the ruck of less competitive men. His temporary disappearance from the American scene, caused partly by the end of Prohibition which created him in the first place and abetted by the sudden burgeoning of the FBI, left a trail of regret, not so much out of love of successful crime as out of a growing passion for the spectacle of will. When Dillinger met his end under a fusillade of G-man bullets in a Chicago alley in 1934, Robert E. Sherwood read the funeral sermon in his play *The Petrified Forest* the following year. Fleeing from the police, Duke Mantee, the gangster in the play, comes to the edge of the Petrified Forest in the Arizona desert. In a last blaze of action, asserting his defiance with a hail of bullets from his smoking gun, Duke is killed and becomes one with the other petrified mummies in the desert, the final relic, the playwright asserts, of a past now finally over. Little Caesar, the equally celebrated character created by W. R. Burnett, passes through an identical experience without ever leaving the streets and gang warfare of New York and comes to an equally dramatic and final end. This generation of gangsters had their successors later, who flourished behind varying screens of respectability or behind the anonymity of crime syndicates in the '40s and '50s, but they never achieved or for that matter even stirred the public admiration accorded to their predecessors. Frank Costello and Albert Anastasia seemed but sleazy versions of indomitable individualists like Dillinger and Capone.

It is the element of rugged individualism, the independent gesture of defiance that is the seedbed of heroism. The amateur felon who acts on impulse like the New York bus driver who drove his vehicle to Florida one fine day when he should have been covering his local route, or the assistant cashier who fleeced his bank of eight hundred thousand dollars which he proceeded to scatter to the four winds with insouciance, arouses the secret sympathy of millions. But the black-marketeer who operates stealthily behind the scenes, the procurement general who tosses advance information on army contracts to his business pals, the burglar who does everything possible to conceal himself, arouse very little interest and certainly no admiration. The concealment robs the act of its psychological meaning, and destroys its usefulness as a symbol. It is shady without being defiant, and defiance is the very trait that lends significance to the violation. An intellectual or spiritual repudiation of an established idea or a pattern of behavior won't do at all; when it does not arouse indifference, it arouses irritation and hostility on the part of those who will yield to the spell of similar action on the physical level. The highwaymen of American history have usually excited greater admiration in their time than the rebellious poets, scientists and martyrs. To the public at large Jesse James is a greater name than Willard Gibbs, Billy the Kid than Emily Dickinson. Al Capone has quickened the pulses of more Americans than all the organizers of Brook Farm put together, and while many have thrilled to the exploits of Pretty Boy Floyd and Baby-face Nelson, few have heard of John Jay Chapman and Randolph Bourne.

Blood brother to the gangster was the tough guy, who took life's cruelest blows and went on fighting. Ernest Hemingway produced a whole series of heroes cast in this mold, men who learned at an early age that the world was a tragic place in which "one's breath was drawn in pain," and who developed a code of endurance and bravery which enabled them to survive in it without losing their manhood. Henley's line, "My head is bloody but unbowed," was the text for their behavior. Jake Barnes, made sexually impotent by a war wound, hangs onto what is left of his life with unyielding grimness. Lieutenant Henry survives the war and the loss of Catherine Barkley without breaking down under the strain even momentarily. Jack Brennan, savagely fouled in the thirteenth round of his last fight, picks himself off the canvas while still in agony and delivers his final riposte. Francis Macomber flees from the wounded lion, yet pulls back from the pit of his own cowardice to stand firm in the path of a charging water buffalo two seconds before his death. The old Cuban fisherman, after hooking his giant marlin, fights to the end in a cause that he knows is a losing one against the sharks that tear at his great conquest. The defiance hurled in the teeth of a brutal universe by the wounded romantic individualist was given new tragic meaning by Hemingway. The "never-say-die" spirit of the Horatio Alger hero was now lifted into a complex level of action by the most influential writer of his time.

A variant of the tough guy has been the hard-boiled private detective, sensual and utterly amoral who, like the males in Hemingway, lived by the quickness of his reflexes rather than by the keenness of his intelligence. He too survived in a bloody world, only because he lost less blood than the opposition and because he had mastered better than they the fine points of Darwinian ethics. Though the detective story as such goes back to Edgar Allan Poe, the tough detective did not appear until well after the first World War. Dashiell Hammett was generally credited with having begotten him in *Red Harvest*. In that early book, at any rate, the private eye went through maneuvers soon destined to become classic. Hired to find some important object (a jade necklace, an I.O.U., an incriminating photograph), our hero, aged thirty to forty and in excellent physical condition, finds himself at the beginning of a maze. He lives from incident to incident with no clear notion until the very end where they are leading him and who the major criminal is. As in the adventures of Cowperwood, slices of erotica and slices of violence are pasted together as far as the eye can reach. On the average he makes love to three or four sexually magnetic women, consumes four or five quarts of hard liquor, smokes cartons of cigarettes, is knocked on the head, shot, and bruised in fist fights from seven to ten times— while groping his way through a dense fog as far as breaking the case is concerned. He has of necessity a short-range view, being able to see no farther than the next menacing face emerging from the mist, and is intent for the most part only on survival. He is no more hampered by scruples than Dreiser's robber baron, and is playing for high stakes (if not in money, then in life) in the same kind of dangerous universe. His relations with the police, who are as tough and unscrupulous as he, are hardly better than with the actual criminals, one of the striking features of his adventures being that there is little to choose by way of moral sense or civilized instincts between any in the cast of characters, no matter which side of the law they may be on.

The center of their existence is the I, bristling with defenses and traps for the enemy. And everybody is the enemy. Moreover, the enmity is curiously detached. It is like the enmity between animals; there is nothing personal in it. It is the competitive spirit in evolutionary survival, the clash of antagonists moved by laws having nothing to do with love or hate, judgment or conviction. This unstained biological egotism, in its literary context, is best seen in a masterpiece of the hard-boiled, private-sleuth genre, Dashiell Hammett's *The Maltese Falcon*. Its central figure, Sam Spade, is a characteristic specimen. When his partner in the detective agency is murdered while on assignment, he is upset not because of any love for the dead man but because if he does not bestir himself to catch the killer, it would be bad for business. Later, he has an affair with a beautiful client, but when he discovers that she is the murderess, he unhesitatingly turns her over to the police. Not because of any love of the police. Or out of a desire to see justice done. Or to avenge his slain partner. But simply to save his own skin; he is reasonably sure that she will not hesitate to murder him some day if it suits her purposes. Everyone in the story, regardless of affiliation, is in eternal pursuit of a "fall guy," a victim who can be tossed to the police if they get too close. This sacrificial offering, so reminiscent of the practices of certain primitive tribes, is accepted procedure which adds no end to the rat race of the hardboiled detective thriller, and gives to the egotism of its participants an even more knifelike and carnivorous edge. The general predatory air infects the police too. They are as ruthless and as prone to using the third degree as are the men they pursue. Fine shadings of law and order tend to dwindle away, until before long all sides, the constabulary included, have acquired the same amoral coloration. The lines between civilization and savagery begin to disappear, so that even the official paid agents of civilization lose their function as it grows blurred to the point of empty formality. The hard-boiled detective story becomes a capsuled version not so much of reality as of Darwinism carried to its ferociously logical extreme.

The tough guy in his most brutalized form, the hero generated by Hemingway, stripped by Hammett and Chandler of much of his dignity and nobility, was incarnated in Mike Hammer, the sadistic monster created by Mickey Spillane. Mike loves to splinter the knuckles of his enemies by pounding them with the butt of his gun; he enjoys shooting women in the guts in order to watch them suffer lingeringly; he threshes his way through a society of degenerate characters, an implacable avenger using hideous methods to purge a corrupt world. The odor of raw violence rises from his adventures in a form so crude that they are turned at once into nightmare kaleidoscopes without any pretense at art or insight. Since their appearance in the late '40s Spillane's books have sold by the millions, chiefly in paperbound reprints. For the price of twenty-five or thirty-five cents, with lurid covers showing Mike pointing a revolver at a half-naked blonde, these reprints supplied, like quick shots of cheap gin, terrific nerve-numbing literary jolts guaranteed to draw some kind of response from every reader. In them the tough guy had reached the end of the road. The myth of his conquest of the universe in purely physical terms now found its ultimate flowering.

The emergence of the military into public prominence during the second World War and the years immediately following turned up generals remarkably like the hard-boiled literary detective, transferred with little change to the arena of military combat. The most typical of these was General George Patton, appropriately nicknamed Old Blood and Guts. He was very tough, very physical, a perfect symbol of anti-intellectualism in its simplest American form. He incarnated a kind of national egotism: arrogant, bellicose, yet petulantly spoiled and naïve. The notorious soldier-slapping incident revealed his flat contempt for the workings of the mind. He was certain that the soldier suffering from combat fatigue was malingering, that nerves were a sign of welshing, and that only two mental states had any real foundation: bravery and cowardice. The rest was trumpery. A person was either fit or unfit. There were no two ways about it, and anybody who thought otherwise was a damned interfering meddler who didn't understand human nature. All this newfangled stuff about psychology and psychiatry was enough to turn a strong man's stomach. Much later, after the firing had ceased, Patton was chosen to administer a section of occupied Germany and ran almost immediately into another hornet's nest over his refusal to admit the existence of ideas. He had difficulty, he said, telling the difference between Nazis and anti-Nazis. In fact, he announced belligerently, he couldn't tell the difference at all. He was thereupon relieved of his post, much to his own expressed surprise. Peace and the problems of peace quite frankly baffled him, and once outside his tank, he was a lost man.

The tank, which was his favorite weapon, suggested the mechanical, physically driving America he stood for, at its best and worst. It was an aggressive, headlong weapon, full of beautiful machinery, high-powered and well-oiled, useless when standing still, fulfilling itself only when knocking down obstacles, when conquering. The world from inside a tank was a simple place, untroubled by issues of politics and morality, and could be managed by simple force if only people who had never been inside a tank didn't come along and muck it up. The general who led the Third Army from within its finely tooled armor viewed his problems through a tank's eyes. In combat his record was something less than an uninterrupted series of glorious victories, but no American general exceeded him in ardor, impulsiveness, bravado, dash and sheer lust for battle. He became something of a hero to those who also had simplified life along his lines, and a great, barbarous villain to those who regarded him as a brutish obstacle to a realization of the humane virtues. To both he was the epitome of the American who did not think and was proud of it. His closest approach to what might loosely be called thought was the composition of very bad poems to his martial God after victory on the battlefield. This streak of literary sentiment, with its overtone of Puritan piety, lent to his otherwise monolithic figure an authentic touch of pure corn.

Lest his type be blamed on the military, reference should be made to another, even more famous American general who went through a similar military education with results almost diametrically opposite. The general was Eisenhower, and the contrast all the more striking because of the intimate relationship between the two. It was Eisenhower who was Patton's superior in Africa, Sicily and Western Europe, who investigated the face-slapping affair, who removed Patton from his administrative post in Germany. Where Patton proceeded by instinct, Eisenhower was open to ideas. Where Patton reduced the condition of man to simple black and white, Eisenhower elevated it to the level where emotional complications and shifting categories played some part. Patton was floundering and disoriented in peaceful times; Eisenhower made the transition from war with sufficient naturalness to become president of Columbia University, commander of NATO, and Republican nominee for the Presidency. One reason for his election in 1952 was the immense respect and affection he had already inspired in millions of Americans of both parties before the campaign had even begun. If a characteristic America emerged in the one, an equally characteristic, though profoundly different America appeared in the other. If Patton was the symbol of bold physical egotism wedded to a boy-scout mentality and jungle ethics, Eisenhower was an example of the modest, unassuming man with obviously decent impulses and a deep sense of moral responsibility.

In the developing pattern of the American hero there have been signs of a movement away from the stark egotism displayed in the primitive environment of the frontier, in the new universe of technology and trade, in the new world of organized crime, and in the arena of war. Men growingly aware of the complex problems of life, conscious of their own inadequacies yet no less resolved to struggle and achieve, began to make their appearance in the public eye. The swashbuckling, flamboyant military egotist of the MacArthur-Patton type was increasingly elbowed out of the picture by men like Marshall, Eisenhower and Bradley who impressed their countrymen with their quiet restraint, who seldom blew their own horns, and in their professional work gave off an air of solid maturity.

A similar change was to be seen in the evolution of the movie hero. Douglas Fairbanks was the matinee idol of an earlier generation. He leaped over ten-foot walls, engaged in rapid and daring swordplay, stormed impregnable ramparts, and performed feats of incredible acrobatic skill much like a cinematic Paul Bunyan, remaining all the while tongueless, uninhibited by flickerings of thought or doubt, and sublimely indifferent to any emotion more complex than the desire to pulverize the villain. He was succeeded by James Cagney and Humphrey Bogart who operated in the same dimensions but used strongarm methods more in keeping with the advancing times. Flourishing with them but functioning in the suave purlieus of polite society instead of the back alleys of the underworld, were Clark Gable and Cary Grant, more polished perhaps but no less effective, who like Fairbanks never entertained the faintest doubt of their unconditional success in knocking over whatever obstacle stood in their way. They, in turn, were followed by a new type of movie hero who for the first time began exhibiting signs of awareness that the problems of life perhaps could not all be solved by a breezy manner, a gun, or a punch in the nose. His manner was diffident rather than brassy; he acquired a worried look rather than a pugnacious one; he tended to hunch his shoulders instead of clenching his fists. Skepticism, anxiety, self-deprecation, shyness, sensitivity, replaced aggressiveness and braggadocio. He moved in a world which possessed psychological as well as physical dimensions. The I was not his all-consuming center, and his successes were stained with the grit, harshness and difficulties of life. Played by an assortment of actors, Henry Fonda, Gregory Peck, James Stewart, William Holden, this new movie hero represented an advance toward reality and maturity. Without eliminating or replacing the earlier heroes, he found his way into their company and flourished in their midst.

The whole American passage from bombast, egotism and self-inflation toward more grown-up and disinterested approaches to experience was seen in an intense form in the writings of Thomas Wolfe. He created two heroes in his own image, Eugene Gant

and George Webber, each as gargantuan in frame and appetite
as Wolfe himself, appropriate somehow to the magnitude and
forward drive of the country itself. Perhaps the greediest of
American novelists, Wolfe devoured himself and everything he
touched; everything in him was puffed up several times beyond
life-size. His craving for food and drink turned into passionate
love affairs, making his addresses to apples, lettuce and sirloin
steak sound like the ardent perorations of an infatuated man to
his mistress. Eugene Gant's thirst for books was so overwhelming that he absorbed virtually the entire contents of the Harvard
library in a breath-takingly brief interval:

> . . . he would prowl the stacks of the library at night, pulling
> books out of a thousand shelves and reading in them like a mad-
> man. The thought of these vast stacks of books would drive
> him mad: the more he read, the less he seemed to know. . . .
> Within a period of ten years he read at least 20,000 volumes . . .
> and opened the pages and looked through many times that
> number. . . . Yet this terrific orgy of the books brought him no
> comfort, peace, or wisdom of the mind and heart. Instead, his
> fury and despair increased from what they fed upon, his hunger
> mounted with the food it ate.
>
> He read insanely, by the hundreds, the thousands, the ten
> thousands, yet he had no desire to be bookish; no one could
> describe this mad assault upon print as scholarly: a ravening
> appetite in him demanded that he read everything that had ever
> been written about human experience. He read no more from
> pleasure—the thought that other books were waiting for him
> tore at his heart forever. He pictured himself as tearing the
> entrails from a book as from a fowl. . . .
>
> This fury which drove him on to read so many books had
> nothing to do . . . with formal learning. He was not in any way
> a scholar and did not want to be one. He simply wanted to
> know about everything on earth; he wanted to devour the
> earth, and it drove him mad when he saw he could not do this.[6]

[6] Thomas Wolfe, *Of Time and the River* (New York: Scribner's, 1935), pp.
91-92.

His hunger for women was at a constant bursting point; when in love, he longed to consume them orally and digest them with his whole self, in the spirit of Havelock Ellis' observation that we secretly yearn to eat the things we love. And so with all else that impinged upon him. The urge to swallow up the world flung Wolfe violently upon the themes and emotions he returned to again and again: the image of a beloved and prematurely dead brother, the American continent with its geological vastness and beauties, slatternly Southern poor whites whom he loathed, opulent Jews whom he hated and admired in alternating waves, loneliness, curiosity and gnawing ambition. His immense egotism was the key to the inflated sentiments, the fury of his lust for self-realization and success, the subjective distortions of his early views of life. In seeking to exploit his own resources, he exploited without cease the resources of others, in the fashion of a noisy cement mixer into which an endless stream of raw material is poured.

For three long novels, this self-love reigned unchallenged, attracting, firing, shriveling everything that came within its orbit. It filled Wolfe's young heroes with pride and gluttony, with rages that bordered on insanity, with a deepening sense of frustration that no success seemed able to allay. No woman, no love however passionate, no literary achievement, could appease them, so great and irresistible was the vanity with which they were hagridden. It was an unquenchable vanity, and was slowly widening the gulf between Wolfe and the world.

However, during the prolonged adolescent nightmare of *Look Homeward, Angel, Of Time and the River* and *The Web and the Rock,* other impulses in Wolfe were struggling for voice—impulses toward truth and clarity, toward seeing the world as it was without twisting it into the false, vivid shapes demanded by an importunate ego, toward union with all men. Their appearance was fitful at first, and for a long time seemed threatened with extinction. Wolfe's very reluctance to let go of anything he felt was probably all that kept these fugitive tendencies alive during this long period.

The course of maturation for Wolfe was as agonizing as everything else in his life. One felt the enormous effort he made to take hold of himself and shake loose from his attempts to conquer the world by mashing it up and jamming it into himself. These attempts continued but with abating violence and, in his last novel, *You Can't Go Home Again,* were punctuated by bursts of writing that were detached, scrutinizing, and free of the maudlin frenzy that clung to the earlier work. When Webber breaks off his relationship with Mrs. Jack, it is as though a last shackle of his heedless youth has fallen from him, and he begins looking about through eyes less fogged with emotional mist:

> . . . he had learned that he could not eat his cake and have it, too. . . . He had learned that he could not devour the earth, that he must know and accept his limitations. He realized that much of his torment of the years past had been self-inflicted, and an inevitable part of growing up. And, most important of all for one who had taken so long to grow up, he thought he had learned not to be the slave of his emotions.[7]

He reveals an unsuspected insight into the foibles of others. He starts thinking seriously about the meaning of the world, and engages in a long correspondence with his editor on good and evil. He feels a growing pull in the direction of humanity. He becomes suddenly aware of the depression and the millions of unemployed, of the approaching world war, of reaction and progress. He feels compelled to take a stand and after months of reflection and debate ranges himself on the side of faith in

---

[7] Thomas Wolfe, *You Can't Go Home Again* (New York: Harper, 1940), p. 6.

men, optimism about the future, and an astonishing belief in the powers of reason.

Where hitherto reality had seemed caught up in a maddening flux, it now begins to acquire permanent dimensions. He begins to think of his art in terms outside himself. From this to a reaffirmation of America is only a short step:

I believe that we are lost here in America, but I believe we shall be found. . . .

I think the true discovery of America is before us. I think the true fulfillment of our spirit, of our people, of our mighty and immortal land, is yet to come. I think the true discovery of our own democracy is still before us. And I think that all these things are certain as the morning, as inevitable as noon. I think I speak for most men living when I say that our America is Here, is Now, and beckons on before us, and that this glorious assurance is not only our living hope, but our dream to be accomplished.[8]

The last stage of his last novel concludes with a reaffirmation of humanity itself:

And the essence of all faith, it seems to me, for such a man as I, the essence of religion for people of my belief, is that man's life can be, and will be, better; that man's greatest enemies, in the forms in which they now exist—the forms we see on every hand of fear, hatred, slavery, cruelty, poverty, and need—can be conquered and destroyed.[9]

Having thus visibly emerged from the suffocating vanity of his extreme youth, Wolfe was now ready for a new approach to life. At this point, with all its boundless promise, death overtook him. His work, though incomplete, constitutes a fascinating record of the fractures and distortions imposed by an ego

[8] *Ibid.,* p. 741.
[9] *Ibid.,* p. 738.

enthroned at the center of the whole personality, and of the stages by which its hold was loosened. This loosening process cost Wolfe something in the way of vitality and exuberance. *You Can't Go Home Again* is a slower, less volatile book than the others, much of it being more philosophical essay than novel. But it is a mirror of the egotistical mind in transition, on its way to emancipation, intellectual independence, maturity.

What happened to Wolfe's characters has been happening to the American hero generally. He started at the peak of an inflationary spiral and began slowly coming back to earth. The emptiness of mere physical size was filling up with psychological gradations. His certainty of absolute victory was replaced by a sobering realization that the world never yields up its triumphs in absolute terms. The epic proportions of myth and fantasy shrank toward the more lifelike proportions of reality. Pecos Bill, bestriding the whole West, had come down to the weather-beaten features of Gary Cooper, just trying to stay alive in the dusty street of some cowtown far from the main line. Frank Cowperwood, pulling off his spectacular financial coups in Philadelphia, Chicago and London, was reduced to George Apley and Harry Pulham, the anxious men of J. P. Marquand who had little trouble making plenty of money, but found that by itself it was not enough.

The deflation of the hero has marched with the deflationary times. The simple grain of life before the turn of the century has acquired shading, depth and a complex texture, making it harder to take hold of, less malleable to the individual will, and increasingly resistant to straight-ahead assault. If the American hero in this later stage has been less of a giant and more of a human being, he is reflecting a change in the atmosphere of the country on its way to a less ingenuous and more sophisticated concept of the nature of experience, the meaning of the universe, and the toughness of the future that looms ahead.

Part III

The
Whole Man

Chapter X

Intuition and Kindred Matters

I

ONE OF THE GREAT ENEMIES OF INTEL-
lect has been intuition, that mysterious indefinable faculty which
its defenders claim is responsible for the great discoveries of science, the vital insights into truth, even our daily hunches on
which so many actions rest. Precisely what intuition is has been
the subject of much speculation, most of which has ended in the
same impatient incoherence as afflicted the Prior in Browning's
poem when trying to define the soul:

> Man's soul, and it's a fire, smoke . . . no, it's not . . .
> It's vapor done up like a new-born babe—
>   . . . .
> It's . . . well, what matters talking, it's the soul![1]

Intuition is most commonly believed to inhabit the persons
of women, children, animals and geniuses, where it behaves
most erratically, coming and going at unexpected moments,

---

[1] "Fra Lippo Lippi," lines 184-5.

often without the conscious intention or knowledge of the person so endowed. For centuries women have been associated with pure feeling, insights beyond the calculations of the intellect, and a special capacity as well as inherent appetite for mystical experience. Pamela North, the sleuthing heroine of the detective stories by Frances and Richard Lockridge, is the intuitive female to the life. She goes off on seemingly irrelevant tangents, scorns the orderly and rational approach, refuses to believe the evidence of her senses, and always solves the crimes. She is the despair of the sensible people around her, who hold her in high affection though they have not the foggiest idea what makes her tick.

Intuitive children and animals come by the bushelful. The child who is wiser than the man, not intellectually, of course, but spiritually, is a popular figure in verse, fiction, films and folklore. Wordsworth's version of him is perhaps the most inflated:

> Thou, whose exterior semblance doth belie
>   Thy Soul's immensity;
> Thou best Philosopher, who yet dost keep
> Thy heritage, thou Eye among the blind,
>   . . . .
>   Mighty Prophet! Seer blest!
>   On whom those truths do rest,
> Which we are toiling all our lives to find . . . [2]

The children in Dickens are filled with intuitive moral judgments, equaled only by their capacity to absorb punishment without going under. The child star in films, from Shirley Temple to Margaret O'Brien, has always displayed an uncanny understanding of where the best interests of its bungling elders

---

[2] "Ode on Intimations of Immortality," lines 109-11, 114-16.

lie, disentangling their emotional problems with an astonishing finesse and finality.

Animals, dogs and horses especially, are reputed to be equally intuitive, although with them where instinct ends and intuition begins is not always clear. Rin-Tin-Tin used to recognize his friends and enemies even before they were introduced. Lassie has always proceeded to his[3] destination in an uncompromisingly straight line, whether it was home five hundred miles away or a friend in danger or a war mission to be accomplished. He is also much wiser than the human beings around him, whom he rescues from a succession of scrapes averaging one per reel. The horses of cinema and legend are as fully equipped with the sixth sense. Every cowboy hero, William S. Hart, Hoot Gibson, Buck Jones, Tom Mix, Roy Rogers, Gene Autry, has had one such noble animal, who not only performed tricks of marvelous agility and dexterity, but also understood the nature of the plot against his master (a feat perhaps not so greatly to be wondered at considering the story line of the average sagebrush opera), passed through the villain's hosts like an avenging scythe and, when the finale called for tenderness and discretion, discreetly withdrew while hero and heroine melted into each other's arms.

As for geniuses, it has long been popularly believed that their creative moments are doused in intuition. All the talk about hard work, discipline, perseverance, routine being the essence of the artistic process, has had little effect on the romantic notion of the artist feverishly turning out a masterpiece in one or a series of incandescent spasms, or the scientist in whose head the solution to the great experiment suddenly explodes like a flashbulb. Poets and composers, for some reason, are supposed to experience this kind of thing more than others.

------

[3] Despite the name, the movie Lassie was played by a male dog.

Poets, flushed, wild-eyed or sometimes, as was long thought to be Coleridge's case, under the exotic influence of opium, dash off their immortal lines in a blaze of ecstasy; while composers sit down at the piano and tear off their symphonies spontaneously, the pieces coming out finished and ready for eternity's applause. Genius is always recognized by such outbursts. The plodding fellow engaged in art who goes about his business soberly like everybody else obviously has no great talent, and lacks the divine spark. The divine spark is a popular and recurring epithet for creative intuition in great men, both words connoting something higher and more significant than appears in the merely rational. It functions best in the disembodied state described in the following passage from V. Sackville-West's novel, *All Passion Spent:*

> Only in a wordless trance did any true apprehension become possible, a wordless trance of sheer feeling, an extra-physical state, in which nothing but the tingling of the finger tips recalled the existence of the body, and a series of images floated across the mind, unnamed, unrelated to language.[4]

The wordless trance, the state of sheer feeling bound up with unnamed images unrelated to language, these are the ingredients of the intuitive process. It has no precise dimensions, undulates in unpredictable directions, and exists in folds of the subconscious. This very fluidity and shapelessness lend it a distinctive fascination. Its detachment from the conscious world of measured responsibilities and fixed demands makes it seem the more ideally suited to the temperament of genius.

The vogue of intuitional and related phenomena in the United States has been and remains enormous. Numerology,

---

[4] V. Sackville-West, *All Passion Spent* (New York: Doubleday, Doran, 1931), p. 170.

phrenology, the playing of hunches, spiritualism, psychic manifestations and mental telepathy—the vast underworld of the
nonrational—flourish in turgid abundance. Belief in witchcraft
remains widespread, and the murder of "witches" is still reported. Astrology, one of the more prolific cults, is almost a
major industry by itself. According to Bergan Evans in his *The
Natural History of Nonsense,*

> There are twenty-five thousand practicing astrologers in Amer-
> ica who disseminate their lore through a hundred daily columns,
> fifteen monthly, and two annual publications. . . . It is even
> said that there is a movement on foot to have a Federal astrol-
> oger appointed as an officer of the government, and, considering
> the official recognition given to other forms of superstition, the
> movement may succeed.[5]

All these practices and beliefs provide a thick superstructure
within which a dark distrust of reason flourishes and against
which logic often beats in vain.

Many of these practices go back to ancient times. Only one,
spiritualism, actually had an American origin.

Modern spiritualism began in 1848 in Hydesville, N. Y. The
mediums were two little girls named Margaret and Katherine
Fox. The story is that a man was murdered in their house.
The spirit of this murdered man would return at night, and call
attention to itself by rapping on the walls and furniture of the
girls' room. The children said that the spirit agreed to answer
questions by giving one number of raps for "yes" and another
for "no." The word of this communicative spirit quickly spread
about the countryside.

The children were taken to the city of Rochester and according to the story, the spirit went along. More and more persons

---

[5] Bergen Evans, *The Natural History of Nonsense* (New York: Knopf, 1946),
p. 272.

now claimed to hear the spirit. Within a few months, the *Rochester Rappings,* as they were called, were a matter of interest throughout the world. Other persons "discovered" themselves to be mediums, and spirits came to rap for them. Thus spiritualism began.[6]

It continued to prosper in the United States, together with crystal gazing, card prophecies and palmistry. Many hundreds of thousands of dollars are paid to an assortment of fortunetellers every year. There has been little differentiation as to wealth or education in the spread of these activities. They flourish among rich and poor alike, among the well-educated as well as the barely literate. Big-circulation newspapers attest to their popularity by running daily horoscopes and handwriting analyses. Police records chronicle the numerous raids on fortunetellers and clairvoyants who practice without license or in defiance of the law. Cultist magazines do a thriving business, as do almost all periodicals dealing with mystic and occult manifestations. The one sure-selling item in bookstores is the volume dealing with the occult and supernatural. "Hexes" and "conjure women" survive in many areas.

The manufacture and sale of good-luck charms is a bustling business that grosses millions annually. Howard Whitman describes this phenomenon in a *Collier's* article:

Americans today are carrying some 10,000,000 rabbit-feet in their pockets. They are purchasing four-leaf clovers at the rate of 3,300,000 per year. An estimated $1,000,000, according to Professor Brewton Berry of Ohio State, is spent annually in Louisiana, Mississippi and Alabama for charms, magic philters, hoodoo bags and similar gimcracks.

In sophisticated New York you can buy "Graveyard Dust" at

---

[6] *The World Book Encyclopedia* (1947), v. 15, p. 7654. Copyrighted by Field Enterprises, Inc. Used by special permission.

fifty cents the vial, a hexing or "Evil Eye" candle for a dollar, and a "Penny from a Dead Man's Eye"—very potent, the superstition peddlers say—for ten dollars.

Our insistent belief in Lady Luck put Charles Brand, of New York City, into the rabbit-foot business in 1938 and has kept him there—at a profit—ever since. Known as the Rabbit-Foot King, Brand processes and ships from his West Side factory 1,000,000 rabbit-feet per annum to all parts of the country. Atlanta, Georgia, is the most avid consumer, followed, in order, by Hollywood, Chicago, New York and St. Louis. . . .

Four-leaf clovers became a big business for Charles Donald Fox, one time Hollywood publicity man, by a stroke of—shall we say luck?—in 1938. . . . To date he has sold 30,000,000 to millions of Americans. . . . [7]

Apart from these large enterprises, there is a vast hole-in-the-corner trade in superstitious tokens, advertised furtively in neighborhood newspapers, personal letters of solicitation, and by word of mouth. They appear in response to fear and insecurity, the desire to escape responsibility by shifting it to agencies outside the self, and the recurring disbelief in the capacity of human beings to solve their own problems. Side by side with the march of science with its accent on rational knowledge, this last motive has acquired a frightening proliferation since 1914.

The intuitional process takes other prominent forms. It lies curled up inside that traditional, long-standing American institution, the hunch. The hunch has a wide range, covering poker, betting on horses, playing the stock market, making business investments, selecting political candidates, deciding on pitchers for crucial baseball games, together with a dozen other basic aspects of life in the United States. "I've got a hunch," "He played a hunch," "Obey that impulse!" are among the

---

[7] Howard Whitman, "Merchants of Luck," *Collier's,* November 27, 1948.

commonest daily expressions in American English. To have a hunch is to feel something in your bones, the bones being a kind of indisputable source of truth and knowledge. Hunches are often excuses for avoiding thought altogether. Like so many devices that begin as decoys, they become in time positive instruments for dealing with the world, and in this way set up shop as rivals to reason. Hunches bear the familiar stigmata of intuitionalism. They leap up unexpectedly out of nowhere or from some bottomless region of the mind without boundaries or dimensions. They strike with sudden impact, carrying with them an eloquence so overpowering that they are often taken for prophetic truth. Hence the importance attached to first impressions or love at first sight. They have about them a peculiar urgency that makes one feel they must be acted on at once lest some great opportunity be lost, an opportunity that will never again recur. Hunches frequently turn up in moments of stress or critical decision, and wrap themselves in the gravity of the occasion so that their voices seem the more pressing and persuasive. Like any bolt from the blue, the very rapidity with which they materialize undermines close examination, and they tend to carry the day with one impetuous rush.

The hunch is often identified with spontaneity, and benefits from this flattering association. Since it is something that bubbles up from inside without conscious effort, it is considered natural and sincere, and therefore all the more deserving of belief. The fact that hunches come from within seems to invest them with a special trustworthiness. There is the large general impression that whatever a person feels impulsively can't be too far off the track, and that it is on the whole unwise to examine feelings too closely. The fear of examination is seldom greater than in the case of a hunch. To examine it is to pause, and nothing, so the claim goes, is more destructive of spontaneity than bringing it to a halt. In the twilight realm of the mystical and intuitional where all is translucent haze, a call for station identification is as painful as the flashing of a sudden sharp light upon a half-wakened eye. The murkiness of the atmosphere, the wraithlike passing of dim shapes and mute impulses that touch the mind with quick ecstasy, are the very antitheses of the rational spirit and the enemies of inquiry. From this moist underworld, existing in some stratified subregion, some deeply grounded catacomb of the soul, comes the hunch, moving with rapidity and electrifying suddenness, appearing and persuading in the same breath, brushing aside *whys* and *whences* with sublime disdain.

II

In the prevailing view, intelligence and intuition seldom appear together. They are in fact opposing elements that tend to cancel each other out. The intuitive person is supposed to be slightly wacky, and there is something more attractive in his wackiness than in the sober, orderly and prosaic conduct of the logically minded. At any rate, he has charm and color, is forever doing the unexpected, and is not bound by routine. These attributes and freedoms are the blessings that accrue to the intuitive, and are secured nowhere else in so pure a form. Since blessings seem more blessed when not generally distributed, they are reserved in this instance to the few: the psychic, the "pixillated," those given to sudden dazzling insights, the uncannily perceptive characters separable from the great majority.

In contrast with such attractions, the conscious, thinking mind has been at a considerable disadvantage. The brilliantly executed attack upon it by Henri Bergson laid down the chief accusations developed by his successors and disciples. In his famous book

Creative Evolution, Bergson identified the intellect with artificiality and ignorance of life. It could deal only with inert matter in a state of immobility:

> ... the intellect, so skilful in dealing with the inert, is awkward the moment it touches the living. Whether it wants to treat the life of the body or the life of the mind, it proceeds with the rigor, the stiffness and the brutality of an instrument not designed for such use. . . . *The intellect is characterized by a natural inability to comprehend life.*[8]

Proceeding from another direction, Bergson strove to demonstrate that mobility is the true reality, and that mobility is the essential characteristic of life. The intelligence, unfit to understand anything but inert matter, was thus severed cleanly from the metaphysical picture, and degraded to a low order of reality. Bergson filled its once exalted place with that prized romantic faculty, the intuition, which he defined as "the instinct that has become disinterested, aware of itself, capable of reflecting upon its object and expanding it indefinitely." There exists a large dose of intellectuality in this definition: the disinterestedness of intuition, its self-consciousness and reflective power. This was a significant tribute to the rational tradition that, though attacked by Bergson, was yet too close to him to be denied utterly. It remained for later Bergsonians to repudiate the intellect beyond the wishes of their master. It was Bergson, however, who among modern philosophers delivered the first blow at the analytic faculties of the mind. Since his time the intellect has been identified by its enemies with artificiality, uninventiveness and hostility to the vital aspects of life.

While Bergson was inaugurating his anti-intellectualism in one form, Eduard von Hartmann, taking his cue from Schopen-

---

[8] Henri Bergson, *Creative Evolution,* tr. by Arthur Mitchell (New York: Holt, 1911), p. 165.

hauer's blind purposeless Will and anticipating Freud, was
conducting the same argument in another. Instead of regarding it in terms of instinct and reason, as did Bergson, he considered it in terms of the conscious and unconscious. Just as the
intuition was Bergson's master passion, so the unconscious became Von Hartmann's *idée fixe*. He referred everything to it,
art, thought, language and sex. The finer these were, the more
deeply grounded were they in the unconscious, and the less did
they depend on the conscious or rational faculties of the mind.
Von Hartmann sought to subordinate reason to the mystical
impulses of the unconscious. Like Bergson, he reacted against
the carry-over of eighteenth-century rationalism into nineteenth-
century science, and deplored the stress that this carry-over
placed on reason. In his *Philosophy of the Unconscious,* he
wrote:

> Conscious reason is never creatively productive, never inven-
> tive. Here man is entirely dependent on the Unconscious . . .
> and if he loses the faculty of hearing the inspirations of the
> Unconscious, he loses the spring of his life. . . . The Uncon-
> scious is, therefore, *indispensable* for him, and woe to the age
> which violently suppresses its voice, because in onesided over-
> estimate of the conscious-rational it will only give heed to the
> latter. Thus it falls irrecoverably into a vapid, shallow rational-
> ism, which struts about in childish senseless knowingness, with-
> out being able to do anything positive for posterity. . . .[9]

Von Hartmann, however, like Bergson, would not destroy
reason utterly, but would train it to be a handmaiden of the
more "productive" and "inventive" mystical faculties of the
Unconscious. He revered artists who created with sudden fire,
and called them men of genius because he said they were in-

---

[9] Eduard von Hartmann, *Philosophy of the Unconscious,* tr. by W. C. Coup-
land (London, 1884), II, p. 42.

spired by the Unconscious. He exalted women above men because women were presumably more "instinctive" and "unconscious" than men:

> ... the genuine woman is a piece of Nature on whose bosom the man estranged from the Unconscious may refresh and recruit himself, and can acquire respect for the deepest and purest form of life.[10]

Among the worshipers of the nonrational soul, distrust of the intellect and admiration of the "pure" idealized woman and the "spontaneous" artist were henceforth to go hand in hand. The merger of the French intuitionism of Bergson and the German mysticism of Von Hartmann provided the philosophical background for the assaults on thinking and reason in other phases of living since the start of the present century.

Bergson's conviction that reality was not to be held up and measured but was a continuously flowing current bearing one along, had its American reverberations. William James, the philosopher of the period of business expansion, the developer of pragmatism with its belief that truth and ethics were to be judged in terms of workability, took up the conviction in his own way. James was concerned with its operations inside the mind, and evolved the theory that there was no single self within the individual but many selves ever changing. The human being, consequently, was different from moment to moment as he was caught up in the flux of life, and must be thought of as an endless series of constantly altering persons. His mind, far from being a positive agent to grasp the essence of experience, was now liquefied to the point where it too was in a state of constant motion, and could no longer function as a measuring or analytic instrument. James's whole system of pragmatism hung on this

---

[10] *Ibid.,* p. 43.

Bergsonian concept of mobility. Since an act that worked well today might not tomorrow, it would be idle to set up permanent criteria of judgment or create fixed instruments by which truth could be evaluated. All judgments were temporary, and partook of the fluidity in which all things were caught up. In any conflict between logic and experience, observed James, he would side with experience. He thus reduced the powers of reason to the needs of the moment, and grounded them in shifting earth. The conclusions these powers arrived at were relative, the truths they sought too elusive to be firmly grasped.[11]

James was in many ways the ideal philosopher for the age of industrial growth. In the life of the country as a whole, the criterion of "Does it work?" was rapidly supplanting the older question "Is it right?", a change which provided people with the moral elasticity to do what they pleased. In cynical quarters this elasticity was called slipperiness; whatever the term, the relativism of James's ethics fitted the new technological order in the later years of the nineteenth century like a well-made cloak. Sharp practices lost their unpleasant edge in the swiftly fluctuating passage of events, and in any case there were no longer fixed frames of reference with which to judge them. Men were measured in terms of what they did rather than what

---

11 These conceptions of a fluid universe were immensely supported by the theory of Relativity. In *The Growth of American Thought*, Merle Curti, quoting from an article by George W. Gray ("No Hitching Posts," *The Atlantic Monthly*, February 1932), described its effects: " 'The General Theory of Relativity brings us to a picture of the cosmos in which space by itself and time by itself have ceased to exist, and the blend of the two has become a supple theater for events. The theater continually changes with the events which it stages. Not only is space-time moulded and transformed at every point by the matter and motion which it contains, but the very rules of the geometry by which its manifold is measured are shown to be relative.' . . . The principle of indeterminism, of uncertainty . . . appeared to be the only principle anyone could be certain of, if indeed he could be certain even of that." (New York: Harper, 1943), p. 723.

Curti went on to list as parts of the same liquefying movement John Dewey's undermining of formal logic, and the insistence of the semanticists that words are no longer to be identified with general principles but change constantly according to their shifting context.

they were, a far easier system in an age of material achievement which had neither the leisure nor the inclination for assaying nuances of character. Life was a huge beckoning sea of possibilities, in which the old landmarks of tradition and ethics had been washed from sight and there were no life lines except one's own resources.

The tide of creative evolution which Bergson had portrayed was reaching a crest in America, unhampered by controls of any kind except the strength and determination of the men who rode it. These men—the entrepreneurs, the captains of industry, the giants of advancing technology—found in the relativism of James with its easy sanctions and flexible rules an ideal metaphysics. It was a metaphysics accepted, indeed eagerly embraced by the great majority of Americans whose dreams of sudden wealth appeared dewy and attainable until the crash at the end of the 1920s. While this view of reality ran its course, the intellect, reduced to a minor element in the scheme of things, passed into temporary eclipse whence it began to emerge along with other neglected faculties during the struggle against the depression.

The stress that James put on environment as a manageable commodity was picked up by the Behaviorists during the '20s. Led by Dr. John B. Watson, this school of psychology with its peculiarly American origin enjoyed a remarkable vogue. Watson claimed that he could take any baby and mold its personality into any shape desired.[12] Since the individual in the Behaviorist scheme was the sum total of his habits, instincts and motor responses, nothing was simpler than to organize these according to plan. Man was no longer a human being; he was

---

12 Which makes him a kind of curious predecessor of Lysenko and the new Soviet geneticists of the late '40s with their subordination of heredity to environment.

an aggregate of conditioned reflexes. Thought was nothing but an activity of the larynx, and the intellect was a fake exploited by discredited schools of psychology—notably the Introspectionists, led by Titchener. It did not exist because it failed to express itself outwardly. Neither words nor movements could be considered its outlets, for they were patterns of habit, and habits were ruts in the nervous system rather than obscure faculties of the cerebrum. According to the Behaviorists, man was an irrational creature at the beck and call of external stimuli. Their theory sought to discredit all thinking that did not manifest itself in movement or was not done with a view to action; in short, all abstract thinking, and with it, the intellect itself.

Their emphasis on action and environment seemed in accord with the facts during the period when action (any kind) paid off and environment was behaving well. But the depression made it plain that action *per se* was not enough. When environment passed out of control, the ensuing miseries shifted the focus back to the individual who was now enduring them, and it became all too painfully apparent that he was something more than a bundle of instincts and muscular habits, that he was indeed a human being with a mind and consciousness, and that without the exercise of his mind and consciousness, environment would never return to the track again. The public was now ready for the replacement of the Behaviorists, who faded from view, by a new school of psychologists more in tune with the times and the fresh conceptions of reality. This school, the Gestaltists, was founded by Wolfgang Köhler who in a series of famous experiments had discovered rationality in apes, an odd thing since Watson had been able to find none in men. The Gestaltists devoted themselves less to environment than to man and his reactions, less to a study of his body than of his mind. The intellect began regaining some of the ground lost during the years of uninterrupted physical prosperity, and the individual, now restored to the possession of all his faculties, resembled once again a whole human being.

The excesses of Behaviorism, which reduced the individual to putty, were equaled by the excesses of Freudianism, which in another way deprived man of his conscious rational self. The doors to the subconscious, over which Von Hartmann had waxed lyrical, were broken down by Freud. There sallied forth from its mysterious depths a legion of impulses, inhibitions, frustrations, dark desires, suppressed instincts, ids and libidos, egos and superegos, a whole *smörgåsbord* of complexes and phobias, equipped with a whole new idiom, ready to demolish the high barriers of convention and tradition that stood in their way. They acquired a swarm of allies from other fields: writers, painters, composers, scientists, amateurs and dilettantes dabbling on the fringes of a dozen professions, who began spreading the new gospel with evangelical fervor.

The first result of the new doctrine was to split the public into two extremist camps: those who were sure that the whole thing was a joke and those who were equally convinced that it was the solution to all problems. The first group, still going strong despite the great advances in psychiatry, jeered at its jargon, scorned its claims to analyzing human behavior, manufactured jokes at its expense, and used every means fair and foul to ridicule it out of existence. Part of this hostility was an automatic reaction against anything new, part was based on genuine outrage at the rubble heap Freudian ideas threatened to make of established theories and mores, and part resulted from the extravagance of the claims made not so much by Freud as by his disciples. These disciples in every sphere, like the early zealots of a new religion (without whom, no doubt, it could not hope to be widely established), began in their enthusiasm to chip away at the conscious mind until it became no longer something to be illuminated by what went on in the subconscious but only a kind of insignificant outer sheath. Its importance dwindled under these constant attacks, and with it all its attendant faculties: reason, logic and the free exercise of choice and will, rational selection of modes of conduct and distinctions between right and wrong.

The more one probed into the subconscious, the more threatening and irrational it became, a tumult of selfish and aggressive impulses in whose grip the individual was helpless. Moreover, they were irreconcilably opposed to society. The terrific pessimism of Freud lay grounded in the conviction that all social institutions were bound by their very nature to suppress the instinctive drives of the individual. Consequently the war between him and society was bound to last forever, a prospect calculated to throw anyone into the deepest gloom. The pessimism and gloom were reinforced by the major events of the century, in which the tensions between man and society became violently aggravated, and his ability to control the increasingly dangerous natural environment which he himself had discovered became growingly uncertain. Freud developed into one of the main prophets of the time not only because of the radical originality of his insights but because of the darkling atmosphere emanating from his conclusions. This atmosphere seemed precisely fitting to the breath-taking calamities since 1914. The disintegration that appeared to be overtaking the external world had its counterpart in the anarchic universe of the subconscious where the civilizing disciplines and restraints were being ground to bits by greedy instincts which had passed beyond control. The Götterdämmerung of the world was being matched by the Götterdämmerung of the psyche.

At their extremes the popularized theories of the subconscious produced in literature piles of ornamental gibberish, starting with the rhythmically idiotic and unintelligible verse of

Gertrude Stein and the frenetic nightmares of Dadaism. Sensation-hunting cults and coteries maggoted in the warm dark catacombs of the psychic interior, and bred faddist poetry, obscurantist painting, and damp philosophical movements shrouded in sleazy mysticism. Many were drawn by the hot breath of promised sexual abnormality, realized even in the pages of James Joyce himself, the great literary master of subconsciousness. The splendidly written erotic monologue of Molly Bloom, which brings *Ulysses* to an end, illustrates the widespread association of the Freudian discoveries with the release of sexual taboos. The impassioned prophecies of D. H. Lawrence springing from the sexual subconscious, the frustrated characters of Sherwood Anderson, the rush of uninhibited feeling that E. E. Cummings advocated as the key to happiness, revealed the far-ranging impact that the Freudian libido had upon writers of the twentieth century.

The literary fruits of Freudian doctrine were most vividly evident in the plays of Eugene O'Neill. These plays dealt with people who faced a hostile world and were driven by inner compulsions which they could not control. Often these compulsions assumed specifically sexual forms, as in *Diff'rent, Desire under the Elms, Strange Interlude* and *Mourning Becomes Electra,* where whole hornets' nests of repressions, Oedipus complexes, adulteries and incestuous relationships swarmed over the characters and brought them to disastrous ends. All the plays record the tragic misfortunes resulting from the rush and frenzy of uncontrolled feelings. O'Neill reduced these feelings to their instinctual core, keeping them free of interference or complication from other aspects of the human personality, notably the capacity to think. Emperor Jones, in the dramatic masterpiece that bears his name, is not without intelligence, but at the first real pressure begins caving in under the weight of his greed and fear, and soon turns into a gibbering primitive, prey to all the superstitions of his race. Yank, hero of *The Hairy Ape,* is incapable of even the most elementary thought. When driven out of the hold of his ship, he cannot come to any terms at all with the ordinary world, and winds up in the final scene inside the gorilla's cage, staring at us with pain-ridden eyes, himself scarcely more than a disoriented animal. The split personalities of *The Great God Brown* are so violently in the grip of their conflicting desires that one is driven to murder the other and is himself released from his obsession only by death. The derelicts of *The Iceman Cometh* are victimized by their emotional incapacities before the play begins. It describes only their twitching movements in the direction of life, before they sink back again into their stupors. Even the seamen of O'Neill's early one-acters, huddled together with their small ambitions and endless dreams aboard the *S.S. Glencairn,* make only the feeblest gestures at pulling out of the floating prison of the sea.

The highlights of the Freudian drama are thus transformed into their stage equivalents: characters at the mercy of powerful instinctual drives that doom them to destroy themselves or one another; the outside world which provides no adequate grooves to fit into and forces them back into themselves; the disasters which are the inevitable culmination of these irreconcilable tensions; the helplessness of the powers of insight and rational will to prevent or even delay this compulsive journey toward destruction. The spontaneous overflow of powerful feelings, that Wordsworth had called the source of poetry, had now in its new context washed away all the civilized landmarks men had laboriously built up through the centuries. They were swept in an overwhelming tide toward oblivion. The victory of instinct over intellect, the uncontrollable subconscious over the conscious, the intuitive sources of action over the rational, the distorted self over the whole self, was given its most shattering demonstration in the work of America's most celebrated and gifted playwright.

III

In the struggle for domination between reason and intuition, intuition has not been the only aggressor. If the intuitionalists have often used pure feeling as a club to beat down intellect, the devotees of rationality have on occasion used pure intellect as a club to beat down feeling and emotion. They have insisted that the intellect is the *sole* faculty by which experience can be comprehended and truth ascertained. Calvin developed an inflexible system of ironclad ideas into which the individual had to fit, at whatever cost to his natural impulses, lest he suffer eternal damnation. Since at best man was regarded as a sinful creature, prey to his "evil" passions and appetites, there wasn't much hope for him in the first place. But what hope there was could be realized only by subordinating himself to a rigid code of behavior prescribed for him in advance. This code, whether applied in Calvin's Geneva, John Knox's Edinburgh, Oliver Cromwell's England, or the Massachusetts of Cotton Mather, had a faultless logic once its beginning premise of the natural depravity of man was accepted. Philosophically and logically the principles of Calvin are among the wonders of the modern world in their supple reasoning, closely textured deductions and derivations, and nobly proportioned intellectual design. But they put men in moral strait jackets, hoping to elevate their minds by suppressing their flesh. In this way, and wholly in the interest of the rational and abstract convictions of a high-minded theology, they imposed a ruthless intellectual tyranny on the many aspects of the personality. The price this exacted from the Puritan pastors and parishioners alike was measured in the anguished sermons of Jonathan Edwards and the morbidly sensitive novels of Nathaniel Hawthorne.

New England Puritanism ran thinner in later generations, but in the 1920s it flared up briefly in the movement called New Humanism. Led by Irving Babbitt and Paul Elmer More, the New Humanists called for a ruthless suppression of the animal in man, and by animal they included every impulse, passion and appetite not immediately rational in source. The higher man, developed through the exercise of conscious intellectual will, held the lower in restraint by means of a self-governing mechanism known as the ethical check. This was the old Puritan conscience and morality operating under another name. New Humanism made few converts, and received a wide hearing only during the depression when a philosophy that urged people to tighten their belts and restrain their appetites seemed peculiarly appropriate to the times. But it was too much out of tune with the generally expanding nature of American life to win real popularity. Its advocates argued and wrote with the frosty aloofness of the intellectual temperament that has gone dry and is devoting itself to finding reasons for holding down the rest of the personality.

The tradition that denies feeling and distrusts emotion in the service of a stratified code of conduct finds its ultimate contemporary expression in the novels of J. P. Marquand. The code is that of the Boston Brahman, going back to the early Anglo-Saxon, Protestant settlers who developed into the ruling aristocracy of Massachusetts. Their taboos, inhibitions, prescribed modes of behavior now hang like a dead weight around the necks of the Marquand heroes, preventing them from living their own individual lives, yet not quite strong enough to keep them from regretting it forever after. George Apley and Harry Pulham fall deeply in love with "unsuitable" young women whom they are forced by social pressure to renounce; they then marry young women from their own class and settle down to a lifetime of dull conventionality, nursing all the while an ache inside themselves which time mutes but does not eliminate. They are the prime victims of a view of life that distrusts and stifles the natural feelings.

In slightly altered situations Marquand's other heroes are similarly victimized. Jim Calder is so bound by ties of caste and family that he allows himself to be exploited and blackmailed by his shoddy relatives. Jeffrey Wilson, married and middle-aged, yields to passion just long enough to discover that he lacks the capacity for it. Bob Tasmin is jilted by his girl friend because in her eyes his proper upbringing has washed out every element of freshness and spontaneity in him. Charles Gray, teetering on the edge of executive ascension, wonders whether the game is worth the candle but goes right on playing it in the midst of continuing doubts. Sid Skelton has money, an assured position, worldly prestige and a satisfactory marriage, yet happiness persistently eludes him.

In these varied contexts Marquand records with penetrating accuracy the emotional price paid by the subscribers to a system whose accent on discipline and self-restraint, however rational to start with, has stiffened into a rigid mold. The Puritan tradition, emphasizing reason over emotion, produced the lifeless conventionality ironically assayed in Marquand's fiction. Its ultimate decline is illustrated in the observation of the doctor in André Gide's *The Counterfeiters:* "Many things escape the reason, and a person who should attempt to understand life by merely using his reason would be like a man trying to take hold of a flame with the tongs. Nothing remains but a bit of charred wood, which immediately stops flaming."[13]

---

[13] André Gide, *The Counterfeiters* (New York: Knopf, 1947), p. 165.

The artificial war between the advocates of intuition and intellect delays progress toward the whole man. The subordination of one to the other, in the name of whatever high-minded and well-intentioned goal, generates within the individual a conflict that can be only damaging and, when carried to an extreme, makes a harmonious and integrated existence impossible. Here once again is a traditional area of hostility where impulses and faculties, fruitful in themselves, assault one another to their mutual loss.

The fruitless tensions, social as well as personal, induced by those who dogmatically assail the intellect as deadening or the passions as treacherous, must be allayed. Only then can the resolution of these ancient disharmonies be achieved. When thought and feeling, reason and emotion, acknowledge each other's legitimacy, not in terms of domination however principled or of unrestrained license, but in co-operative equality, then one road to the fulfillment of man's nature will be unblocked.

Chapter XI

Flights from the Unavoidable Self

ONE OF THE ROUGHEST HURDLES IN THE struggle for maturity is the acceptance of the self and its responsibilities. Not one's self as other people would have it or as standardized pressures require, but the real self, expressing the individual's special drives, qualities and temperament which make him unique. This involves doing one's own thinking, making one's own decisions, assuming responsibility for one's own actions.

Since our real selves are necessarily imperfect and complex, we are under constant pressure to substitute for them other selves, simpler, more perfect, easier to live with. Our willingness to yield to these attractive substitute images and live according to their lights rather than our own, pulls us away from reality and in this way from our emotional growth. Yet in the long run we can no more avoid our selves than we can escape our bodies or minds.

The acceptance of the real, the unavoidable self, however difficult and even painful, is a basic measurement of our advance to maturity.

224

I

The American can endure almost all states except solitude. At home in the world of material objects and gadgets, eager for the company of others, he is restless and uneasy in the company of himself. His society is crammed to the bursting point with clubs, groups, associations, lodges, fraternities and sororities, organizations of every description which he joins in great numbers less to be with his fellows than to get away from himself. He is an Elk, Oddfellow, Shriner, Moose, Eagle or American Legionnaire. He is a Rotarian, Kiwanian, Mason or Knight of Columbus. He attends church for reasons more social than religious. He joins societies that seek to protect ownerless animals or aim at world government or rehearse the operettas of Gilbert and Sullivan. He attaches himself to the countless booster clubs that dot the civic landscape with posters advertising Belleville as the town of industrial opportunity, or Dead Lick as the biggest little city in the country. He attends innumerable conventions with unflagging enthusiasm. Bars, taverns, bowling alleys, poolrooms, gymnasiums, country clubs, are social centers that attract him in large clusters. When he is not in formal contact with others, he is listening to the radio, or sitting in front of a television set, or watching a movie, one in a dark crowd. He is never alone if he can help it.

From her listening post on the campus of Smith College, Mary Ellen Chase reports, in *Woman's Day*, the same flight from solitude: "I am particularly impressed by the repeated aversion, which countless girls express, to being by themselves . . . I hear . . . every morning . . . frenzied appeals for company. 'Wait for me! I'm coming!' 'Don't go without me.' As we stream onward by scores across the campus, I overhear the same desolations repeated again and again: 'I had the most boring evening. Not a soul came to my room.' 'I can't possibly go alone. It would be just too awful.' 'I don't think there's another girl in this college from Idaho (or Dakota, or Montana). Whatever shall I do after Chicago, all that train ride alone?' 'If I only had a roommate, it might help some. At least I'd have someone to talk to at night.' 'She's nice, you know, but she must be a bit queer. She's forever going off all by herself!' "[1]

Moreover, solitude is associated with failure, a pattern traced by Karen Horney in her last book, *Neurosis and Human Growth:*

> . . . he must feel accepted by others. He needs such acceptance in whatever form it is available: attention, approval, gratitude, affection, sympathy, love, sex. To make it clear by comparison: just as in our civilization many people feel worth as much as the money they are "making," so the self-effacing type measures his value in the currency of love, using the word here as a comprehensive term for the various forms of acceptance. He is worth as much as he is liked, needed, wanted or loved.
>
> Furthermore, he needs human contact and company because he cannot stand being alone for any length of time. He easily feels lost, as if he were cut off from life. . . .
>
> The need for company is all the greater since being alone means to him proof of being unwanted and unliked and is therefore a disgrace, to be kept secret. It is a disgrace to go alone to the movies or on a vacation and a disgrace to be alone over the week end when others are sociable. This is an illustration of the extent to which his self-confidence is dependent upon somebody's caring for him in some way. He also needs others to give meaning and zest to whatever he is doing.[2]

A key word in American life is popularity, the tense pursuit of which has crushed many a youthful spirit. One source of

---

[1] Mary Ellen Chase, "Are We Afraid To Be Alone?" *Woman's Day*, October 1949.

[2] Karen Horney, *Neurosis and Human Growth* (New York: Norton, 1950), p. 227.

Willy Loman's tragedy in *Death of a Salesman* was his anguished desire to be not only "liked," but "well-liked," and not
just by some people but by everybody. Since popularity implies
not being by oneself, it makes the exclusive company of that
self difficult to bear with comfort and painful to contemplate.
The process begins early. Babies who do not respond visibly
to the hovering presence of strangers are less cooed over. Children who do not play readily with other children arouse the
concern of parents and the pity of neighbors. Teen-agers out of
the high-school swim are supposed to be wretched. Young people without dates are either unattractive or queer. Men who
are not one of the boys, women who keep to themselves, are
treated as snobs or dismissed as failures. From the earliest age
the American is taught to be gregarious, to function in high gear
in the company of others, to seek his success through fraternities, lodges and associations. Movies dealing with campus life
have rescued any number of retiring students (male and female
both, spotted instantly by their shell-rimmed glasses) from their
shyness by teaching them jive or maneuvering them into a romance or discovering in them unsuspected athletic ability—
that is to say, working them into one of the approved social
activities on the campus and weaning them as fast as possible
from an unhealthy attachment to their studies. Studiousness is
regarded as the biggest possible drag on a young person's success at school. The same ideas are disseminated in magazine
stories where the simple homebody never gets her man until she
primps up a bit, displays a little sex appeal, and strikes out for
herself. The solitude of study or laboratory may be all right
for the occasional genius, though even he has rough going during his lifetime, but for most people it is one of the lowest and
least satisfying forms of existence.

The quest for popularity carries the individual away from his
own identity. He tends to cultivate not those qualities which

are uniquely his, but those which he thinks will make him popular. If these qualities are alien to his nature, he will strive all
the more desperately to assume them. The gap that thus grows
up between his actual self and his "popular" one not only produces tensions that become more and more difficult to resolve
but keeps him from growing into his full stature as a whole
human being. The result is a society of people who are more
and more collectively alike and less and less individually different—a society which, contrary to the democratic ideal, contracts rather than expands the area in which its members can
assert their own unique potentialities.

One of the chief aspects of the "popular self" is physical
attractiveness.[3] Fantastic quantities of money, time and energy
are spent by both men and women to achieve a flawless complexion, well-groomed hair-dos, clothes which set one off to
best advantage. Tooth-paste manufacturers warn their female
clients in print and over the air that if their teeth do not sparkle
their telephones will stop ringing. Soap dispensers picture
otherwise unobjectionable young men being shunned by pros-
perous-looking employers and well-shaped young women because they give off indelicate body odors. Blurbs for facial
creams suggest that no pretty debutante, no matter how well-
launched, is likely to make a prize marital catch unless she has
"the skin you love to touch." Beauty parlors are as ubiquitous
as gasoline stations and have replaced sewing circles as gather-

---

[3] This emphasis on surface attractiveness appears elsewhere in American life.
We tend to stress the visual appearance of things at the expense of quality, and
to equate the biggest with the best. André L. Simon, President of the Wine and
Food Society, describes in *The Atlantic Monthly* the effect of this on our food-
growing habits: "It is particularly disastrous as regards fruits and vegetables.
There are some truly beautiful cherries, as large as Mirabelles, with the shortest
possible stalks . . . but also with so little juice and so little flavor that they are
best left in a silver dish in the center of the dining-room table as decoration. . . . I
am certain that watermelons would be much better flavored if they were picked
before they have reached the huge size of those one sees in all the shops." "U.S.A.
Retasted," *The Atlantic Monthly*, November 1948.

ing places for women. The whole fashion industry is geared to
the cultivation of artificial standards of social success; those who
do not keep up appearances are considered out of the running.
The anxieties bred in people striving frantically to keep up with
the remorseless standards of attractiveness and the sense of
defeat and inferiority aroused in those who feel that they are
unable to attain them, create one of the large areas of disturb-
ance in American life.

But it is not enough to be attractive and fashionably clothed.
One must also be young. Youth is the time when the flesh
counts most and mind least, and is the period of maximum
popularity. The glorification of youth in America ranks as one
of the major manias in history, to which our conceptions of
love, our popular arts, and the advertising media have made
persistent contributions. It is not so much the spirit of youth
that is glorified as its physical energy and surface attractiveness.
Middle age has become a bogie which scares millions into con-
cealing its telltale signals when they appear. Whole industries
have been built on the fear of baldness in men, wrinkles and
gray hair in women. Massages, girdles for men, an enormous
beauty-parlor trade equipped with superb machines, diets,
weight-removing salons, rejuvenation fads, and a host of other
devices to dam the inroads of age, flourish throughout the
country.

This passionate quest for youth is accompanied by a feverish
pursuit of health. The popular magazines are crowded with
articles on diseases and their cures. One of the most lucrative
sources of newspaper advertising is the patent medicines with
their reassuring promise of relief from pain. Laxatives, blurbed
in print and over the air, are sold by the millions of bottles to
ease the American past his chronic bouts of overeating. The
one subject of conversation that never flags is the state of the
body, from its operations and ulcers to its vaguest, most inde-

terminate aches and pains. The problems of the mind, by contrast, lag far behind in national attention and interest. Edwin R. Embree describes one aspect of the uneven race between body and mind:

> Recent reports show that certain of our leading universities are spending one hundred times as much each year on the education of each prospective doctor enrolled in their medical schools as on the education of each prospective teacher enrolled in their schools of education. . . . The sums put into the natural sciences at all our leading universities and research institutes are in glaring contrast to the meager funds available for the human studies. . . . Amid all this generosity we have so neglected the study of mental health and personal growth that we are in danger of maintaining robust bodies simply to house sick souls and dull minds, and we have so neglected social studies that society is in danger of destroying itself by its own scientific miracles.[4]

The body is the key to popularity, and popularity the key to success. This is a major tenet of the advertising industry, with its daily barrage of coaxing, wheedling, threatening, fear-producing, envy-arousing messages. The whole pull of the industry is from the inside out, a terrific centrifugal force drawing the individual away from the center of himself to the periphery and beyond. As such, it is clearly a latter-day product of all the forces in the United States which have shied away from meditation and self-searching, and concentrated on go-getting in the world of flesh and space unstained by thought. Seen from this side, the life of the American is one long unbroken flight from his inward self. Abetting him in this flight has been the literature of advertising, itself as much a symbol of the mechanical side of American civilization as refrigerators and automobiles. Enormous care, patience, design, energy, fusion of painting,

---

[4] The New York *Times*, December 1, 1949.

prose and music, are lavished on it daily. Tons of print have been devoted to boosting the fabulous powers of advertising, and reams of invective have appeared assailing its vulgarity and banality. Yet for all the barrages pro and con, little attention has been paid to advertising as a divisive force, which rejects people as they are and induces them to strive after what they are not and can never be. The split is between man as he is and the illusory not-man created by the perpetual and hypnotic snobberies of the high-voltage blurbs. Back in 1922, at the very start of the era of the big blurb, J. Thorne Smith observed with satirical insight:

> ... advertising is America's cruelest and most ruthless sport. ... The comforts and happiness it holds out to the reader are forever contrasted with the misery and misfortune of another. Thus, if I ride in a certain make of motor, I have the satisfaction of knowing that every one who rides in a motor of another make is of a lower caste than myself and will certainly eat dust for the rest of his life. There is a real joy in this knowledge. Again, if I wear a certain advertised brand of underwear, I have the pleasure of knowing that my fellow-men not so fortunately clad are undoubtedly foolish swine who will eventually die of sunstroke, after a life devoted entirely to sweating. Here, too, is a joy of rare order. If I brush my teeth with an advertised tooth paste, my satisfaction is enhanced by the knowledge that all other persons who fail to use this particular paste will in a very short time lose all of their teeth. In this there is a savage, but authentic delight.[5]

But the contrast is not only between those who use and those who use not. It is more deeply a contrast between what one is and what one is tantalizingly and unrealizably made to feel one should be by the high-pressured bombardment of advertising

---

[5] J. Thorne Smith, "Advertising," *Civilization in the United States,* edited by Harold E. Stearns (New York: Harcourt, Brace, 1922), pp. 383-4.

appeals. Tantalizingly because it seems so temptingly within reach, like the carrot before the proverbial donkey; unrealizably because there is never any end to the demands imposed on the consumer, which makes his attainment of a given sequence futile since it is immediately replaced by a fresh sequence that makes the previous one instantly out-of-date. There is no end to this treadmill, to which nearly every newspaper, magazine, billboard, radio and television program in the country contributes zealously every day. To set real men against one another in painful contrast is serious enough, but it is at least encompassable and in part remediable. To set up the same contrast between men and a mythical entity that bears all the lineaments of reality but lacks its substance and is perpetually beyond reach, is to create a far more serious schism since it is neither encompassable nor remediable, and consequently imposes a burden which can never be set down.

II

The impulse to flee from oneself also finds expression in the desire to become lost in something outside of and larger than the individual. America is full of movements which provide this kind of escape. One such movement, found in the more sequestered areas, is revivalism. With its mixture of religion and hysteria, revivalism has flourished not simply among the superstitious but among those to whom life for one reason or another has not been satisfactory, the emotionally undernourished, the sexually frustrated, those who can no longer endure reality. There are no exact statistics on the revivalist public but there seems little doubt that it includes millions. Its social structure is as varied and fluid as the American social structure everywhere, running from the huge gaudy temple of Aimee Semple McPherson in Los Angeles to folding tents in the remote hinterlands of the Bible Belt. It ranges from the millionaire properties of Father Divine in New York to the nickels and dimes of fly-by-night itinerant preachers living out of suitcases and sweating tiny collections from the writhing poor in the back country of Kansas. The revivalist program is the same in essence regardless of plush or penurious surroundings. The spellbinding voice of the preacher (Huey Long had such a voice, and he used revivalist tactics in his political oratory), the swaying congregation, the warm comforting mass, the ecto-plasmic presence of the Lord wavering just out of sight in the darker shadows of tent or temple, exercise an immensely magnetic pull away from the anchors of the rational, conscious, fully aware self into the vortex of a whirling, mystical current where release from individual identity, the abandonment of anxiety, a final emotional anesthesia, come in a suffusing flood.

In this orgiastic state anything can happen. The preacher can roll with the girls in the bushes as Casy did in *The Grapes of Wrath*. He can get folks to beat their heads on the ground moaning for forgiveness and absolution for sins whose nature they are but dimly aware of. He can induce in his listeners all sorts of physical manifestations, from jerks and muscular contortions to the babbling speech divorced from thought known in the trade as the "gift of tongues." He can even persuade his listeners to allow themselves to be bitten by poisonous snakes, and make them believe that those who died were lacking in faith. The voluntary abandonment of personality, which is the end product of revivalism, is a sacrificial self-yielding into the hands of someone else, a kind of triumphant suicide very strange indeed within the bosom of a democratic society, where the individual personality is, in theory, a most precious possession. So desperate a craving for otherness is a potent sign of how tedious, unpleasant or unendurable one's own self has become.

Of the many ways in which the individual can lose himself,

revivalism is perhaps the most glandular and frenzied, and comes close to defining contact with the Almighty as a kind of ecstatic oblivion. But Americans are not only a God-pursuing but also a devil-conscious people. Not the devil in the shape of Lucifer with a handsome swarthy face and horns, or the symbol of evil, dark and overpowering, prayed to in secluded groves by cults of Satanists who have, in some miasma of mind, bound themselves into his service. Nothing so romantic, literary or primitive. The devil rather as scapegoat, on whose single shoulders manifold troubles can be heaped, the "fall guy" of the detective story whom we can offer as a sacrifice to the powers unleashing miseries upon us, whom we can blame for errors we subconsciously refuse to acknowledge as our own. Thurman Arnold, in his searching book *The Folklore of Capitalism,* has studied the devil-hunting proclivities of the American people in politics. For a long time, the government was the devil responsible for all ills, and its agents, the politicians, were crooked, conniving and corrupt characters who leeched upon the population. With the collapse of 1929 and the new role of the government as rescue agency under the New Deal, the devil became the big businessman, the "economic royalist," as Franklin D. Roosevelt called him in a memorable epithet, who had brought about the depression as a consequence of his greedy policies and who was doing all in his power to block any attempts at recovery not under his sponsorship. This was a carry-over from earlier days when that traditional American bugaboo, Wall Street, was dusted off during election campaigns and blamed for everything that had gone wrong.

In foreign affairs during the 1930s fascism was the devil. After the end of the second World War, it became communism. Both were, of course, responsible for incalculable barbarities and created vast disturbances in the world, making it all the easier to blame them for everything else that went wrong, for all the ills of existence. The convenience of having a ready-made monster around made it all the easier not to think about individual problems and situations as they came up. It was far simpler and hence irresistibly tempting to blame the devil. Discontent among racial minorities, the restlessness of labor, the drive for civil-rights legislation, even the campaign for public housing—to take a few examples at random—were on frequent occasions attacked as being communist in origin. Any controversial movement which aroused strong partisan feelings tended to be devil-labeled to the point where the hunt for communism was pursued with microscopic intensity in every remote as well as relevant aspect of national life. All this in a country where Marxist ideas had taken virtually no hold, where the bulk of the labor movement was notably lacking in class consciousness, where the native Communists were probably the most absurd, incompetent and ineffectual of all the Communist parties in the world.

However large a percentage of contemporary troubles can be attributed to the Communists, not all of them can be so ascribed. Some are due to other causes or are of our own making, and will not disappear merely because we refuse to acknowledge them. Our refusal is as much a flight from ourselves and reality as is revivalism, the more dangerous because it is a collective and not simply an individual matter. The end of the communist tyranny, when it comes, will relieve the world of much of its trouble; but the world will not then be in a utopian state, any more than it was with the overthrow of the fascist empires. Other difficulties, other baffling dilemmas will appear, whose solutions can only be postponed by piling them patly on some single outside source. The devil, in his numerous appearances in history, has been useful in this respect: without him the burdens of living would shift back the more heavily on individual man. The devil, always at hand in one form or another, has been rampant in America since the Puritans brought him over wrapped in the traditional motley of fire and brimstone. In no form, however, has he wielded a more potent influence than as a cloak for troubled conscience, a social lightning rod to deflect danger in other directions, and as a convenient evasion of self.

Another symptom of the same evasion is the national faith in experts, and the eagerness to believe them without qualification or reserve. The enormous specialization that accompanied the spread of scientific and technical knowledge broke life up into smaller and smaller segments, and made the custodian of each segment growingly important. In due course this custodian developed into the professional expert who, by virtue of his total knowledge of a single area (and often total ignorance of everything else), set up shop as middleman between his area and the public at large. His very concentration on a single sphere at the expense of every other kind of knowledge was a strong element in his functioning as an expert. The man who claims familiarity with more than one field is looked on with suspicion, regarded as spreading himself out too thin and forfeiting all claims to depth. The jack-of-all-trades, at one time the darling of the American scene, has passed into limbo. In the days of the frontier, when survival required one man to do many things, he was the backbone of a society expanding in space. With the new era of machine technology he lost his function and faded from view; in his stead the new man of the new era, the specialist, put in a formidable appearance and is apparently here to stay.

Belief in the expert is more than a tailored product of our complicated age. It has been immensely stimulated by our reluctance to think for ourselves and to accept responsibility for what happens.[6] The expert is a convenient mechanism for doing our

---

6 Among other industrialized countries of the West, there is little glorification of the expert in England and France. He has, however, been idolized and enthroned in Germany, much more so even than in the United States. Significantly, the Germans are, of all Western peoples, the ones least willing to think individually for themselves and accept responsibility for their actions.

thinking for us and a superb scapegoat when things go astray. This is perhaps why we never cease to belabor him and yet believe in him no matter how wrong he proves. Combining in a unique way two of the adult functions of which we long to rid ourselves, he is a wonderfully useful device to perpetuate moral and intellectual adolescence, all the more useful because he fits so well into the institutions of the machine age.

On the great events of recent times the experts have been wrong with impressive consistency. Less than two years before the Battle of Britain, Charles Lindbergh stated flatly that the Nazi Air Force was invincible. Major George Fielding Eliot, the military expert, was certain when war broke out in 1939 that Germany had no chance against England and France. Nearly every military expert was positive that Japan, hopelessly inferior industrially, would never attack the United States. The number of wrong statements about the last depression were too numerous to tally. Virtually no one (among bankers, economists, industrialists, politicians and other *cognoscenti* who had the ear of the public) anticipated the stock-market crash, the collapse that followed, its length, its intensity, the stages by which the country recovered. And so with most other affairs of the day.

We listen eagerly to the voices of the experts. When the wrong tune is called, they, not we, absorb the blame, and since this is a process with manifest advantages for both parties, it is repeated over and over. Suspicious of every form of physical and political authority, America is laden with a vast bureaucracy of authority in the areas of health, aesthetics and personal conduct.[7] The expert flourishes as briskly in child care and interior decorating as in market analysis, in sports as in diet and

---

[7] A contradiction that extends elsewhere. In his book *The American Character* D. W. Brogan comments on it with regard to war: "The American people . . . have always been anti-militarist but never anti-military. They have combined a rational and civilized horror of war's waste and inhumanity with a simple and . . . natural pleasure in the trappings of war." (New York: Knopf, 1944), p. 56.

nutrition, in weather forecasting and elections as in every branch of the exact and social sciences. He slices up the human being into every arguable segment of his life: from etiquette, gardening and the mixing of martinis to marriage and the forecasting of future trends.

America's enshrinement of the expert is illustrated by our persistent embracing of the public-opinion polls. These have become firmly established in the country and, despite the severe battering they received in the election returns of 1948 and 1952, show few signs of yielding ground. The polls are made authoritative by their scientific trappings. The careful sampling of opinion from a representative cross section seems valid enough, and suggests the authentic atmosphere of the laboratory. The listing of results in neat tabular columns appeals to an age that reveres statistics. The whole air of impartiality, reinforced by such terms as Institute, Associates, Foundation, attached to the names of the leading firms, is impressive and designed to persuade. The predigested opinions supplied by the polls make it that much easier for the individual to avoid the effort of arriving at his own conclusions.

They have led a charmed life in America, and seem almost disaster-proof. The great debacle of the *Literary Digest,* which predicted with dogmatic assurance in 1936 that Landon would defeat Roosevelt for the Presidency, put hardly a crimp in their growth. The *Literary Digest,* true to its pledged word, ceased publication when Roosevelt defeated Landon in a landslide, but the other polls and polling organizations went cheerfully on with scarcely a pause. They claimed their methods were better than the *Digest's.* And indeed their predictions for the twelve years that followed were sufficiently close to the mark to make their post-mortem on their luckless colleague sound reasonable. This interlude, however, lulled them into a feeling of false security, for with the campaign of 1948 they forgot their caution and became as dogmatic in their proclamations of a Republican victory as ordinary citizens with no claim to being experts. They were proved wrong on every issue that was subject to any kind of variation. The votes for Dewey and Wallace were overestimated in about equal proportion, those for Truman immensely underplayed. Only the strength of J. Strom Thurmond, the Dixiecrat, the one candidate whose area of influence was static and hence calculable in advance, was gauged accurately. The staggering nature of their error was dramatized two months before the election by the statement of Elmo Roper, one of the leading pollsters, that he would not bother to take further samplings since the results in favor of Dewey were so assured.

When the roof fell in on Roper and his colleagues (as well as on the collective heads of all the political correspondents, columnists and poobahs), it seemed certain that the polls had at last received their comeuppance and would be heard from no more. The suicide of the *Digest* would now be followed by the suicide of Gallup, Crossley, Roper and the rest. This expectation, however, like all the others, backfired. For a few weeks after election day the polls were deluged with a storm of jeers from every quarter, discredited as institutions and cussed out by those who had set personal store by them. The objects of these attacks went into conspicuous public mourning, accused themselves of carelessness and inaccuracy, and announced their determination to discover wherein they erred, inviting a whole corps of social scientists to help them in this task (so vital to the national interest, they implied). Back they came in the campaign of 1952, took their samplings and, having been overbold in their predictions of 1948, were now supercautious. The election would be a hairline one, they concluded unanimously, to be decided by the narrowest of margins, so close indeed that no one could possibly forecast the outcome. Anyone taking their reports seriously could only have been overwhelmed with astonishment at Eisenhower's more than six million vote margin and his even larger victory in the Electoral College.

Samplings of public opinion, like the comments of experts, have their legitimate uses, but not when they turn into commercialized guesswork, or when given exaggerated credence by gullible persons only too eager to let someone else do their thinking. And there are apparently enough such people left who long to peer into the future, and with short enough memories of the past, to provide the pollsters with a fairly solid social base on which to continue operations.

III

If one form of self-abdication is allowing experts to tell us what to think, another, more inclusive form is allowing strong leaders to tell us what to do. To have faith in sound leaders is a natural and healthy principle, but not when it involves a voluntary renunciation of personal responsibility and decision. Although by theory and tradition the *Fuehrer* principle has been alien to American life, the willingness to yield to others authority over oneself has always been present.

The dangerous instance of Huey Long, who headed the fastest-growing American demagogic movement in the 1930s, revealed how viable was that willingness, how swiftly exploitable. It was not Huey's promises alone that won him his large and mushrooming following in his native Louisiana and in the neighboring states of Texas, Arkansas and Oklahoma. Many other demagogues had promised to share the wealth, give every man, woman and child two hundred dollars a month and more—and got nowhere in particular. Come-ons were clearly necessary but they were just as clearly not enough. Huey rose from the swarm of promise makers through his resourceful and intelligent personality, oozing with eloquence and humor. He was in instinctive rapport with the same dissatisfied lower middle class of the towns and the dissatisfied small tenant farmers of the country that provided Hitler with his mass base in Germany. Where Hitler's speeches were sullen, monotonous and full of rant, Huey's were anecdotal, varied, full of provincial shrewdness, and always easy on the ears. It was the impact of this magnetic personality, with its enormous assurance, perhaps even more than his invitation to quick wealth, that held those who flocked to his banner. The flight from self is never more easily achieved than to the arms of some bold fellow who persuades you (since you are only too willing to be persuaded) that he knows all the answers. Americans, while less susceptible to this form of persuasiveness than certain European peoples, are nevertheless more prone to it than naïve libertarians conceive.

Another ruthless and aggressive leader, contemporary with Huey, was Father Coughlin. Working the anti-Roosevelt and anti-Semitic sides of the street for all they were worth, Coughlin built up a considerable following during the middle and late 1930s. Only the fact that he was a Catholic priest in a largely Protestant country prevented it from being much more considerable. The Christian Front bands, organized with his blessing, held their street meetings in the large cities, distributed their noisome literature, beat up stray onlookers who looked like Jews, while the eloquent pastor of the Church of the Little Flower orated through a radio microphone from his pulpit at Royal Oak, Michigan, about social justice. The pull that Coughlin exercised on those who came under his spell, educated and ignorant alike, transcended doctrine and became a matter of personality, in his case full of venom, energy and absolute, infectious, doubt-destroying assurance. Coughlin's doctrine, as a matter of record, turned out to be a hash, beginning with an ardent advocacy of Rooseveltism, then running a whole gamut of pro-silver, anti-gold tirades and anti-New Deal reform, until it became indistinguishable from the slightly more uncouth program notes of Gerald L. K. Smith, George Deatherage, William Dudley Pelley and Fritz Kuhn, among the small-fry American fascists. It was a doctrine held together by a few violent prejudices and a dominant personality which was the vital force of the Coughlinite movement. He exercised a hypnotic spell that underlay the whole shifting tangle of confused and often contradictory ideas.

Political demagogues and regressive orators are not the only ones who exercise a spell. The powerful figure on the liberal side, whether he wishes to or not, exerts a similar influence. Franklin D. Roosevelt acquired after a time a hold on the affection of millions of his constituents that far transcended the specific ideology of the New Deal. He assumed the role of the Great White Father soon after his advent to the Presidency, when conditions began to improve. The feeling that all difficulties could be solved simply by leaving them to the man in the White House grew stronger, and acquired an existence independent of the ebb and flow of economics, so that even when business again declined and the approaching war filled the country with alarm, his popularity scarcely diminished, his pulling power at the polls remained unchecked.

An idolatrous cult arose round Roosevelt, as passionate in its way as the cult of Roosevelt-haters (less numerous but no less emotional). It prospered on the mystical assumption that so long as Roosevelt remained President, all was well, and the storm of grief that greeted his death had overtones of hysteria as though the world itself had come to an end. His name, his personality, the attitudes he stood for, remained potent assets in America and the world as a whole years after his death, as the contention among various political persons and groups to appear as his legatees indicated. There is no evidence to suggest that

Roosevelt had dynastic ambitions, despite the accusations of his enemies, or even wished to serve as an all-protecting father to millions of insecure Americans. But he served as such, whether he wanted to or not, to the millions who were no longer willing to rely on themselves emotionally in the ceaseless struggles with the problems of life.

These yearnings for self-relinquishment do not of course dominate the American political scene, but they characterize it. When not visible at any given moment, they lie under the surface out of sight, waiting for a magnet to appear. They bestrew the road to maturity, cutting off access to those farther reaches of the mind where the making of decisions and the bearing of personal responsibility reside. Fortunately the structure of our government and political system is such that the compelling figure, ambitious for unrestricted power, seldom gets a chance to operate freely. The hero-worshiping instinct, for the most part on half-rations here, has been deflected to other, less dangerous fields.

What a flowering it has enjoyed in these other fields! Few Presidents have won the popularity or have been so widely publicized as Rudolph Valentino or Clark Gable. Or generated as much interest as night-club entertainers and habitués. Or aroused as much discussion as did the feats of Babe Ruth, Jack Dempsey, Bill Tilden, Red Grange or Bobby Jones.[8] The lumi-

---

8 The public enthusiasm aroused by the great athletes is in direct ratio not to their skill or artistry but to their aggressive and muscular drive. Few people went to see Babe Ruth because he was a beautifully co-ordinated ballplayer, blessed with an uncanny sense of anticipation in the field and a great throwing arm, as well as being a powerful figure at the plate. They went to see him hit a baseball farther than any man who ever lived. Gene Tunney was a splendid boxer but never drew large crowds except in his two fights with Dempsey. Ty Cobb's artistic feats as a ballplayer were drowned out by his aggressiveness, flying spikes and generally ruthless play. Ted Williams, a sulky unenthusiastic figure except when at the plate, was one of the game's great drawing-cards because of his astonishing batting feats. The long drivers in golf, the hard hitters in tennis, the rough bone-crunching body checkers in hockey, are the big gate attractions, while the artists and stylists depend on the appreciation of the relatively few connoisseurs.

naries of the sports world, professional and amateur, have been the petted darlings of the public since the end of the first World War, but they are mere satellites in the terrific luminosity of the movie stars. The lives of the stars have had almost as great an impact, and to many fans are as fascinating and important, as the movies themselves. This is more than normal curiosity about spectacular figures; it amounts to frenzy. No obscure or intimate corner of their daily existence is free from its blinding light.

To satisfy this hungry curiosity, a swarm of magazines have arisen, parasitical growths on the lives of the actors and entertainers, from whom they exact a constant tribute. These sheets, swollen to enormous circulation, specialize in personal notes, gossip, biography, detailed announcement of romances, marriages, divorces, and a persistent concentration on the cruder forms of "human interest." But their interest is for the most part inhuman. Woe to the actor who refuses to co-operate or talk about himself frankly or is reserved about his private affairs! An unfavorable article may appear about him; his pictures may be reviewed coolly; he may even be accused of that most damaging misstep, "going Hollywood." The effect of such treatment can well be catastrophic, and so thoroughly is this understood that few performers are bold enough to do anything but put on their sweetest smiles when the movie-magazine editors (and columnists who, in their gossipy syndicated newspaper chats, operate similarly) come for their interviews.

So large and inveined a system of blackmail can be sustained only by the fanaticism of the movie-going public. The enormous volume of fan mail, the prolific spread of favorite movie-actor clubs, the adulation of the bobby-soxers, suggest the scope of the movie craze as a social phenomenon. They suggest even more sharply the lineaments of the American passion for otherness, the deliberate creation of the glamorous personality in whom the ordinary citizen can live more richly than he can in himself. As fast as one hero fades, another springs up in his place. The cults of Lindbergh, Greta Garbo, Jack Dempsey, have been duplicated dozens of times in identical fashion, the great deed or the glamorous action being relived multitudinously.

Such fervor denotes the need to submerge one's real self as completely as possible, and creates a gap into which the spectacular self being worshiped can flow. One exit from the self which, being real, is imperfect and hence unacceptable to the immature, is toward what Karen Horney has called the "idealized image." This image may be a perfect combination of all the qualities of prestige and success which the real self is felt to lack. The glamorized stars satisfy the terrific hunger for the idealized image because they embody it, if only vicariously, in a dazzling and concrete form. This process has a universal range, and it would be absurd to regard its habitat as exclusively the United States.[9] But the shapes it assumes in America are indigenous; not the least of them is the extraordinary, movie-worshiping cult, fittingly revolving around an art form created in America and enjoying here its largest efflorescence.

But the self, no matter how many doors are slammed upon it, remains unavoidable. The flight from it, for whatever reason, sooner or later reverts to the starting point. The harder the individual tries to get away from it, the more reduced is his capacity to cope with himself. What has happened in America is a partial atrophying of this capacity as a result of our abundant supply of escapes, glitteringly ornamented, temptingly displayed, made the more seductive by the application of the

---

9 The craze for movie celebrities has become one of America's chief cultural exports. It is already well established in England (where it has been a source of chronic complaint among Britain's cultural purists). And it has begun to take root in Italy. The wedding in Rome of Tyrone Power and Linda Christian was almost swamped by mobs of Italian girls seeking a glimpse of "Ty the Magnifico."

technical skills developed in the country farthest advanced on the machine highway. Yet the more the world presses in upon us, the more urgent grows the need to face it with ourselves as we are instead of as we would like to be in our persistent hunt for otherness.

Our maturity as individuals and as a nation depends in part on our ability to master the impulses carrying us away from actuality instead of being mastered by them. Unpleasant, imperfect, inadequate though the real self and the real world may appear to be, they must be recognized and accepted on their own terms before we can move forward. On the already arduous journey toward self-realization, this acceptance is an indispensable and unavoidable preliminary.

Chapter XII

Premises We Live By

T HE WHOLE SOCIETY, LIKE THE WHOLE MAN, rests on premises which require constant restatement. The individual, on his way to integration and maturity, strives to bring into working harmony the many impulses that he feels burgeoning powerfully within himself: drives toward self-preservation and self-expression, cravings for love, acceptance and recognition, the often divergent needs of body and mind. He wants to be secure, yet also to sense that life is full of opportunity. He becomes aware of the dangers of the closed or biased mind, and of how easy it is for him to relapse into cynical despair as a way out of unresolved conflicts. If one or another of his legitimate impulses is stifled or deflected, he is set back on his journey toward full growth.

What applies to the individual is true of a democratic society, whose many groupings in the ideal state live together in mutual respect, enjoy freedom of expression, and keep open the opportunities for self-realization. The premises underlying this ideal state, as expressed in the basic documents of the Republic, are threefold: 1) the oneness of man ("all men are created equal"); 2) the fluidity of his modes of expression and behavior ("Congress shall make no law respecting an establishment of religion,

or prohibiting the free exercise thereof; or abridging the freedom of speech, or of the press; or the right of the people peace-
ably to assemble, and to petition the Government for a redress
of grievances"); 3) the improvability of his nature and the
nature of his society ("We the people of the United States, in
order to form a more perfect Union . . . ").

I

The premise of the oneness of man, or human indivisibility,
has been under attack from many quarters. The Nazis were its
most flagrant disavowers, with their theories about superior and
inferior races. The racist *mystique,* American style, has flourished
in various locales and periods, with assorted victims: Jews,
Catholics, Negroes in the South, Mexicans in the Southwest,
Chinese and Japanese on the West Coast, and Indians everywhere. The voices of its advocates have even been heard on
the floor of Congress. Former Representative John Rankin and
the late Senator Theodore Bilbo held forth for hours on the
"mongrel" Negro, the superiority of white civilization, biological differences in blood, and a racial mumbo jumbo com-
pounded of sexual hysteria and economic fear.

But from whatever quarter, the nature of the attack is nearly
always the same. It begins with an unproved premise: one race
is superior to others, or a particular religion is poisonous and
infects any society in which it manages to take root. This
premise is repeated boldly and dogmatically, the very act of
repetition becoming after a time an equivalent of proof. Hate
is the principal driving force of the purveyors of racial categories, and is of all emotions the most native to an irrational
darkness of mind. In this atmosphere, conditions and criteria
can be created at will, judgments formed and suspended, sen-

tences executed, life partitioned into any pattern, at the whim
of the racist. Truth and reality are just condiments to be added
or omitted according to his requirements. Of all the forces then
victimized, reason is the first. With the subjugation of reason,
or its perversion, the path is clear for the conquest of persons
and objectives whose first line of defense has been breached.

The racist scorns logic. It is enough to feel. If one feels hard
enough and long enough, the truth about the mongrel races
will become clear. While nothing is less contagious than
thought, nothing is more contagious than feeling; it spreads,
especially in crowds, like wildfire and, as a result, seems to come
more "naturally." Wherever racist demagoguery triumphs, the
divisionalist camp has scored a victory over reason and the
oneness of life.

The annals of modern literature are also veined with attacks
upon this oneness from the most widely assorted writers. When
T. S. Eliot indulged in anti-Semitism for carefully worked-out
philosophical reasons, he belonged in the same camp with the
early Wolfe and the early Faulkner who derided the Negro out
of an unreasoning contempt, and with the proletarian novelists
of the 1930s who caricatured the factory owner as a depraved
monster helpless to keep himself from exploiting his employees
even if he wanted to be humane. In each instance the separation
of human beings into the inherently good and bad was done
without qualification or possibility of reprieve, and hence cate-
gorically excluded segments of humanity from the joys and
privileges of the full life, whether in the given present as with
Negroes and Jews, or in the revolutionary communist future as
with the employing class.

T. S. Eliot gave his anti-Semitism a philosophical rationale.
In a lecture at the University of Virginia, while discussing the
attributes of healthy and unhealthy cultures, he delivered himself of the following:

You are hardly likely to develop tradition except where the bulk of the population is relatively so well off where it is that it has no incentive or pressure to move about. The population should be homogeneous; where two or more cultures exist in the same place they are likely either to be fiercely self-conscious or both to become adulterate. What is still more important is unity of religious background; and reasons of race and religion combine to make any large number of free-thinking Jews undesirable. There must be a proper balance between urban and rural, industrial and agricultural development. And a spirit of excessive tolerance is to be deprecated.[1]

Eliot's poetry is tainted with uncomplimentary references to Jews. In "Gerontion" they are identified with the international moneyed power responsible for the ruin of Europe.

> My house is a decayed house,
> And the jew squats on the window sill, the owner,
> Spawned in some estaminet of Antwerp,
> Blistered in Brussels, patched and peeled in London.[2]

In "Burbank with a Baedeker: Bleistein with a Cigar," a poem contrasting the grandeur of Venice in the past with the commercialized tourist town of the present, the Jews are associated with the decay of that great city.

> But this or such was Bleistein's way:
> A saggy bending of the knees
> And elbows, with the palms turned out,
> Chicago Semite Viennese. . . .
>
> The rats are underneath the piles.
> The jew is underneath the lot.
> Money in furs. . . .[3]

---

[1] T. S. Eliot, *After Strange Gods* (New York: Harcourt, Brace, 1934), pp. 19-20.

[2] T. S. Eliot, *The Complete Poems and Plays* (New York: Harcourt, Brace, 1952), p. 21.

[3] *Ibid.*, p. 24.

Eliot's harsh and proscriptive attacks had been heard in other intellectual quarters, notably in the work of Stuart P. Sherman who felt that the immigration waves had muddied the stream of American letters—Theodore Dreiser, of German stock, was his particular *bête noire*. But these attacks had nowhere been made with so much learning and trenchancy. Eliot's later embracing of that formidable triangle, the High Church in religion, classicism in literature, and royalism in politics, did not release any perceptibly larger flow of the milk of human kindness. If anything, it only increased the paradox of a man of great talent, so influentially devoted to the service of culture and civilization, splitting his good society into those with certificates of good standing and those denied admittance altogether.

Anti-Semitism in literature has been pitched in a variety of keys. Its American forms often go back to English prototypes. Traces of anti-Semitism can be found in many light English novels, from the casual detective story where the Jew is nearly always an unctuous moneylender to the average romance of country houses and county gentry, where he assumes his other British configuration, a *nouveau riche* with vulgar manners and a pushing disposition. The books of Anthony Trollope contain Jews who are either greasy moneylenders or shady characters like Ferdinand Lopez in *The Prime Minister,* treacherously imposing themselves on honest, native-born Englishmen. These literary portraits reflect the long and heavily documented record of discrimination against Jews in various aspects of our social life, in education, employment, housing, all the way down to the small humiliations involved in hotel and resort practices.

The divisive attitude is not always expressed in a derogatory way. Many of the sympathetic portraits of Jews have been awkward and unbelievable idealizations where the authors, in all good faith, have gone whole-hog to the opposite and equally nonhuman extreme, a viewpoint seen in *Ivanhoe,* George Eliot's

Daniel Deronda and John Galsworthy's *Loyalties*. In American fiction the pro-Semitic idealization is typified by those two pamphlets masquerading as novels, Arthur Miller's *Focus* and Laura Hobson's *Gentleman's Agreement*. Both extremes are to be found in Thomas Wolfe, where they coexist side by side, sometimes even in the same book.[4] Jews are seldom treated as human beings, without that self-consciousness which puts them into categories different from their fellow men.

Anti-Semitism, wherever and however it appears, represents a denial of the oneness of mankind, and loosens an essential prop of democratic life. This denial is far more evident in the life of the Negro and the literary treatment he has received. Here the range of tone is even wider, from the ingenuous simplicities of cowboy fiction to the complex theories of racial degeneration of William Faulkner. The following passage from Zane Grey's *Arizona Ames* is characteristic of the first. Arizona Ames, the hero, is in the process of denouncing the villain (who is white), and arranges his insults in order of climax: " 'Grieve, you're a drunkard—a sot!—You're a black-faced buzzard! . . . You're shore a nigger! An' you've got the soul of a nigger!' "[5]

The deepening shades of contempt, pity, painful tolerance, outright hostility toward the Negro after one gets beyond the sagebrush saga are very numerous, and all are to be seen knotted intricately together in the novels of Faulkner. The Negro who is just a Negro and exists outside the structure of white life, is at first regarded by Faulkner with indifference or with contemptuous disdain. In *Sartoris* he compares the Negro with the mule: "Misunderstood even by that creature, the nigger who drives him [the mule], whose impulses and mental proc-

---

[4] For a detailed account of Wolfe's feelings about Jews and Negroes, see my book *The Angry Decade* (New York: Dodd, Mead, 1947), pp. 151-9.

[5] Zane Grey, *Arizona Ames* (New York: Grosset & Dunlap, 1932), p. 144.

esses most closely resemble his . . . "[6] Later the Negro who knows his place in the white world and keeps within it draws Faulkner's approval and even affection. These are the emotions aroused by Dilsey, the faithful family servant of the Compsons who in *The Sound and the Fury* holds herself together while her white masters disintegrate around her.

The Negro who has an admixture of white blood and hence has broken into the framework of white life, preoccupies Faulkner intensely and has swelled into one of his major themes. For a long while, this figure was a source of unrelieved tragedy in Faulkner's early fiction, bringing misfortune to the whites and disaster to himself. Two of the novels were devoted almost wholly to detailing the unhappy results of miscegenation. In *Light in August* Joe Christmas, of mixed blood, took revenge upon the white world by murdering his white mistress. In *Absalom, Absalom!* the racially "tainted" Charles Bon proposed to marry his white half sister who did not know his identity, by way of securing the same revenge. Jim Bond, in the same novel, a degenerate of mixed blood, was Faulkner's warning of the hideous consequences that racial intermingling would bring upon white civilization.

But from 1936, the year of *Absalom, Absalom!*, to 1942, when Faulkner's next full treatment of the race question appeared in *Go Down, Moses*, his attitude toward the Negro underwent a profound transformation. He created in Lucas Beauchamp a man of mixed blood who, unlike Christmas and Bon, was not tormented by his situation, indeed was extraordinarily and nobly beyond it.

Yet it was not that Lucas made capital of his white . . . blood, but the contrary. It was as if he were not only impervious to that blood, he was indifferent to it. He didn't even need to

---

[6] William Faulkner, *Sartoris* (New York: Harcourt, Brace, 1951), p. 279.

strive with it. He resisted it simply by being the composite of the two races which made him, simply by possessing it. Instead of being at once the battleground and victim of the two strains, he was a vessel, durable, ancestryless, nonconductive, in which the toxin and its anti stalemated one another, seetheless, unrumored in the outside air.[7]

Since Faulkner inflates his characters far beyond life-size, Lucas becomes as abnormally calm and heroic a figure as his predecessors had been violently haunted and guilt-ridden. So calm indeed that when falsely arrested for murdering a white man in *Intruder in the Dust,* he scarcely lifts a finger to help his white defenders gather evidence on his behalf. He has at any rate the secret of heroic tranquillity, of inscrutable wisdom, and represents at his polarized extreme Faulkner's first acceptance of the Negro as a human being, however idealized.

His creation coincides with the appearance of another noble figure of mixed blood, Sam Fathers, the leading spirit of Faulkner's marvelous story "The Bear," central to the *Go Down, Moses* collection. Sam is an even more "miscegenated" creature than Lucas, for he has Indian blood as well as Negro and white. He stands for the incorruptible spirit of the old wilderness now being overrun by the factories and lumber mills. It is he who teaches the boy Ike McCaslin the meaning of the ancient verities, and is the symbol of the glorious and eternal past upon which Faulkner's imagination forever broods. This idealization of the Negro continued in *Requiem for a Nun,* the novel that followed *Intruder in the Dust.* Here the colored servant who murders her mistress's baby to keep the lady from running off with another man and ruining everyone's life, is portrayed as acting from the purest of motives, and goes to her own death with the

---

[7] William Faulkner, *Go Down, Moses* (New York: Random House, 1942), p. 104.

same unhurried serenity that marked the demeanor of Lucas and Sam.

Civilized life rests on a belief in the essential indivisibility of mankind, which derives from the theory that men are created spiritually equal. However diverse intellectually and culturally human beings may be, the theory of ethical oneness holds that all men have equal moral value and an equal right to liberty and happiness. Faulkner's viewpoint as it affects the Negro has marched full circle from rejection to acceptance. Since he possesses one of the extraordinarily fertile and powerful narrative talents of our time, the impact of this change is all the more profound.

A somewhat similar change has taken place in the projection of the Negro by the movies, despite their tendency to freeze their views of human nature into fixed attitudes. At first, beginning with *The Birth of a Nation* in 1915, the film classifications of the colored man seldom varied. In comedies he was a good-natured, slightly imbecilic, wholly irresponsible creature who stole chickens and watermelons and got entangled in mild scrapes because of his slow-wittedness. Stepin Fetchit used to play this role with a marvelous leisureliness of movement, and as a result became popularly associated with it. In serious dramas of the South, the Negro was invariably a faithful servant, whose loyalty to the family he served was by far his strongest emotion. If the period predated the Civil War, he was a contented slave; if after, he stoutly resisted all attempts by carpetbaggers to "improve" his lot in life. As a male, he was gentle and docile. In female form, as portrayed by Louise Beavers or Hattie McDaniel, she was the old mammy played broad, on whose ample bosom the white heroine flung herself for solace in moments of crisis, and who delivered little lectures in monosyllabic language designed to buck up the flagging spirits of her "white folks."

In musicals the Negro was either a hot jazz player with more animal rhythm than would perhaps be decent in a white man, or a member of the Hall-Johnson choir singing beautiful spirituals while picking cotton with a carefully stage-managed swaying motion that removed all sense of hard labor and filled the scene with purely aesthetic vibrations. In juveniles the colored kid was always cute as a bug (Farina in the *Our Gang* comedies), but a little slower mentally than the white children and considerably less responsible as far as the practical world was concerned. For a long time the Negro was never shown committing murder or violence, arson, robbery (except petty thievery of a whimsical kind, and even this was later abandoned), or doing anything immoral. Neither was he shown in love nor involved in any real way with the problems of life. Hollywood, in short, eviscerated him as a human being, stuffed him with sawdust after removing all nerves and emotions, hoping in this way to avoid exacerbating the sensibilities of any influential portion of the white world, pro- as well as anti-Negro. As an exhibit in cinematic taxidermy, this portraiture was superb. As a comment on the working of the popular arts in a democracy, it could be regarded only as appalling. The more appalling because it was perpetrated without conviction,[8] unless sensitivity to box-office returns can be equated with conviction. This too helped muddy the waters from which our culture draws its sustenance, and was a factor in the assault upon its wholeness.

After the second World War, when a wave of strong feeling about the segregated status of the Negro swept the country, Hollywood produced a number of pictures which portrayed the

---

[8] With the marked exception of *The Birth of a Nation,* where D. W. Griffith, a Southerner by birth and conviction and a great creative artist by temperament, portrayed the Negro as an inferior creature because he genuinely regarded him as such.

Negro in a maturer light. Films like *Home of the Brave, Lost Boundaries* and *Pinky,* though scarcely distinguished, succeeded in breaking out of the narrow pattern on issues of race which had for so many years stifled Hollywood's approach to the subject. Produced more under outward pressure than inner conviction, they have not yet solidified into a permanent shift in attitude; yet they represent a hopeful beginning.

Even films not primarily concerned with Negroes have begun to portray them as human beings rather than racial types. There appeared in 1952 a mediocre movie called *Red Ball Express* where Negro soldiers played only a minor role, yet were presented not only realistically but without any trace of that self-consciousness whose mere presence is a sign of differentiation. The movement to establish Negroes as Americans and as full-fledged members of the human race has been gathering momentum in other spheres. A large and prominent group of Negro Americans published a political advertisement in the New York *Times* on October 24, 1952, stating their urgent desire that they be regarded and addressed in the Presidential campaign and at all other times not as Negroes but as Americans. This, too, was an expression of the indivisibility of man.

Racial and religious prejudices have not been alone in attacking the wholeness of American culture. There is also the divisionalism based on stratified theories of class, region and intelligence, a divisionalism with multiple forms. It is promoted by the Communists who proclaim all bosses wicked,[9] by employers who proclaim all labor (particularly unionized labor) dissident and greedy, by Northerners who proclaim all Southerners bigoted and prejudiced, by Southerners who consider all Northerners carpetbaggers and "nigger-lovers," by farmers who think all urban workers radical, by workers who

---

[9] Except during the brief period of the Browder "heresy," when some influential capitalists were regarded as "progressive."

regard all farmers as grasping and reactionary, by the small-towners who look on the big cities as sinks of iniquity, by the big cities which look on the small towns as provincial goldfish bowls, by the citizenry that is cynically sure all politicians are rascals, by the politicians who are cynically sure their constituents are cranks and fools. It animates the thinking of those who espouse the doctrine of the elite: that some are born to lead and others to be led.

The proletarian writers of the 1930s built an entire literature on arbitrary group labeling in which individual variations were impermissible. In the proletarian formula no factory owner, no matter how kind or decent he might be personally, could avoid exploiting his workers, hiring spies to report on their activities, engaging efficiency experts to speed them up inhumanly, condoning police brutality against strikers and picket lines, hiring strikebreakers, and even joining fascist organizations like the Black Legion if the workers refused to yield under the other pressures. On the other side were the workers, especially the unionized ones, and of the unionized ones those sympathetic to the Communist party, who were blessed with the virtues of courage, intelligence and integrity. Most important, they had justice on their side and were fighting a heroic war for economic freedom. The occasional worker who weakened under the strain and "ratted" on his fellows by stool-pigeoning for the boss, was cast aside sorrowfully but firmly. One or two strikers were invariably killed but this served only to spur the others on, until at last, bursting through police lines, they gathered by the thousands in Union Square with banners waving, faces stalwartly forward in a massive demonstration that a new world was a-coming.[10]

---

[10] This formula appeared as late as 1948, in Howard Fast's novel *Clarkton*. Here, Fast was still identifying as the villain a weak, neurotic employer who almost against his will yielded his power to a professional strikebreaker with smooth manners and Machiavellian morals; and still identifying as dyed-in-the-wool heroes all union organizers, particularly those who were Communists.

This setup, dramatic in itself, was given a surface plausibility by the events of the depression, the growth of the C.I.O., the sit-down strikes; yet it soon became tiresome and mechanical, and collapsed partly because the proletarian movement in the arts failed to produce or attract sufficient talent, but chiefly because it could not grow and expand on the basis of an ethic and a psychology so unrelievedly black-and-white. The same was largely true of proletarian criticism and drama, which suffered equally from the ruthless classification of human beings according to the requirements of an abstract theory. As an example of the iron operations of the divisive mind, the whole proletarian aesthetic supplied a revealing case history.

The bias of class (any class[11]), of religion and race, has its counterpart in the bias of intellect, which in its own special way weakens the acceptance of the inherently equal moral value of all human beings. The intellectual snob begins with a conviction that few deny: people are of unequal intelligence. From here, however, he proceeds to the sequential conviction that the more intelligent are the more valuable members of the community, and should therefore be given more authority. The slogans and epithets dramatizing this attitude are numerous: the masses are stupid, people are ignorant, most folks want to be told what to do, human beings are sheep who will follow any strong leader, there's a sucker born every minute, the majority prefers not to think, the road to political success runs through the stomach of the electorate, not its head. The split that is thought to exist between the thinkers and the nonthinkers stratifies into dogma and becomes, presently, a whole theory of life.

The more serious and philosophical of its defenders seek to justify the split with a variety of arguments and rationalizations.

---

[11] At various times, the aristocracy or the middle class was glorified. In the 1930s, it was the proletariat. And one remembers how the simple primitive man of the soil was held in a mawkishly romantic esteem by Marie Antoinette, George Sand, Wordsworth, and, in its modern form, D. H. Lawrence with his quest for the rhythm of the primitive consciousness.

Plato argued that recognition of the right to leadership of his philosopher-kings was best for the state. Carlyle was sure that the mass of common humanity would be much happier working at the jobs for which they were fitted by nature, leaving the very difficult matter of governing to the intelligent elite. Shaw's supermen are creatures of superior brain power who in the name of order and reason would lead the less gifted to the blessings of Fabian socialism. H. L. Mencken's aristocracy would restore dignity to living by doing away with the vulgar and clownish stupidities of the "booboisie." The philosophy of the elite is further expressed in the essays of T. S. Eliot, in the proclamations of Southern agrarians and members of the New Criticism led by John Crowe Ransom, Allen Tate and Robert Penn Warren, and has found powerful clerical spokesmen like Dean Inge and Canon Bernard Iddings Bell.[12]

Whether in the name of the welfare of the state or the happiness of the mass or the virtues of rational orderliness or the dignity of human behavior, a society based on the rule of a special brainy class seeks to justify itself in terms other than the rude essential one that the majority, being stupid, should submit to the intelligent minority. This program is always softened and sheathed in some glowing account of the benefits that will accrue to mankind if it is rationally applied. Yet all the softening of which the imagination is capable does not conceal the ruthless dichotomy imposed by the tyranny of the intellect.

Nor is it concealed by the usual insistence that the privileges enjoyed by the superior intelligence carry with them attendant responsibilities and strains. The philosopher-kings had to devote

---

12 Canon Bell, in his book *Crowd Culture* which appeared in 1952, coined the curious and internally contradictory phrase "democratic élite," referring to a leadership group to be drawn from the mass of people themselves. But however dressed up in palatable phrasing, it derived from the author's expressed belief that most people are dolts and can be led around by the nose, and that the leading had better be done by a body of trained, dedicated and brainy men.

the first thirty-five years of their lives to a grueling training program of mind and body. The later supermen would be bent beneath the cares of state, the strain of having to do everybody else's thinking, and the prospect of being held to account if things went wrong. But no matter how paternalistically or benevolently conceived such a structure would be, it remains irrevocably schismatic and delivers as hard a blow at spiritual equality as does the racist concept of white supremacy.

Intellectual snobbery, like every fundamental human attitude, has a dynamic of its own. It tends to equate intellectual superiority with valuableness. Valuableness to what does not much matter. To the state, to society, to the world, even to oneself. Once the idea of greater valuableness acquires full growth, the concept of the moral equality of human beings is swept away, and the path paved for dictatorship, benevolent or otherwise, of the valuable minority. Since all groups, whether they have risen to influence through brains or through force, seek to perpetuate themselves in power, such a minority would use any means at its disposal to maintain its position. Because in the opinion of this minority most persons are not valuable, a callousness to human life would be inevitably bred, and all the instruments of oligarchic rule would soon put in an appearance. How cleverly and lucidly these instruments would be employed is beyond anticipation, but that they would work toward a stratification of the relationship between rulers and ruled seems beyond question, a state that would assure the eventual corruption of the one and degradation of the other. The stewardship of an elite of the brain appears temptingly rational and right; yet there is nothing in the workings of the advanced intelligence which *per se* immunizes it to the temptations of self-glorifying power. The conspicuously intelligent have their role to play; but despite the seductiveness of the prose of Shaw and others, it is not that of a ruling hierarchy.

A final assault on the premise of indivisibility is xenophobia. Given its first political formulation in America by George Washington in his warnings against entangling European alliances, it dates back to the first immigrants who left the Old World to settle the New. It is a Hydra-headed emotion, assuming as many forms as there are foreigners. Every wave of immigration, with the exception of the original English and Scotch-Irish, created at first impact an intense and prejudicial dislike, so that by the time the rigid clamps on immigration were imposed in the early 1920s, a thoroughgoing antipathy to the Irish, Italians, Jews, Puerto Ricans, Mexicans, Chinese, Japanese, Poles, Hungarians, was firmly established.

Xenophobia, unlike racism, does not summon arguments to "prove" the inferiority of certain peoples, and indeed makes no special point of their "inferiority." It fixes instead upon their differentness, their otherness, and in some cases, their "malevolence." Here once again it is just something one "feels" and, like all presumably deep, inner, instinctive feelings, plainly beyond the understanding of reason, beyond the artificializing grasp of analysis. The xenophobe simply "feels" that Mexicans are greasy, Irish clannish and bellicose, Jews grasping, Poles and "Hunkies" thickheaded, Orientals cunning, Italians dirty and numerous, Puerto Ricans backward on all counts, and Britons slick at inducing others to pull their chestnuts from the fire. He senses it intuitively, feels it instinctively—to him the surest sources of knowledge. No other criterion is admissible.

All this applies with special force to aliens, the first targets of suspicion in any crisis of foreign affairs. Despite the fact that most of the resident spies and agents of history have been citizens of the country they spied on, the absence of formal citizenship papers is an oblique mark of guilt often more difficult to explain away than the possession of incriminating tangibles. The word alien evokes a vague antipathy, a slight shrinking away from a somewhat untidy image: an un-American fellow still smelling of steerage and the old country, whom, except perhaps for business reasons, one had best avoid. Being an attitude locked within an emotion which is in turn wrapped inside a psychic haze, it is not something that can be inspected in the light of day and indeed, if so inspected, might become too tenuous to be seen. Like many nonrational convictions, it travels without visible credentials, and explodes in indignation if challenged.

The split between feeling and reason, so contrary to the concept of the whole man, is constantly emphasized and encouraged by those who look on the oneness of man with aversion or regard reason as innately bloodless and cold. The prejudiced, in the ordinary rather than Machiavellian sense, accept without thinking the accusations launched against thought. Ironically, they often do so within the bounds of the prejudice while remaining perfectly rational in other matters. Yet the boundary between reason and unreason is not a static one, and encroachments from one side upon the other are constant. In this state of flux, the mind with its cargo of attitudes and convictions wars within itself along lines that shift, sway, break and re-form continually. Prejudice has the great tactical advantage of being difficult to dislodge once it takes root, and yields ground only before the most persistent campaigns of reason and reasoned experience. If unchallenged, it spreads out like an aggregate of tumorous cells into adjoining territory. The dislike of aliens, racist mythology, class hatred, oppressive discrimination of whatever kind, drive a wedge into the organic framework of the democratic state.

II

Second among the premises of that state is its fluidity. When freedom of movement, thought or expression is unduly restricted, democracy has to that extent been injured.

The struggle between conformity and individuality, orthodoxy and heterodoxy, thought control and the right to dissent is, of course, eternal. A healthy democratic culture resists every tendency to close or stratify. It defends nonconformism within the limits of its own physical self-preservation, and does not use the legitimate needs of national security as a pretext to smother unpopular opinion. It leans to the heterodox rather than the orthodox, and employs its powers to protect the privacy of its individual citizens. Nothing is deadlier than the society where everyone thinks or is compelled to think and behave exactly alike. None is more life-breathing than that which stimulates variety in habits, customs, opinions and modes of thought.

Such a society seeks to prevent monopolies and cartels from closing up the economic pores of the country, machines and lobbies from doing the same to the political. It encourages the widest possible circulation of ideas, and strenuously resists witch-hunters, doctrinaire fanatics, flag-waving jingoists, pressure groups of both extreme right and extreme left, who would restrict this circulation to their own advantage. "We proclaim 'freedom of enterprise,' " said Christian Gauss, "when we mean only freedom for money-making enterprise, and forget that science, scholarship, literature and the arts, teaching, public service, free discussion, are also enterprises which must have equal freedom unless our society is to become . . . a plutocracy."[13]

No damage done by free speech—except when it constitutes what Justice Holmes called "a clear and present danger" to national safety—can possibly be as great as that inflicted by the censorship of such freedom, whether that censorship be exerted by legislative fiat or outright force. This is the lesson driven home by our whole civil experience since President John Adams'

---

[13] Christian Gauss, "Can We Live with our Enemies?" *The American Scholar,* Winter, 1948-49.

Alien and Sedition Laws in 1798, and our whole international experience in this chequered and violent century. The maintenance of the free flow of movement—political, economic, intellectual—through the numerous channels of society, is as necessary to its civilized well-being as light and air.

The demand for orthodoxy in all matters of opinion and belief is forever on the alert in America. It is an active and aggressive combatant with nothing less than the organizing of the national mind as its goal. It has its touchstones by which conformity can be measured. Loyalty oaths are regarded as guarantees of fidelity, criticism of established institutions as un-American. Foreign dangers, domestic crises, patriotic appeals of all kinds, are used as screens for assaults on heterodox opinion. Only in extreme emergencies, as during the great depression, when society is threatened with breakdown are enough chinks created in the orthodox armor for unconventional and challenging ideas to gain entry and set up shop for varying lengths of time. But the main current is against them and soon absorbs them, though not without being influenced and altering itself somewhat in their direction.

Rigidity is characteristic of the orthodox temper regardless of doctrine, conservative, liberal or radical. Right or left, orthodoxy demands an unreflecting faith from its devotees and, at the very least, lip service and a proper obeisance to its symbols from the hosts of unbelievers whom it seeks to drive into line. Whatever the context, the proposed effect is always to atrophy the mind and its active faculties of skepticism and resistance.

Orthodoxy is not only political or economic. It extends into the corners of everyday existence, into manners, morals and etiquette, into home furnishings, entertainment, dress and every routine activity. Its classic pattern appears in Sinclair Lewis's *Main Street,* where nearly everybody in Gopher Prairie does things in the same way until Carol Kennicott arrives. The novel deals with what happens when she proceeds to flout the local orthodoxy. She dresses differently, gives parties differently, talks vivaciously to men other than her husband, hires servants differently, acts on impulse, displays an interest in drama and literature, and—most frightful of sins—insists on thinking for herself. The ensuing uproar raises enough dust, noise and confusion to animate the book, and provides an object lesson in the smothering weight of conformity. At the end Carol, weary from the losing battle, not only surrenders unconditionally but talks herself into believing that it is all for the best. Since no believer is more zealous than a convert, we may be sure that she will henceforth outconform the natives. Before this happens, however, the sharp thrust of the conformist doctrine has been acutely felt.

The tendency to harden into a rigid code is endemic to every system of ideas that acquires power. While basic matters are occasionally open to discussion in the early stages, they are seldom so in the later. Bolshevism is a good example of this. At first, Marxist concepts were subject to analysis and debate. Later, however, the irrevocability of Marxism, the infallibility of Stalin, the fixed coupling of Soviet actions with the welfare of humanity, passed beyond argument and had to be accepted as true with blind intensity. Doubters and disbelievers were vilified, pursued and liquidated with a ferocity reminiscent of the treatment meted out to medieval heretics.[14] Similar mindless obedience marked the regimes of Lycurgus and Nero, Genghis Khan, Hitler and Ivan the Terrible, Mussolini and Henry VIII. The social content of their respective programs may have differed, in some instances profoundly, but each demanded a strict suspension of individual thought, and crammed

---

14 "Trotskyite swine," "Fascist beasts" (the epithet most commonly applied to schismatic Marshal Tito), "degenerate class collaborators," "deviationist wreckers," "corrupted enemies of the people," are among the milder terms of opprobrium in the Communist lexicon.

into the vacuum thus created the predigested principles prepared by the tyrant.

The tactics of American orthodoxy have nothing in common with those employed by the totalitarian movements of Europe and Asia. By contrast, American tactics are negative and mild: ostracism, whispering campaigns, obstacles in the way of economic success, blackballing, with lapses into physical violence conspicuously rare. Yet in intent and psychology there is little difference. Orthodoxy moves toward the ideal of the closed circle, organizes life in terms of the monolith, insists on unanimity. Within the orthodox fold, an umbilical warmth and comfort prevail; outside it, there exist only enmity and isolation. The reward for conformance is security, with the purchase price, as elsewhere, the yielding up of the right to think and do for oneself.

A microcosm of this process is the growing trend on the part of many American corporations to supervise and organize more and more closely the private lives of their executives. This extends to examining carefully the prospective employee's wife who must meet certain tests of social attitude and personality set up by the corporation. Once he is employed, the couple must fit into a carefully controlled hierarchical framework of houses, clothes, clubs and cars. In exchange for conformity and proper behavior, the corporation guarantees them advancement and economic security. Typical of what conformity and proper behavior signify is the remark made by a top executive's wife about her community: "It's a very worth-while bunch we have here. Edith Sampson down on Follansbee Road is sort of the intellectual type, but most of the gang are real people."[15]

If the orthodox norm in America seems to bear a conservative stamp, it is because we are essentially a conservative country, not simply in politics but in community life. The liberal waves, of

---

15 William H. Whyte, Jr., "The Wife Problem," *Life,* January 7, 1952.

whatever shading, have nearly always been on the defensive, and
require critical times and extraordinary men (Lincoln and the
Civil War, the depression and Franklin D. Roosevelt) to sweep
into power. And then their tenure has been relatively brief.
Andrew Johnson and Harry S. Truman were much closer to the
average temper than their illustrious predecessors. Even under
Roosevelt, the period of New Deal reforms endured for less
than half his twelve years in office, and the reforms themselves
were under constant and in some instances effective assault.
Had the social climate of the country been different and the
liberal viewpoint the prevailing one, in all probability this viewpoint would have established an orthodoxy of its own, equipped
with an equal drive to unanimity and an equal desire to deal
with humanity in mass lots. The mystical veneration of Roosevelt that flourished among some sections of the public was one
sign of what might have developed in another atmosphere.

Of all the agents of orthodoxy, the most immediate menace
to the open society are the professional thought-controllers, full
of brisk plans for the suppression of independent ideas. Not
content with letting the established laws of the land dispose of
traitors and fomenters of violence, these vigilantes seek to prevent the expression of any opinions they find unpalatable. They
campaign against dissidents everywhere, from those who express
unpopular opinions on specific questions of foreign policy to
those who depart from the norm on issues of private taste. The
thought-controllers jam through laws like Michigan's Callahan
Act in 1947 which makes it a crime to advocate any policy that
might benefit a foreign power, strict enforcement of which,
according to the *New Republic,* "could mean prosecution of
persons favoring another loan to Britain and of travel agencies
who urge tourists to spend money abroad."[16] They set up censorship bodies that seek to determine what books, movies and

---

16 *New Republic,* September 22, 1947.

plays the public shall be exposed to.[17] They prowl about in quest of ideas which seem heretical and pursue their advocates with gimlet-eyed intensity. Like the cultural commissars of the Soviet Union, they seek to establish themselves as official guardians of thought. They aim not simply at limiting the areas of thought but at relegating it to limbo in its entirety. They are the bully boys in the great modern business of organizing opinion for use as a battering ram in the imposition of an unquestioning unanimity or for the achievement of power.

Their local and regional operations are as energetic as their national. The white Southerner who speaks out too boldly for Negro rights is apt to receive one of their calling cards. The Californian who suggests that the Japanese-American is as decent and reliable a human being as anybody else invites their instant displeasure. The small-town merchant who implies that a labor strike is perhaps not wholly unjustified is likely to be honored by the kind of visit that Babbitt, under similar circumstances, was paid by the sinister Vergil Gunch, a visit that caused him speedily to change his mind.

The apostles of thought-control have taken root almost everywhere, opposing the free play of thought and the uncensored flow of expression. The conformity they impose, wherever it operates, reduces the flexibility of our lives and restricts that sense of individuality which has always been one of the great ideas and achievements of American democracy.

III

A society which is whole, a democratic society, not only accepts the spiritual equality of its members and maintains the

---

17 An example of this was the refusal of the Chicago police chief to permit Sartre's *The Respectful Prostitute* to be shown in his city because of its title. When invited to see the play, he declined, claiming that it would make no difference in his decision.

greatest possible flexibility of action and thought. It also believes in an improvable future. If man is not an improvable animal, if he is doomed to remain locked forever in his present dilemmas, then the future has no meaning and the struggle toward the better life central to the democratic idea becomes hopeless from the start.

In its theological form the issue goes back at least as far as the dispute between Augustine, who claimed that man was burdened with original sin, and Pelagius, who argued that he was not. Modern pragmatists like William James and John Dewey denied that man is burdened with anything he cannot free himself of through the trials, errors and efforts of living, while powerful contemporary pessimists like Dean Inge and Reinhold Niebuhr stress the evil in him, his helplessness, his capacity for destruction. Psychiatrists are similarly split. Freud was profoundly pessimistic about the future of man because he could see no way out of the eternal war between the subconscious drives striving for expression and society which, in sheer self-preservation, had to suppress them. A whole school of younger psychiatrists—Karen Horney, James Plant, H. S. Sullivan, Erich Fromm—while acknowledging their debt to Freud, were convinced that perpetual disharmony between the inward man and the external world was by no means inevitable. Karen Horney, who went farthest along the line of asserting the affirmative future, found in self-realization and understanding and the emotional responsiveness of the individual all the powers needed to help him toward the mature and integrated life. She became convinced, furthermore, that society, especially the democratic society she found in America, was in no sense the deadly obstacle to psychic well-being Freud had felt it to be.

The disbelief in human improvability has been strongly maintained by our writers as well. The early Hemingway, the man who published in the 1920s *The Sun Also Rises* and *A Farewell*

to Arms, those superbly written novels devoted to the thesis
that life is empty and meaningless, rejected the idea that things
can get better. The world which his characters inhabited was
bleak, indifferent to them and unchangeable. It inflicted upon
them senseless tragedies like the wound that made Jake Barnes
impotent or Catherine Barkley's death in childbirth, which only
accented life's pointlessness. In this universe of purposeless
pain, Hemingway's early figures survive only by tightening their
belts, stripping themselves of hope and expectation, and getting
rid of every illusion. When Lady Brett Ashley says to Jake,
with whom she is hopelessly and unrequitedly in love, "Oh,
Jake, we could have had such a damned good time together," he
replies, "Yes. Isn't it pretty to think so?"[18] The rain that falls
continually through *A Farewell to Arms* suggests the desolation
of the cosmos through which pass Lieutenant Henry, the hopeless, endless war on the Italian front, and the love affair that
comes to a meaningless, irrelevant end. Harry Morgan, the
smuggler of *To Have and Have Not,* lives with courage but his
life, too, comes to a bitter, designless close. Many of the characters in the early short stories continue living, but in a crushing
spiritual emptiness which is the psychological equivalent of
death.

The consequences of this point of view are shattering. They
impose upon humanity the most painful of sentences: that which
is at once irrevocable and undeserved, irrevocable because there
is no exit, undeserved because implicit in Hemingway is Rous-
seau's old dogma that man is born good into a world that has
grown corrupt. Furthermore, the action within this closed system seems never to change. Trapped in the same maze, the figures go through the same gestures of courage which come to
nothing. The monotony in Hemingway is not only a matter of

---

[18] Ernest Hemingway, *The Sun Also Rises* (New York: Scribner's, 1926), pp.
258-9.

style; it is a monotony of feeling and behavior as well, to which the unvarying style is so admirably suited. Nothing is more calculated to trumpet the accents of doom. Hard-boiled, tight-lipped, extravagantly monosyllabic though this barren-surfaced art appears to be, it bears a startling resemblance, as far as will and freedom and doom are concerned, to Dante's *Inferno*.

Contemporary with the gloomy impasse of Hemingway was the moist nostalgic pessimism that was characteristic of F. Scott Fitzgerald in the 1920s, during the first period of his career. Fitzgerald was another superb craftsman who, while attacking the foundations of the rich and leisured society which so fasci-nated him, contributed to our understanding of it. Where the characters in Hemingway are battered from the outside, Fitz-gerald's are defeated by their own inadequacies. They are brittle and crack under strain. They have extravagantly youthful illu-sions about the world, which blow away at the first puff of reality. Like Gatsby, they have an inflatedly romantic concep-tion of what life should be, and when the absurdity of this con-ception becomes plain, they unravel at the seams with alarming rapidity. Fitzgerald describes the unraveling process, its fre-quent alcoholism and occasional mental breakdowns, with poig-nant fidelity and unremitting skill, his figures being broken up at the end into powdery fragments that nevertheless retain their fragrant exhalations to the last.

Anthony and Gloria Patch, hero and heroine of *The Beautiful and Damned,* are beautiful to start with and damned at the end. The rich boy in the story of the same name, the Buchanans, Jordan Baker and Gatsby in *The Great Gatsby,* the assorted fig-ures in "May Day," begin at the pinnacle and slide downhill. To the early Fitzgerald life is marvelous for a brief period in extreme youth; its only direction afterward is down. Far from believing that the future was full of possibilities, he believed it to be full of impossibilities. Far from accepting the improvability of man, he could see only the lines of his degeneration. Through the rhythms and idiomatic locale of the jazz age which his fiction records, one sees this closed view of human nature, a view that shuts out hope, and because it is lacking in large dimensions and even, as in Hemingway, a capacity for endurance, results finally in disheartening the reader.

A tragic view of man as such is not incompatible with a faith in his potentialities; indeed tragedy in the deepest sense rests on that faith. But suffering in a work of art, as in everyday experience, can be endured only if there is a way out; otherwise it becomes a pointless and therefore intolerable burden. Shakespeare and Dostoevski, to mention two supremely relevant examples, cause us pain. But there is an exit from pain in each, and in the exit an assertion of the powers of man. The function of the surviving characters in the Shakespeare tragedy who pick up the corpses, promise to profit from the unhappy events and make the concluding flourishes, is to suture the vicarious wounds in reader and spectator. Hence Horatio is our exit from Hamlet's grief. With Dostoevski it is redemption through Christian penance. Raskolnikov is redeemed in Siberia for the murders he committed in St. Petersburg. Alyosha redeems the other Karamazovs by the shining example of his goodness and his eventual entrance into a monastery. But Fitzgerald leaves his characters and ourselves with no way out, moving swiftly toward extinction.

This is felt even more sharply in the work of John O'Hara, Fitzgerald's chief disciple in the next generation. O'Hara picks up the narrative thread just at the point where Fitzgerald leaves it, with the characters having made the turn downward but not yet having reached bottom. In O'Hara they reach bottom. They are the same people a few years older. Mainly in their twenties in Fitzgerald, they have now reached their thirties, but still belong to the youngish country-club set, suffer from serious emotional disorders having little to do with their environment which is as favorable as money and background can make it, and as a result are drinking themselves to death. The first stages of their disintegration—after O'Hara takes hold of them—reveal the logic of Fitzgerald's premises when carried to their extreme. O'Hara feels no tenderness or compassion toward them as Fitzgerald did, but regards them with a cold clinical stare. He is absolutely merciless in setting down their aberrations, without any show of feeling or hope of salvation. This is humanity in the boneyard, with the writer picking his way—and O'Hara does so very skillfully—through the wreckage, classifying it with scientific detachment. It is to the great benefit of Fitzgerald's art that he was not coldly detached, that his figures were not yet that far down. But they were already headed in that direction under his impetus. Where they were headed and how they looked both on the way and after they got there, is made heartlessly clear by O'Hara. The pattern of life created by the two of them, the second an extension of the first, works out into one of the destructive philosophies of contemporary literature. By comparison, Hemingway is sweetness and light, for his people hang on no matter how adverse the circumstances. Fitzgerald-O'Hara's lose this capacity for survival even under the most favorable conditions.

The sense of futility communicated by these writers is part of the widespread defeatism present in our century. The conviction that human life is a nightmare springs from Freud and Franz Kafka, from Oswald Spengler, Robinson Jeffers and Eugene O'Neill, from gloomy theologians, psychologists and historians. All of it attacks man's ability to handle life and is contrary to the premise of improvability without which democracy, resting on a belief in man's power to develop, cannot function. The dream of building "a more perfect union" depends on a conviction that improving it is possible. If beyond reach, the game is up before it starts, and why then strain to be better citizens and more successful human beings? This defeatist view also undermines our intellectual resources. Why struggle to use one's reason and intelligence if they are certain to prove vain? And if the effort toward self-rule, arduous at best, is vain, the society based on self-rule at once loses its motivation and its very reason for existence.

But man is an affirming creature. He does feel the urge to improve himself and to develop his institutions. Never content with past achievements or the *status quo,* he drives on to higher and more complex forms of living. Our whole history in America is a record of the persistent energy with which we have worked toward creating a freer and more abundant society, and hence belies the paralyzing conviction that the future, in terms of human betterment, is an illusion.

The triple premises of democratic civilization give purpose and meaning to our efforts, charge them with creative energy, and direct them toward a more advanced maturity. Whatever strengthens or obstructs these premises strengthens or obstructs the foundations of our society and determines, therefore, the texture and character of life in America.

Chapter XIII

The Decline of Optimism and Pessimism

ONE OF THE NUBS OF THE CULTURAL question in America during our time is the relationship between the pursuit of property and the achievement of justice. The period that began with the Revolution and concluded with the end of the Civil War was weighted in the direction of justice. The growth of industry since the Civil War just as clearly weighted the social equation more and more heavily in the direction of property at the expense of justice. When opportunities to make money in dazzling, new and rapid ways outrun the powers of the public conscience to regulate them, social and cultural disturbances of the profoundest sort set in. Such opportunities arose during the 1870s and '80s, the era of Rockefeller, Harriman, Vanderbilt, Gould, and company, the era of the robber barons in Matthew Josephson's expressive phrase, of the Great Barbecue as Vernon L. Parrington called it. The disturbances that were then shot into motion have been defined in a variety of ways, depending on the angle of approach. To sociologists they have represented in a dramatic form the age-old lag of social organization behind technics; to theologians, of morality behind materialism; to artists and writers, the frustration of the American dream.

276

It is among these last that the nature of the disturbances can be seen most poignantly and plainly. Mark Twain's nausea at the bric-a-brac phoniness of life among the newly rich in the 1870s was recorded in *The Gilded Age*. The rebellious outbursts of the realists of the 1890s and early 1900s were directed at the heartlessness and injustice of the new industrial order. In *Maggie* Stephen Crane fictionized his indignation at conditions of life in the slums. In *The Octopus* Frank Norris recorded the brutality with which the Southern Pacific Railroad juggernauted the homesteaders who stood in its way. William Dean Howells was moved to embrace socialism in his later years as a protest against exploitation. In *The Financier* and *The Titan* Theodore Dreiser—not without a certain admiration for his hero, Frank Cowperwood—described the corruption with which fortunes were now being acquired. Upton Sinclair launched with *The Jungle* his crusading and pamphleteering novels exposing the harsh working conditions in one large industry after another. A school of muckrakers, as Theodore Roosevelt described them with contemptuous vividness, arose to hammer away at the iniquities of the new industrialism. Its leading members, Lincoln Steffens, Ida M. Tarbell, Gustavus Myers, David Graham Phillips, burrowed into every phase of oil, the press, the political machines, steel, coal and finance with indefatigable zeal, and emerged with indictments, on moral grounds, of all of them. Even Frederick Jackson Turner, the calm and detached historian, was to warn in his essays on the frontier against the rapacity and public irresponsibility of the latter-day tycoons, traits summed up as "the curse of bigness," in the famous comment of Louis Brandeis.

The poets were not far behind. Their major reappearance in the second decade of the twentieth century, after a long interlude of comfortable late-Victorian gentility, was ushered in on varying notes of criticism, bitterness, outright repudiation and militancy. The militancy was largely supplied by Carl Sandburg; the criticism, restrained and semiphilosophical, by Robert Frost; the bitterness, with complex overtones of irony, by T. S. Eliot; the outright repudiation, *ex cathedra,* from his cliff in California, by Robinson Jeffers. Sandburg picked up a bludgeon, belabored the rich and apostrophized the poor with so obviously muscular an enjoyment of the game that his invectives against injustice were bathed in a radiant and paradoxical optimism. Frost quietly concerned himself with the ancient issues of right and wrong, life and death, and carefully disengaged himself from the hideous urban industrialism which his absorption in the rural simplicities of New Hampshire seemed by example to reject. Eliot's famous accounts of the sterility of the contemporary world, woven through "The Love Song of J. Alfred Prufrock," the Sweeney poems and "The Waste Land," were scrupulously pessimistic and ascetically erudite. Jeffers combined Sandburg's energy and Eliot's bitter irony, added to these a certain twisted passionateness, and emerged with surely the most uncompromising repudiation of the machine age and all its values extant in our poetry.

Many of the lesser poets expressed their recoil from the times just as positively but in other moods and different timbres. Wallace Stevens wove his spiderwebbed verses, full of delicate traceries and glittering tiny filaments, the very texture of his work embodying all the qualities of subtlety, sensibility and miniature size which a society dominated by magnates, high-powered salesmen and advertisers so aggressively lacked. E. E. Cummings fled on occasion into perverseness and obscurity, though all his mockingly eccentric verbal acrobatics did not fully hide his wounded feelings and rebellious spirit. This was even more painfully true of Hart Crane—without the perverseness. His inability to cope with the world lent his writing an intense wounded vitality and also helped induce his early suicide.

These numerous literary testaments cast sharp lights on the split that took place between an advancing, overriding technology and the sense of social responsibility. This sense had been lost in the shuffle or regarded as a hampering element while laissez-faire industrialism was under a full head of steam in the sixty years between 1870 and 1930, when the depression brought it to a temporary but immensely significant stop.

These changes and conflicts generated intense emotional responses. The great economic expansion in the last part of the nineteenth century may have left more sensitive spirits with the feeling that America had somehow gone off the track; but it produced in most Americans an easy and unthinking optimism, reinforced by the successive advances and final conquest of the frontier. Though punctuated by the brief setbacks of the panics of 1893 and 1907 and by the tragic despair that settled on the post-bellum South, this optimism grew and swelled until it became a commodity recognized the world over.

After reaching its apex during the boom of the 1920s, it blew up with a tremendous roar in the stock-market crash of 1929. Four depression years altered it unrecognizably. By alloying optimism with elements of uncertainty and fear, that disaster in our national life produced a new emotion altogether. Optimism in its naïve form disappeared and was replaced for a time by an equally naïve pessimism. But with the partial recovery under the New Deal and our later emergence into a role of world leadership, both eventually merged into a new and more complex point of view. Existence, we now realized, was no longer the simple thing it had appeared to be at the turn of the century but a difficult, tortuous, often painful process. A dawning awareness of the tragedy of life and of the necessity for struggle in the perpetual effort to master it now began to filter into the consciousness of the American people.

Optimism and pessimism were still present, but mingled

together in a new, more realistic and more mature way. That brash confidence with which every crisis had been met before was now neither so brash nor so confident. The sense of stability and permanence, the planning of one's life on a long-range basis, thinned out alarmingly. Hence the paradox which so many commentators have noted,[1] that with the coming of greater material abundance, the morale of the country has gone down and not up. The average citizen lives more from day to day, less from one end of his lifetime to the other. In the past, the future may at times have seemed dangerous but it was always relatively clear. Now it looks very dangerous indeed, and cloudy. This striking change has been dramatized by the atom bomb and its terrors, yet the bomb was only the most recent of a series of shocks that began, in their modern phase, with the Industrial Revolution.

The change in temper had been sensed long before by writers and intellectuals, novelists, poets and crusading journalists, upon whom the psychological and spiritual impact of an age manifests itself early and most sharply. The first stage of this change in temper—the passage from rosy cheerfulness to blank despair—gave rise to the prolonged record of protest, bitterness, disillusionment, realism carried to the mechanical and dehumanizing extreme of naturalism, preoccupation with evil, a growing doubt about the existence of free will or, for that matter, the significance of the individual personality. These became synonymous with modern American literature. Despite the complaints of many who found this literature abhorrent, and were hence out of sympathy with the major literary trends of the day, it was not created out of whole cloth, from the frenzied imagination of the professional writer disposed to look on the gloomy side of things. If his faith in free will had been

---

[1] Lloyd Morris' *Postscript to Yesterday* was devoted to a documentation of this paradox.

shaken, so had the faith of men generally in a time when depression and war seemed less and less controllable by the will of nations, let alone the will of individuals. If his prevailing mood was disillusionment, it was surely more the product of political and economic breakdown, the growth of rampant nationalism, the spread of antihumanism over large areas of the world, than of his own private maladjustments and defeats. If he was moved by anxious skepticism more than by simple faith, it was less from perverseness on his part than from his reflection on experiences common to nearly everyone. Jarring though all this may have been to readers nourished on the settled values of the nineteenth century, it is imperative to recognize this literature for what it was, a profoundly genuine reaction to a profoundly unsettled time.

But the writers did not remain locked in their despair any more than did the country as a whole after the depression. Many of them reached out for new affirmations and passed from a paralyzing pessimism to that maturer state of mind where one accepts life in its complexities and goes on living as resolutely as possible. T. S. Eliot went from the despair of his early Prufrock-Wasteland period to the reacquired faith of "Ash Wednesday," "Four Quartets" and *The Cocktail Party*. John Steinbeck moved from *The Grapes of Wrath*, that remarkable piece of literary sociology which showed the Joads all but crushed by a hostile world, to *East of Eden* with its insistence on man's capacity for survival. Sinclair Lewis satirized Main Street in the 1920s and defended it in the '30s and '40s. John P. Marquand began in *The Late George Apley* and *H. M. Pulham, Esq.* with a skeptical analysis of Boston Brahmanism with its inhibitions and incapacity for the full life, but finally emerged in *Melville Goodwin, U. S. A.* with a portrait of a hero living with sureness and decision. The characters in Ellen Glasgow's *They Stooped to Folly* and *The Sheltered Life* were unable to make the transition from the values of old Virginia to the new; the later characters in *Vein of Iron* and *In This Our Life* succeeded in doing so. Even Thomas Wolfe, who had thrashed about rebelliously in *Look Homeward, Angel* and *The Web and the Rock,* began embracing democracy and humanity during the concluding stages of *You Can't Go Home Again.* The spoiled young rich lovely darlings who populated F. Scott Fitzgerald's early novels were almost invariably defeated by life; in the later works, he was beginning to portray characters like Nicole Warren, Charley Wales and Monroe Stahr who, despite continuous pressure, refused to concede defeat. In the work of Hemingway and Faulkner the movement from the negative toward the positive is equally marked. With Hemingway the aborted relationships of *The Sun Also Rises* and the tragic futility of the world in *A Farewell to Arms* were eventually succeeded by the affirmation of *Across the River and into the Trees* and the exaltation of *The Old Man and the Sea.*[2] The dark and tormented universe created by Faulkner in *Light in August* and *Absalom, Absalom!* was at last supplanted by the growing light of *Go Down, Moses* and *Intruder in the Dust.*

The writers were registering the emotional atmosphere in advance of their contemporaries. There has been a long-standing and plainly futile controversy over whether literature shapes

---

[2] This affirmative strain, implicit in Hemingway, was missed by Bernard De-Voto when he wrote: "Hemingway has always attacked the life of the mind, the life of the spirit, and the shared social experience of mankind. . . . His disdain of intelligence, contempt of spirituality, praise of mindlessness, and adoration of instinct and blood-consciousness" connect him with "the manias of doom that obsess Mr. Faulkner" and the "clotted phobias . . . of Robinson Jeffers." *The Literary Fallacy* (Boston: Little, Brown, 1944), p. 107. In his zest for the sweeping and striking generalization DeVoto confused Hemingway with D. H. Lawrence. Far from holding spirituality in contempt, for example, even Hemingway's earlier characters struggle toward it: Jake Barnes calls himself "a bad Catholic" but is always attending church. Lieutenant Henry tries to establish a fruitful relationship with the priest who is constantly baited by the other soldiers. As for attacking the "life of the mind," Robert Jordan and Robert Wilson are supreme illustrations of men who think analytically and clearly. In these and other ways Hemingway is dissociated at once from the "clotted phobias" of Jeffers.

public opinion or is only symptomatic of it. Plainly futile since both sides of the argument are true, and the question of which is truer is indeterminable. The antiwar novels of the '20s *(Three Soldiers, A Farewell to Arms, All Quiet on the Western Front,* etc.) did not create the strong tide of pacifism which gripped the public at the time, but certainly confirmed and strengthened it. Similarly, *Uncle Tom's Cabin* did not produce abolitionism but surely inflamed it;[3] the novels of Dickens did not of themselves manufacture public indignation about the mistreatment of children, the wretchedness of debtors' prisons, the brutality of schoolmasters, but they did much to crystallize it. The condition of the Dust Bowl victims had been known before Steinbeck wrote of them, but *The Grapes of Wrath* dramatized it to the point where the Federal Government was moved to set up camps in California for migrants from the stricken areas; the early crusading career of Upton Sinclair, beginning with *The Jungle,* illustrates how the romancer can successfully advertise inequity.

Before the depression the disenchantment of the writers had little visible effect. With the economic collapse, and the loss of confidence in the leaders of industry and finance, the disenchantment of the public made Crane, Norris and Dreiser seem like minor prophets living in advance of their time, and prepared the way for what then seemed the radical reforms of the New Deal. After 1929 it was no longer so easy to dismiss the writer as simply a dispenser of groundless gloom, as a protester without cause for protest, as a dealer in abnormal psychic tensions in a society doused in serenity, as a purveyor of growling jeremiads in a time of unclouded peace. The experience of the public began catching up with the insight of the artist and when the country started to pull out of the emotional pit of the depression, it did not revert back to the simple confidence

---

[3] This was implied in Lincoln's comment to Harriet Beecher Stowe: "So you are the little woman that caused this great war."

of earlier times but, like the writers, moved forward to a growing acceptance of the difficulties of life in a troubled century.

Getting the banks back on a sound basis and putting the unemployed back to work were only the immediate emergency aims of the New Deal. It sought through the Wagner Labor Relations Act to give the trade unions bargaining power at least equivalent to that of their employers, after a long period when the individual worker had been helpless in the hands of the giant corporation. The Securities and Exchange Commission was designed to shore up the stock market against future collapses and so protect the investing public. The Federal Deposit Insurance Act succeeded in doing the same for the banks and their depositors. The Social Security Act strove to provide for old age. The TVA harnessed hydroelectric power for the benefit of the community. The Rural Electrification Commission, as its name implied, was created to bring the benefits of the new technology to the farms. There were incidental movements to reduce racial discrimination and encourage conservation of natural resources, all adding up to a vigorous, if completely improvised, impromptu and patchwork effort at increasing the privileges of the underprivileged and providing some security for the hitherto insecure. Nor does an awareness of the waste of the New Deal, its frequent administrative inefficiency, the great and consciously intended political dividends that accrued to President Roosevelt as a result of the lavish expenditure of government funds and the growth of the Federal payroll, obscure its fundamental nature, which made it one of the most significant and, at the same time, one of the most buoyant movements in American history.

Some of its experiments turned out to be radically opposed to its conceptions of democracy,[4] while others died for lack of

---

[4] Notably the NRA, with its price-setting, wage-fixing codes for each industry, which in its structure bore an embarrassing resemblance to Mussolini's corporate state. It was declared unconstitutional in 1935, to the relief of almost everyone.

careful preparation. But the atmosphere it created and sustained of being open to suggestion, of being willing to try almost anything if it made any kind of sense and might conceivably do some good, generated the very freedom of action which would lend substance to Roosevelt's own dictum that "we have nothing to fear but fear itself." That the New Deal had its crackpot personalities and crackpot ideas is not to be denied, but these did not invalidate the premises to which it was committed. Its heyday from 1933 to 1937 was full of crackling optimism, rapid movement, a sense of things being done and old injustices being set to right. By increasing the purchasing power of the poor, by giving labor a voice more nearly equal to that of management, it helped restore to our economic life the equitable balance which had been written into our political institutions from the start. Once more the harmony between property rights and human rights was being established. But even if the New Deal accomplished nothing else, it changed the mood of the country from the inert despair of the depression to a revival of self-belief more characteristically American.

The coming of the second World War, however, brought the New Deal to a formal end, shifted the attention of the country to events abroad, and complicated still further the advancing mood of the country. With the end of the war the United States became locked in a coldly bitter struggle with a Soviet Union eager for world conquest. Coming so soon after the high tide of the fascist empires, this added to our growing sense of life as a permanently complex process.[5] Nor was Russia our only concern. There lurked in the back of our minds the fear of another crash. Here too, our immense wealth seemed of little avail,

---

[5] The concept of life as a hard, persistent struggle against difficulties was the keynote of Adlai Stevenson's campaign for the Presidency in 1952. In speech after speech he held up the possibilities of future success only after we recognized the problems of life and strove unremittingly to overcome them. A similar note had been struck by Winston Churchill in his celebrated "blood, sweat and tears" oration after the disaster at Dunkirk.

its very immensity being a factor in hastening the dreaded event. The more top-heavy the national income, supported as it was by an inflated price structure and maintained by aid to Europe and defense expenditures, the higher the perch from which it might one day fall. Whether this humpty-dumpty psychosis proved groundless or not, it shook self-confidence and easy optimism still further.

Obviously the problems involved in settling the difficulties of the world were going to be more involved than any we had faced before. Cheerfulness and physical aggressiveness had been enough to transform America from a wilderness to the leading industrialized wonder of the modern world. They were clearly not enough to transform an infinitely more complicated planet into a state of peace and prosperity. There began settling on the American mind a world view for which its whole previous history of ocean barriers and continental expansion had left it profoundly unprepared.

The key element in this new outlook was the cold war with Russia that began almost as soon as the shooting war with Germany and Japan had ended. Here too the American past had yielded no precedent. Previous wars had been followed by periods of relative peace. Even after the first World War it had been possible for the United States to retire into continental isolation after repudiating the League of Nations, and pursue its own domestic affairs without outside distraction. The whole Anglo-Saxon tradition of warfare with its roots in chivalry, had indeed dictated the pattern of a winning conflict. After you knocked the other country down until he cried enough, you helped him to his feet, shook hands, dusted him off, and parted company without hard feelings. If he was badly damaged, he could come to you for financial help, which you were always glad to supply. You might have to fight him again in twenty years, but both of you were assured of an interlude of peace in the meanwhile. The rules of tournament jousting still obtained. Even when the other side fought dirty, as the Nazis and Japanese did in the second World War, it did not make any essential difference. They would have to be sat on a little harder and a little longer—that was all.

The behavior of Russia, however, dealt a body blow to tournament rules. A war crisis as a direct continuation of a winning war was a new experience, unpleasant, intensely against the grain, but another factor deepening our awareness of the somber and difficult nature of things. One suspects that to Russia, indifferent to Western concepts of warfare, for whom life and history have been for a long time one continual crisis, this state of affairs was not nearly so unsettling. To the United States it was one more unhappy assignment in the pressing task of learning to readjust old modes of behavior to the world's new ways. As with every learning process the early stages were accompanied by a mounting frustration. But our discovery that frustration as a part of life had to be accepted and endured before it could be overcome, contributed to our growing maturity of outlook.

Those who lamented the lapse of the old brashness, who argued that the loss of our traditional assurance at a time of unexampled military victory, material supremacy and world power, was a sign of a psychic ailment all the more serious because it came at so critical a period, missed the essential point. These mingled feelings of uncertainty and anxiety had regenerative powers imperative to the metamorphosis of the American from the cocky and rapacious frontiersman of the nineteeenth century to the mature citizen of the world the atomic age so obviously and strenuously demands. Such a metamorphosis was impossible without a transitional interlude during which old ways were sloughed off and new ones adopted. Certainly the questions raised by the existence of the atom and hydrogen bombs alone were more complicated and ticklish than any in our history, and made even the Civil War issues, which involved killing one's own countrymen, seem simple by comparison. Courage and determination were no longer enough. Wisdom and intelligence, on a larger scale than have ever been required before, were being painfully and slowly shaped, despite the increased assaults upon the public by the belligerent agents of obscurantism and irrationality. The self-doubt that was the source of so much melancholy speculation may well have beeen a maturing agent for the American as a person and as a member of the global community.

The writers, who were the first to prefigure this state of mind, were participants in a profound national experience and, as has often been true of the artist, they heralded the experience, gave it shape and voice before it settled on the public generally, and proved themselves sensitive and accurate barometers of the emotional life of the people. Far from being isolated from the climate or the responsibilities of the time, they have been remarkably perceptive indicators of feeling and mood, which they projected in advance, and dramatized with clarifying intensity and exaggeration so as to make their work a stage on which the sensations of the audience could be worked out. They have, in a word, been antennae for society as a whole, and all the obloquy that has been heaped on them for their severally embittered or tortured visions cannot obscure the tenacious, if belated and not always acknowledged, harmony that came to exist between them and the country. Far from being misleading fabricators about what was going on,[6] they were in many ways remarkable for their anticipation of what was to come and the depth of their responsiveness to it. All this without assuming the mantle of prophecy or pretending to a factual or historical

---

[6] Bernard DeVoto, in *The Literary Fallacy,* is the chief exponent of the idea that writers are notoriously inaccurate guides to their times.

wisdom they obviously did not possess. All this while the great flood of commercial literature in the popular magazines was continuing to retail the pabulum myths, the saccharine and unproved optimisms, the wishful popular dreams in their most unreal configurations, and proffering to the writers the temptingly quick rewards which their own serious muses so often denied them.

For a long time the dominant stress on money and the acquisition of material goods tended to relegate those who devoted themselves to other tasks to a subordinate place in the scheme of things. Since the serious writer, painter, composer, scholar, was thus devoted, his public rating remained low until such time as his aims and the aims of the public came closer together. One effect of the catastrophes of the century was to force the American, as he grew more involved in them, to embrace a view of the world in which complexity and pain were major attributes. He was driven to accept the existence of values beyond those attached to physical property, and thus establish closer contact with those who pursued those values professionally. The result was a lessening of the historic suspicion of thinking and intellectuality and an inclination to grant creative men a higher prestige than they had hitherto enjoyed. Since their acceptance has long been an integral part of the experience of the West European, culture in Western Europe has long since acquired an honorable place in public opinion. In America, however, the whole weight of folklore and, until the depression, the whole weight of national experience has been against the idea that people and groups concerned with "things of the spirit" were of primary importance to the survival and prosperity of the nation. A common fallacy as late as the 1920s was that all problems could be solved by the acquisition of enough money. Everything that has happened since 1929 has weakened this belief. We are now richer and more powerful in the material sense than any nation on earth, yet we are no longer certain that this superior economic and technological prowess alone will solve our problems. While our physical resources were the decisive factor in winning the war outright, they have not established the *modus vivendi* which the winning of every previous war automatically established.

From these painful uncertainties the new American temper is being forged, in which more frequent pauses for thought and stocktaking, a growing sense of the tragic element in life, are the chief configurations. Unqualified optimism and pessimism as uniquely reigning elements are now growing into a new emotional fusion, in which neither one nor the other but both simultaneously are preparing the way for an adult response to the dilemmas of the age.

Chapter XIV

Toward the Whole Man

I

THE GREAT EVENTS SINCE 1914 HAVE PLACED
on America a strain more continuous and sustained than the
country has ever before endured. The simple responses of
earlier times have no longer proved adequate to the new occasions. Instead, the hard challenging face of the twentieth century is demanding of us a degree of understanding, a complexity of behavior, a maturity of outlook that will in large measure
determine the course of our future.

Where once an alternative existed between thinking and not,
the issue now is between thinking one way and another way.
The age of anxiety, as Auden called it, jogs the intellect as
well as the nerves, and there is no dodging it. Even living from
day to day requires analysis, meditation, all the stages and processes of thought. These have become all the more necessary
for the country as a whole to cope, however sketchily, with the
astonishingly rapid kaleidoscope of capitalism and communism, democracy and tyranny, the unification of Western Europe,
the seething movements of Africa and Asia, and scores of overbearing issues leaping out of the overheated, supercharged air
of the time.

The earth has now become so crowded and overrun that

hardly a physical refuge remains. Matthew Arnold's complaint in "The Scholar-Gipsy" nearly a hundred years ago, to the effect that there was literally no place to escape to from civilized life as there had been back in the seventeenth century, sounds comically nostalgic today. The planet of the 1850s was swarming with places where one could get away from it all. Like the free land in the American West to which men could flee from the difficulties of life on the Eastern seaboard, picturesque havens dotted the earth beckoning to the nerve-worn. Pierre Loti, in his exotic novels of the Middle East, evoked the mysterious and seductive colors of Turkey, Syria and the Eastern Levant. Charles Daughty and later T. E. Lawrence made the Arabian Peninsula equally alluring. Then came in rapid sequence a stream of other romantic paradises which tempted and titillated the imaginations of men longing to escape, if only temporarily, from the anxieties of civilization. There were Tahiti and the islands of the South Pacific, the first infected and finally degraded by white men's diseases, the second despoiled and deglamorized by the hideous island-jungle combat of the recent war. Tibet had its moment in the escapist sun, as did India, Peru and Mexico.

But so shrunken have the dimensions of the globe become that there is scarcely anywhere left. The free land of the West was swallowed by the advancing population, and the picturesque havens were driven off the market or out of existence by science, familiarity and war. There still remain other planets and other bodies in interstellar space, to which all the rumored experiments with rocket ships destined for the moon, projectiles to Mars, space stations suspended above the stratosphere beyond the reach of gravity, bear spectacular testimony. But these are vague and speculative, and offer scant comfort for the imagination in search of a way out. The hard fact is that physical exits no longer exist, that escapology is a dead art, that the present has become unavoidable, that the past is beyond reach and the future of no practicable use as a life raft.

Since crises can no longer be side-stepped, they must be faced. It has been proved over and over again that force and wealth alone will not solve our problems or cause them to vanish. The immense prosperity of the '20s did not avert the crash. The immense potential strength of the United States did not keep Nazi Germany from defying us or Japan, with one seventh of our steel production, from assaulting us. Our emergence as the greatest armed and industrialized power on earth has not kept the Soviet Union from encroaching on the free world everywhere. As the age of scientific power reaches a climax, it becomes clear that power is no longer enough, that the kind of *Realpolitik* which supports one tyranny to resist another is a mere temporary expedient, that the playing out of national life on the primary basis of physical strength perpetuates danger rather than averts it. Power has become powerless unless allied to principle. Since principle cannot be formulated without rational thought or sustained without its constant encouragement, an atmosphere of intellectual suppression is inimical to the national interest. The relationship between the free exercise of the mind and the carrying forward of democratic policies on the largest scale must be intimate and deep-flowing. The recognition of this is one of the pressing imperatives of our time.

A powerful challenge to our maturity as a people is indeed our attitude toward freedom of thought and expression. It is generally acknowledged that the Palmer raids after the first World War, the expulsion of elected Socialists from legislative chambers, the repression of free speech with its corollary restriction on free thought, hindered the advance of democracy. Since the end of the second World War the relationship between security and freedom has dominated the domestic scene. Each has its legitimate interests and clearly each must learn to live with the other if the country is to survive while preserving its democratic life.

At a time when the free world is menaced by Soviet imperialism, our campaign—in the name of security—against dissenting expression has been growing stronger. This situation has been exploited by ambitious politicians who have busied themselves assaulting liberal opinion having nothing to do with communism, and inquiring into personal beliefs in areas remote from the sensitive operations of government offices and atomic laboratories. If unchecked, such assaults will induce that very atmosphere of timidity and spiritual contraction which in its extreme form marks the totalitarian society we are so anxious to resist. But as pressure against unpopular views increases, it generates pressure in the reverse direction. The rights of persons accused of subversive opinions are defended through every court in the country, and powerful voices have been raised against the suppression of the freedom to think. The contending forces for maximum and minimum free speech sway back and forth in the struggle that began with the founding of the Republic. Today the issue around which this traditional struggle centers is the intensely contemporary one of physical security versus intellectual liberty. Espionage, sabotage, treason are no more permissible than robbery and murder, and our laws governing illegal actions must be stringently enforced. In this area security needs clearly come first. But where matters of thought, opinion and expression are concerned, the requirements of intellectual liberty ought surely to prevail. When these are encroached upon, the operating wholeness and balance of our life becomes distorted. In the eloquent words of Judge Learned Hand:

Risk for risk, for myself I had rather take my chance that some traitors will escape detection than spread abroad a spirit of general suspicion and distrust, which accepts rumor and gossip in place of undismayed and unintimidated inquiry.

I believe that that community is already in the process of dissolution where each man begins to eye his neighbor as a possible enemy, where nonconformity with the accepted creed, political as well as religious, is a mark of disaffection; where denunciation, without specification or backing, takes the place of evidence; where orthodoxy chokes freedom of dissent; where faith in the eventual supremacy of reason has become so timid that we dare not enter our convictions in the open lists to win or lose.[1]

Here again the prime objective should not be security *versus* liberty but security *and* liberty. As with our other destructive antitheses the goal of a maturing society is to establish between them a harmonious, mutually supporting coexistence.

II

Because of the agitations of mind and spirit induced by the tremendous changes of our epoch, the intellectual outlook is more wide-ranging and advanced than at any previous point in the century. We have developed, for example, a whole new philosophy of national well-being. Under McKinley in 1900 the government was scarcely more than an adjunct of business. Planning was in disrepute, politicians were regarded as unavoidable evils, and government was of little use in solving social problems. Society rocked along achieving equilibrium or disequilibrium at random. Corruption, venality, cutthroat profiteering, abuse of natural resources, exploitation of labor, went on with no more serious interference than an occasional, easily evaded antitrust law or passing remark by Theodore Roosevelt about "malefactors of great wealth" that would ruffle the

---

1 The New York *Times,* October 25, 1952.

tempers of the tycoons of the day[2] but have little effect on their activities. The Federal government, decentralized to the point of insignificance, had abdicated its function of serving as guardian of the national interest, above considerations of group or class. The scattered voices that were infrequently raised in behalf of centralized direction sounded hopelessly out of tune.

The change that has occurred in the intervening period, especially under the aegis of Woodrow Wilson and the second Roosevelt, has been very great. The ideas of planning on a national scale, Federal responsibility for the welfare of the whole citizenry, application of organized and systematic intelligence to the problems of government, have become widely accepted. A supremely successful example of this application is the Tennessee Valley Authority which harnessed the powers of a great river in the interests of the people living in its basin, and did so in an efficient, self-sustaining and businesslike way. Even unreconstructed spirits rarely bother to challenge the TVA any more. Conservatives who resisted the New Deal are now concerned with the extent and efficient administration of its principles, not with the principles themselves. It would be ingenuous to believe, however, that long-range planning, though generally accepted, is solidly co-ordinated, that Federal responsibility for social and economic ailments beyond the control of the individual, though a part of our working philosophy, is perfectly ordered and equitable, and that co-ordinated intelligence working on the canvas of the whole nation, though widely sanctioned, operates smoothly and keenly. All are halting and zigzag, sometimes conspicuous by their total absence, often inefficient. Government rolls and personnel have grown to gi-

---

[2] In *The Robber Barons*, Matthew Josephson referred to J. Pierpont Morgan's pique at T.R. Upon being informed that Roosevelt was off on a big-game expedition in Africa, the great financier remarked: "I hope the first lion he meets does his duty." (New York: Harcourt, Brace, 1934), p. 451n.

gantic size, and have correspondingly magnified the unwieldiness of bureaucracy. But however inefficiently administered at times or erratic in their manifestations, these ideas have arrived, been incorporated into laws that few would dream of overthrowing, and have represented in the political sphere a first-class triumph for the adult mentality.

Another advance in the maturity of the American people can be measured by the decline in prestige and influence of the political boss. A carbuncular and hitherto chronic growth on the political body of the country, preserving himself in power by the most dubious methods, he has been an institutional fixture for a century. For a long time the public has known all about his ways of doing business, to the point where most machine bosses made no bones about it, and abandoned whatever attempts at concealment may have been made at the start. Back at the beginning of the century, when Lincoln Steffens wrote his famous exposé *The Shame of the Cities* about the corrupt tie-up that existed among political bosses, big businessmen of the community, and the criminal element, he was astonished at the readiness of certain bosses to talk freely about their own unsavory practices. This candor sprang from their widespread acceptance by the electorate, and a confidence, seldom misplaced, in the permanence of this public attitude.

They were more than accepted; they were frequently regarded with admiration or at least respect. The awe inspired by Boss Hague in Jersey City exceeded for more than thirty years the civic indignation he aroused. Boss Crump of Memphis won the respect of so liberal and skeptical a journalist as John Gunther, whose chapter devoted to him in *Inside U.S.A.* contained more praise than censure. Boss Pendergast of Kansas City elicited expressions of loyalty from President Truman himself even after landing in the penitentiary as a result of Federal prosecution. The Kelly-Nash machine of Chicago worked in closest harmony with the Roosevelt Administration, a tribute both to the machine's instinct for the winning side and Roosevelt's tactical genius (or lack of principle, depending on how one looked at it) in political matters. In their time Croker, Tweed and Murphy of Tammany Hall, Penrose of Philadelphia, Hanna of Ohio, and a crowd of lesser luminaries flourished for long periods with little interference. When the individual boss eventually fell from power, as he nearly always did (usually because his machine petrified or corruption grew so outrageous that it became too much for even a complacent public), another, seldom very different, soon took his place, and the system itself went on seemingly impervious to the changing times.

Even intellectuals were seduced from time to time by the powerful image of the boss. The most noteworthy case was the preferential treatment given Huey Long in Robert Penn Warren's magnificent novel *All the King's Men*. After carefully documenting all the immoralities committed by this political demagogue and the heavy price paid by the people for the benefits conferred on them (Huey in real life did wonders for rural education in Louisiana and built miles of new roads), the author still rated him as a social asset, with the good he did measurably outweighing the evil. His assassination at the end is thus turned into a genuine tragedy that moves the reader despite his doubts and better judgment.

In the period following the second World War, however, the machines, at least in the old-line sense, steadily dwindled in power. The defeat of Hague in Jersey City was engineered by a former disciple who made no attempt to rule the city in the dictatorial fashion of his predecessor. The Republican machine in Philadelphia was overthrown after generations in office. In New York City, Tammany Hall fell on progressively hard times. The televised investigation of the Kefauver Crime Inquiry delivered sharp blows at the already dwindling status of the city machines. All over the country they were failing to deliver the vote. The rise of the independent voter, the grow-ing nausea with political corruption, the increasing sense of political awareness and civic responsibility, were making it difficult for the boss to survive.

The social conduct of the public has matured as well. The prejudice against Americans of German descent that marred our civil behavior in World War I was almost entirely absent during World War II. Delicatessen store windows were no longer broken by jeering jingoistic mobs. The German language was not legislated out of the curricula of schools and colleges. Brahms, Wagner and Beethoven continued to be performed without interruption. Nobody suggested that sauerkraut be changed once again to liberty cabbage, and no university facul-ties published blue books—as happened at the University of Wisconsin during the first war—denouncing German culture in all its phases. Treatment of the Japanese was harsher, but even it lacked the pathological note of the previous war.

On larger issues of discrimination, the emancipation of the Negro has been heartbreakingly slow, but it has nevertheless proceeded forward. Anti-Semitism still exists but consciousness of and opposition to it have grown stronger. The quota systems enforced by many universities are under attack, and movies like *Gentleman's Agreement* and *Crossfire* reach wide and sympa-thetic audiences. The living standards of the Puerto Rican, Mexican and Indian minorities remain shocking, yet even with regard to these less publicized groups public conscience is be-ginning to stir. Jim Crow still rules in the South but the issue of civil rights enforced by the Federal Government shakes the country. A Negro can now be elected captain of the Yale foot-ball team, colored ballplayers have played for the first time in the company of whites on the baseball diamonds of Georgia, mixed fraternities are appearing in the colleges, and FEPC laws have been enacted by several states.

This does not mean that the millennium is at hand, and all

Americans will live together henceforth in peace and brotherly love. Nor that progress is everywhere uniform and steady. As the 1949 report of the National Committee on Segregation in the Nation's Capital indicated, the Negro living in Washington, D.C., is worse off today than in 1900. Moreover, tens of thousands more pieces of anti-Semitic literature are distributed than two generations ago. But though the line of progress is ragged, it is largely forward, and suggests a degree of maturation in one of the most difficult of all social relationships.

Signs of independent thinking on the part of the citizenry abound. Our organs of communication and propaganda have developed enormously in this century, yet it is plain that their ability to control the reactions of the public, if it has grown at all, has not increased proportionately. While the great majority of newspapers and magazines have supported the Republicans in Presidential campaigns since 1932, the electorate has for the most part voted Democratic. The campaign of 1948 was a notable example of a citizenry that refused to be bulldozed, band-wagoned or stampeded. Despite the editorializing of the newspapers, the confident predictions of the pollsters and the experts, the voters exercised their own independent judgment.

Big-scale advertising, whatever its initial effects, has bred in the public mind a thickening core of resistance, so that skepticism is as likely to be the response evoked as credulous belief. A whole spate of popular novels, of which *The Hucksters* was the most celebrated, have devoted themselves to exposing the excesses of the advertising business, noting how often it has overreached itself and undermined the faith of its vast clientele. Henry Morgan created his comic radio personality partly by poking fun at his sponsors and their products. Consumers as a whole have become more wary of advertising claims, and of the differences that often exist between these claims and the actualities. The dockets of the Federal Trade Commission are crowded with cases of prosecution for advertising fraud, news of which, in however small a way, has seeped into the general consciousness.

In many ways then, the American is less credulous, less likely to take things at their face value, than he once was. As a result of the bruising experiences of recent history, the abuse to which his trust has been subjected, the promises made and broken, he is a harder fellow to convince than in the past. The very weight of the machinery of persuasion that has sprung up under the spur of technology has created in the public a countermachinery of disbelief, and made it much less the gullible, superstitious mass that Mencken accused it of being a generation ago. There is evidence indeed that the American people are brighter than their leaders. According to William A. Lydgate, in his book *What America Thinks:*

I am prepared to defend the thesis that the American people are not only generally right in their thinking about public issues, but that they show more common sense than their leaders in Washington. That thesis is based on a close examination of the results of public opinion surveys. Those results show that the voters are, most of the time, ahead of Congress and the Administration. In fact, the evidence is such as to raise the real question of whether the leaders have been leading the people, or whether it is the people who have led the leaders. Public opinion studies show but few instances when the majority of our people were not in favor of doing something long before either the legislative or executive branch of the government got around to doing it.[3]

III

Along with the growth of the American people politically and socially, there has been an enormous expansion of their cultural activity. More and more civic symphony orchestras are

---

[3] William A. Lydgate, *What America Thinks* (New York: Crowell, 1944), pp. 2-3.

coming into being. The sale of classical records as well as jazz has reached astronomic proportions. Local theater groups have spread over the country. Concerts by the great performers are making their way into the smaller as well as larger cities. Norman Cousins summarized these burgeoning activities in *The Saturday Review:*

. . . some increase in the nation's intellectual maturity must be indicated by the fact that 65 per cent more Americans are college trained than in 1925. The phenomenal increase in attendance—reaching "mass" proportions—at concerts and art exhibitions must be more than a mere cultural fluke. The high sales figures of many serious books, such as Toynbee's "A Study of History," must have their origin in something deeper than a desire to collect literary furniture. The growth of the community forum, the increasing participation by parents in the formation of local educational policy, the maturing effect of the war on millions of young men and women—all these fit into the pattern of an America far more advanced than it was only a quarter of a century ago.[4]

In these and many other areas the taste of the public, as well as its responsiveness to meaningful cultural activities, has moved far beyond the dreary provincialism prevailing at the turn of the century. Although the bad movies, the diluted corn of the digest periodicals, the slickly tailored sentiment of the mass-circulation magazines, and the bulk of the programs on radio and television have attracted some audiences, it has been only at the cost of repelling others, usually the more enlightened. The public's occasional failure to respond to mature creative work has obscured the times, more numerous in our generation than for a long while past, when it has responded overpoweringly. The tremendous reception given Arthur Miller's *Death of a Salesman*

[4] *The Saturday Review,* February 4, 1950.

and Tennessee Williams' *A Streetcar Named Desire* provides a glimpse into the hunger for art that deals with recognizable human experiences. The reaction was all the more remarkable since these plays made no concessions to "popular" taste, offered no nostrums and were unrelievedly tragic. Shakespeare may have seemed like a dead horse at the box office but the excellent movie version of *Hamlet* produced by Laurence Olivier grossed several million dollars. Grand opera seemed like impossibly highbrow fare but the broadcasts from the stage of the Metropolitan have attracted an immense nationwide audience and evoked a profound response.

Yet the producers of our popular arts continue for the most part to dole out stale and unrewarding hokum. Here and there an isolated figure among them will appeal to the adult potential of the general public, but on the whole there has been little improvement and no sustained advance toward emotional maturity in the popular media. With rare exceptions the leaders of opinion in general still operate under the conviction that the American people have the mental capacity of backward teenagers. In a famous attack on the arrested-mentality myth *Fortune* observed:

With varying degrees of flagrancy, the press and the radio, the advertising profession and the moving-picture industry, have confronted our uncomplaining people with an appalling amount of enervating drivel, deliberately tailored for mass minds of sub-adult levels. Worse, many of our political leaders have proceeded on the same timid assumption, with the result that the typical political campaign is fought out on thoroughly irrelevant—if often thoroughly entertaining—issues. The political value of the unvarnished truth has not been explored for a generation. . . .

There is a persistent tendency to talk down to the people, write down to them, as though they really were children of thirteen, with limited understanding, a minimum sense of responsibility, a congenital distaste for reality. . . . In addressing us in this fashion, our opinion makers are not only undermining public faith in the written and spoken word, but are also failing to draw upon the national intelligence to the full limit of its . . . value. . . .

If you ask people questions—tough questions that require thoughtful answers, questions that call for a realistic appraisal of large issues, questions that concern the future of the nation and the world— . . . [their replies] show a pattern of logical, cohesive thought. . . . The vast majority . . . answers reasonably, with the reasonableness of a man competent to vote, to make his own laws, to formulate for himself the kind of society he wants to live in.[5]

The public may not be the fount of all wisdom which the *mystique* of democracy sometimes claims, but neither is it the stupid philistine mass that culture snobs and reactionary critics often claim. Large sections of it are surely alert to art and expression that are not bogged down in obscurantism. The unrelenting pressures of the age of technology have shaken everyone to the point where, side by side with the most ingenious forms of escape, an unprecedented curiosity about the meaning of life has been generated. It is this curiosity, rising from the ruins of the old credulous faith in the power of muscle and money to solve all difficulties and dissolve all crises, which provides the solid basis for a great expansion of creative work in America.

And the artist? In terms of money the creative arts in America are still largely part-time occupations, pursued in one's spare time after working at a purely bread-and-butter job. During the general rise in the standard of living since 1900, made possible by the enormous advance of technology, only a few meager crumbs have sifted down to the American artist. But

---

[5] "American Man-In-The-Street," *Fortune,* December 1942.

in the vital matter of prestige and artistic recognition, the advance of the creative worker has been notable. American musicians, painters, writers and dancers are attended to now as never before. The works of American composers are now included more and more in the repertories of the great symphony orchestras, where a generation ago they appeared only rarely. Serious choreographers like Agnes De Mille, Hanya Holm, Tamiris, are engaged to direct dances in musical plays produced on Broadway. What started as a daring experiment in the commercial theater with the production of *Oklahoma!* in 1943 was received so warmly by a public only too eager for a change from the stale routines of the musical-comedy chorus line, that it has now become accepted practice to include first-rate dancing in the theater. American literature, once an unimportant adjunct to European, has in our century grown into a leading center of creative expression. Writers like Hemingway and Faulkner are regarded by the Europeans as among the giants of the age.

The immense growth of these arts since the beginning of the century has not been accidental or capricious, but has stemmed from a genuine advance in their community standing. For a period during the 1930s they were even supported by public funds, inconceivable a generation or even a decade before. Whole squadrons of important figures in the several arts have made their way, slowly overcoming the chilling indifference and tacit contempt of their potential audience. Sloan, Marin, Benton, Wood, Curry, the Soyers, Shahn, among the painters; Copland, Shuman, Diamond, Barber, Creston, Della Joio, among the composers; Sandburg, O'Neill, Lewis, Hemingway, Wolfe, Tennessee Williams, Arthur Miller, to mention only a few among the writers; creative and influential dancers from Ruth St. Denis, Martha Graham, Doris Humphrey, Charles Weidman, to a score of vivid young ballet dancers—have wrested accolades from a public which a scant fifty years ago was thoroughly resistant.

This new receptivity offers the most viable hope that the economic status of the artist will improve. Since Americans have always been willing to pay generously for what they wanted, whether it was luxury plumbing or light entertainment, an increase in the seriousness of their appetites would mean a corresponding increase in the prestige and financial rewards accruing to artists and men of ideas. The process is already at work in American business, which in recent years has displayed a growing awareness of the importance of art in industry. The use of modern and at times superbly beautiful architectural design in many industrial and office buildings—the Lever Brothers structure in New York and the General Motors Technical Center in Detroit are spectacular examples—is a sign of the extraordinary possibilities that stem from a fusion of the aesthetic and the mercantile. The fabulous success of designers like Raymond Loewy in improving the visual appearance of hundreds of commodities used in daily life indicates how the age-old hostility between art and commerce is by no means inevitable. The whole trend toward bringing painting, architecture and sculpture into the movements and objects of everyday existence points to the integration of beauty and practicality, attributes which in the past have all too often been thought of as irreconcilable. The fusion of culture and commerce is further illustrated by the Pepsi-Cola and other business-sponsored prize contests for painting, the movement for the organized financial support of liberal-arts colleges by the business community, and the immense sums spent for intellectual activities by the Rockefeller, Guggenheim and Ford Foundations. Ford Foundation money has even set up an Institute for Philosophic Research in San Francisco.

Businessmen are beginning to acknowledge the importance of intellectual training and liberal education to the conduct of business itself. "The success or failure of every business enterprise is traceable to one source, and one source only, namely, somebody's mind," said H. W. Prentis, Jr., Chairman of the Board of the Armstrong Cork Company, "for no one has yet invented a machine that can think. And the present economic and political confusion at home and abroad constantly calls for minds of larger and larger caliber if American business and industry are to discharge their full social responsibility in this sorely troubled world." Such minds, he went on to say, cannot be produced by narrow professional or vocational training but only by the broadest kind of education:

The inability to see a situation in the large, the hesitancy of the vocationally trained mind to indulge in flights of imagination and thereby enlarge its scope are not infrequently the result of . . . professional education too closely focussed and too narrowly applied. President Lowell of Harvard was right: "Dealing with the concrete does not lead to knowledge of the abstract." Consequently, we see too often electricians instead of electricial engineers; surveyors instead of civil engineers; pettifogging attorneys instead of lawyers; hack writers instead of real journalists; draftsmen instead of architects; pedagogues instead of professors; and impersonal, hair-splitting specialists instead of the old family doctor who was capable of sizing up a patient as a human being, not as a conglomeration of separate organs and glands! So by all means let us go as far as we can in the teaching of business as a profession, but in the same breath let us realize the vital importance of resourcefulness, constructive imagination, and vision in modern business; then intensify the development of these characteristics through the broad stimulus that a liberal education affords.[6]

---

[6] H. W. Prentis, Jr., "Liberal Education for Business and Industry," *American Association of University Professors Bulletin,* Autumn 1952.

IV

The recent upsurge in social esteem enjoyed by the atomic physicist further illuminates the change in public values. So long as the scientist was only a queer crank working harmlessly in a laboratory, he was of no consequence. The moment his basic research resulted in the discovery of the atom bomb, capable of blowing the hardheaded practical man and all his properties to smithereens, he became a formidable figure. It began to dawn on a good many people who had regarded basic research, and indeed all theoretical speculation, with contemptuous indifference, that the pursuit of theory was so formidable a process, so immensely practical indeed, that it might at any moment shake the foundations of the universe.

Even the military man, long in a backwater of American life, has come in for his share of prestige and influence. Since the second World War, army generals have become Secretaries of State, received important appointments as ambassadors, occupied crucial positions in the administrative structure of the government, and been elected to the Presidency. Great universities seeking new heads have bidden for their services. Newspaper and magazine columns have been thrown open to them for the publication not alone of their wartime experiences but of their comments, warnings and prognostications on the affairs of peace. This may appear a dangerous process to some, alien to our civilian traditions, though thus far most of our conquering generals have proved a restrained and sober lot. Dangerous or not, it is a process that indicates how fluid is the present situation as regards positions of leadership, for a long while the exclusive monopoly of men engaged in trade and finance.

The trade unions, too, have won their place in the sun, and by removing some of the vast concentrations of power from the grasp of capital, have advanced the cause of democracy, which rests on the division of power and its distribution over as multiple and widespread an area of the people as possible. The greater the number of elements and groups sharing power and responsibility, the better for the well-being of the Republic. American society has not been in so great a state of fluidity as regards public influence since the end of the Civil War, when preachers, poets, professors, eighteenth-century aristocrats, nine-teenth-century agrarian reformers were ousted from positions of leadership and replaced by entrepreneurs. How far into this promising situation men of ideas, regardless of profession, can again make their way remains to be seen.

Their opportunity has not been so bright for a century. The remarkable campaign waged by Adlai Stevenson in 1952 demon-strated this. Addressing himself to the highest capacities of the public rather than, as more commonly happens in politics, to the lowest, Stevenson defined the complex problems of our time with an intellectual penetration, humor and magnificence of phrase that marked a re-entry into the national scene of the thinking man. He did not win the election, but he attracted the votes of more than twenty-seven million people and made an overwhelming impression on millions more of both parties. The fact that such a man, demonstrating the power and range of the free mind operating under the spur of all its faculties, could be the candidate of a great party and run a Presidential race with-out compromising with either himself or the electorate, was in itself an extraordinary event in the maturation of the country.

The flexibility of American institutions, which have been equal thus far to all the strains put upon them, is the most specific insurance that new avenues of approach will remain open. A similar flexibility is evident in our economic system. J. K. Galbraith, in his remarkably illuminating book *American Capitalism,* describes how our economic structure has developed a process of checks and balances such as that built into our political system by the founding fathers. In his theory of "countervailing power," he traces the growth of bargaining strength and economic independence on the part of labor, the farmer, the consumer and other major groups in the population which had once been relatively helpless to protect themselves. A society which under its own momentum distributes economic power among all its constituent parts has provided the material foundation on which higher forms of democracy can flourish. So long as this malleability survives, all changes are possible, even radical alterations in the present, still parlous state of the thinking man.

Our national life requires the free play of its component parts, cultural no less than economic and political. Technological efficiency is vital and rewarding but so are art and creative thought. Materialism may be the unavoidable bedrock of existence but it cannot become enlightened unless joined to organized reason; maximum human well-being results from their co-operation. When the balance between them is upset—as it has so often been—the effects are as injurious as if one branch of our government were subordinated to another, or if in our economy either labor or management were allowed to dominate the other. Hence the elimination of the artificial gap that has grown up between ideas and action is essential to our interests. The healing of the split between highbrow and lowbrow, that Van Wyck Brooks defined many years ago, must be a major item on the national agenda. When they are freed from the hostility in which they have been locked for so long a time, when they exist once again in a state of fusion and mutual respect, a long step will have been taken toward securing the wholeness of American life.

The inescapable pressures of our time are already beginning to force the contending sides together. In the completion of that process lies the hope that the nation will face the crises ahead with renewed integration. With it, too, the release of the mind in all its thinking, functioning powers may be achieved at last. That release will signal, as much as any other single event, a healing of the schisms in American culture, a forward movement in the direction of that larger democracy at whose center flourishes the whole man.

In Lewis Mumford's words: "The final question is 'What kind of human being are we trying to produce?' Not the power, not the profit man, or the mechanical man, but the whole man must be the central actor in the new civilization."[7]

This is the objective beckoning us in the generations ahead.

---

[7] The New York *Times*, September 15, 1948.

INDEX

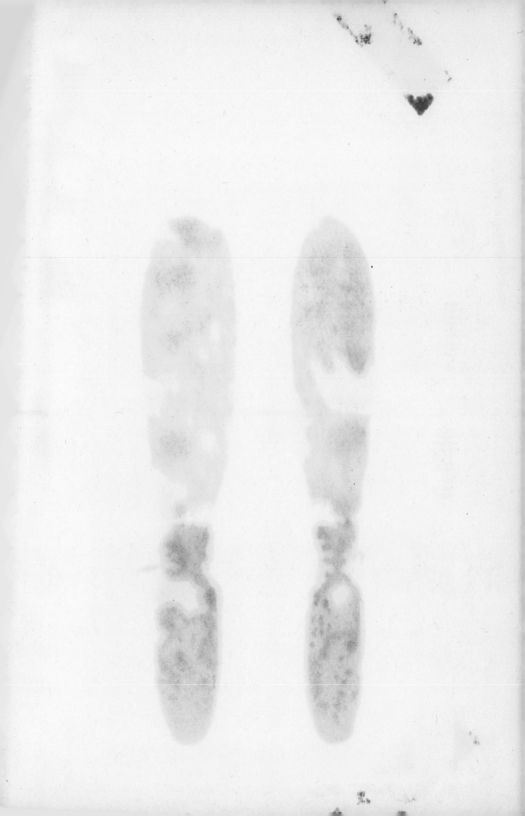

2/4/54

DATE DUE

GAYLORD   PRINTED IN U.S.A.